E N D I N G S

SPEP Studies

in Historical Philosophy

General Editors John McCumber
David Kolb

ENDINGS

Questions of Memory in Hegel and Heidegger

Edited by
Rebecca Comay and
John McCumber

Northwestern University Press
Evanston, Illinois

Northwestern University Press
Evanston, Illinois 60208-4210

Printed in the United States of America

ISBN 0-8101-1506-9 (cloth)
ISBN 0-8101-1507-7 (paper)

Library of Congress Cataloging-in-Publication Data

Endings : questions of memory in Hegel and Heidegger / edited by Rebecca Comay and John McCumber.
p. cm. — (Northwestern University studies in phenomenology & existential philosophy)
Includes bibliographical references.
ISBN 0-8101-1506-9 (alk. paper). — ISBN 0-8101-1507-7 (pbk. : alk. paper)
1. Heidegger, Martin, 1889–1976. 2. Hegel, Georg Wilhelm Friedrich, 1770–1831. I. Comay, Rebecca. II. McCumber, John. III. Series: Northwestern University studies in phenomenology & existential philosophy.
B3279.H49E53 1999
193—dc21 98-49938
CIP

The paper used in this publication meets the minimum requirements of the American National Standard for Information Sciences—Permanence of Paper for Printed Library Materials, ANSI Z39.48-1984.

Contents

Acknowledgments

"Heidegger-Hegel: An Impossible 'Dialogue'?" by Dominique Janicaud first appeared in Janicaud, *A nouveau la philosophie* (Paris: Albin Michel, 1991). It first appeared in English in Janicaud, *Rationalities/Historicities*, trans. Nina Belmonte (Atlantic Highlands: Humanities Press, 1997).

"The History of Being and Its Hegelian Model" by Michel Haar first appeared in Haar, *Le chant de la terre* (Paris: L'Herne, 1987). It first appeared in English in Haar, *The Song of the Earth*, trans. Reginald Lilly (Bloomington: Indiana University Press, 1993).

"The Hegelian Legacy in Heidegger's Overcoming of Aesthetics" by Jacques Taminiaux first appeared in Taminiaux, *Recoupements* (Brussels: Ousia, 1982). It first appeared in English in Taminiaux, *Poetics, Speculation, and Judgment*, trans. and ed. Michael Gendre (Albany: SUNY Press, 1993).

"Stuff • Thread • Point • Fire: Hölderlin on Historical Memory and Tragic Dissolution" by David Farrell Krell first appeared in Krell, *Lunar Voices* (Chicago: University of Chicago Press, 1995).

Portions of "Stone" by John Sallis first appeared in Sallis, *Stone* (Bloomington: Indiana University Press, 1994).

Introduction: Transforming Thought

John McCumber

The Story of Things

According to an ancient story which (because of Hegel and Heidegger) we are now able to remember, there were once things called "things." Things were independent of other things, so they had no problems; and they were stable, so they had few possibilities. They ruled the world. In fact, they *were* the world, for everything was a thing. Even philosophers, when they appeared on the earth, were things.

As time went on, things grew more and more thingly: more and more independent and stable. Their commerce with other things came to be restricted to a relation called "causality," which grew progressively thinner until—with Hume—it vanished altogether into a mere habit of the knowing subject. The relation of things to such knowing subjects was also increasingly impoverished (though it was only intermittently held to be a "causal" relation). Interaction between knower and known, indeed the creation of either by the other (as the participants in a Platonic dialogue, for example, erotically create each other), was generally banished. Knowing finally became, even for things of the sensory world, what Aristotle had claimed it to be in the case of the intellectual realm: a mirroring of one thing by something else totally independent of it. Nothing was changed simply by being known (and rarely enough by knowing). The sole relation between knower and known had come to be correspondence, and its sole virtue was accuracy. Truth had captured logos.

At the very beginning of the story of things, two thinkers sketched out the main paths it would take. Plato and Aristotle would never be surpassed in this, for they found and occupied the two most radically opposed positions one can take on the issue of the independence and stability that constitute a thing. Plato held that the stable independence of a given thing—its nature—was to be found beyond its borders. In fact, he placed it in a wholly different world, the world of the most thingly things, of unchanging and independent Forms (*eide*). Aristotle, by contrast, held that form was immanent: that a thing possessed within it a principle of stability and independence (*energeia*).

It was from these two starting points that the whole story unfolded, over millennia. For medieval Platonists, things were stable and independent of each other because the sole ultimate source of their existence was God. For medieval Aristotelians, what things received from God was a unitary act of existing, which enabled them to be just as God (alone) had created them to be. And so for a Platonist such as Augustine, it was easy to explain why things were stable, but hard to see how they could be independent: freedom of the will, its independent capacity to change, was a major problem. For an Aristotelian like Aquinas, it was easy to see how things were independent, but difficult to show why they were, in their inmost natures, static.[1] The efforts persisted well into modernity.

Today we live in a world not of things but of radical changes: transformations, *metabaseis.* Protons decay, the globe warms, and species proliferate. Relationships explode, empires disappear, and the Internet proliferates. History has replaced the cosmos as the horizon of ultimate meaning, and the logos has been recaptured by time.

The change can be dated, I believe, from Kant, who in his Third Antinomy destroyed both the Platonic and the Aristotelian stories once and for all. He did this not by refuting them with a new argument, or even by making them refute each other: for time had certainly shown them to be irrefutable. Rather, he showed that the two accounts of the thing *turn into* each other. The Platonic story of the thing as determined from outside will not allow itself to be told about everything without postulating, at some point, a thing undetermined by anything outside itself (such as a Form of the Good). And the Aristotelian account, on which a thing has its own immanent source of stableness and independence, will not allow itself to be told about everything without at some point appealing to causality from without (such as the eros with which the cosmos seeks the Prime Mover). So, Kant discovered, the Platonic account transforms itself into the Aristotelian and back. Kant's truly radical move, the creative one which followed on this destruction, was to say that it was not the stories, but these transformations in them, that were basic. Logos, in other words, is not static but fundamentally self-transforming.[2]

This view could not easily be confined to logos. For if the aim of thingly thought was faithfully to portray its objects as stable and independent things, truth now had to become impossible. There is no way for thought which is in constant self-transformation to portray correctly a static universe. Either the universe itself is a set of radical changes, or thought can no longer portray it. Even if the universe shares with thought the feature of being radically self-transforming, there is still no way for thought to mirror it. A mirror can, of course, mirror at the speed of light—but only if it itself remains stable and independent of what it mirrors. Thought could capture transformations only if there was some level, some stable structure, some tain to the mirror,[3] which remained stable and independent. The self-transforming thought of Kant's Antinomies—what he called Reason—dispensed with any such tain: its activity was the free creation of its own content, i.e., of itself.[4] Only the Kantian Understanding itself retained a stable tain, in the form of its twelve categories; and it was, by no accident, the Understanding alone which achieved cognition of external reality. Kant's doctrine of the categories enabled him to maintain that, amidst and in spite of all transformations, the mind itself was a stable and independent thing. Even if it no longer merely mirrored nature, its transformative power was clearly bounded.

But Kant, who thus showed the way into the threatened land of postmodernity, did not enter it himself. It was Fichte, of course, who put paid to what Kant had so laboriously salvaged, by showing the categories of the Understanding to be, like Ideas of Reason, free creations of the mind. And with this, the notion of "mirroring" was finally undone; transformation took its place. Today, thought no longer mirrors reality, but transforms transformations from which it does not itself remain distinct.

This is suggested by today's well-known "crisis of science." Much contemporary science seems increasingly trapped between the radical transformations exhibited by its own history and the stability of the truth it traditionally seeks. In this condition, science cannot attain truth—but cannot abandon the concept altogether without sacrificing its own ancient essence. Philosophy of science thus comes to wrestle with the following trilemma: either it must continue to maintain, in the face of mounting evidence to the contrary, that science actually delivers definitive truth; or it must show why, if science can never reach it, truth remains a relevant goal; or it must articulate what science is without appeal to an overall conception of truth, which means solving dozens of "demarcation" problems. This trilemma is as old as Hegel's post-Fichtean encounter with Kant's noumenon (for surely stable truth has come to be no more empirically accessible than things in themselves), and has been vigorously explored since Karl Popper.

My point in mentioning this particular set of problems is not to solve any of them, but merely to note that it is *philosophy of* science which must discuss issues such as these. This means that the nature of science is no longer clear of itself. There is no clearly identifiable set of people and practices that are so obviously "scientific" that philosophical reflection can simply assume their scientific status and explicate that. Rather, to philosophy of science increasingly falls the burden of showing what is and is not science, what science itself is and is not. From that point of view philosophy of science no longer mirrors and explains science; it is increasingly interventionistic and transformative. As the introduction to a recent and comprehensive anthology in the field puts it, "there is an appropriate and dialectical interaction between research in the philosophy of science and research in the various special sciences."[5] What can this mean but that science and philosophy of science have become mutually transformative? And what can that mean but that they are now conditions of each other's existence?

Art, writes Hegel, "died" when reflection on it became a condition of its existence. If philosophy of science is nothing other than reflection upon science, the day may come when we say of empirical science what Hegel said of art:

> Thought and reflection have spread their wings above [science]. Those who delight in lamenting and blaming may regard this phenomenon as a corruption and ascribe it to the predominance of passions and selfish interests which scare away the seriousness of [science] as well as its cheerfulness; or they may accuse the distress of the present time, the complicated state of civil and political life which does not permit a [researcher] entangled in petty interests to raise [herself] to the higher ends of science. . . . We may hope that [science] will always rise higher and come to perfection, but the form of [science] has ceased to be the supreme need of Spirit.[6]

Thought does not mirror, but transforms its objects—which are themselves, paradigmatically, transformations. We are (once again), like it or not, in a new era, and need new conceptions of thinking.

It seems that (once again), two thinkers stand at the beginning of a new order and sketch out its possibilities: Hegel and Heidegger are to the story of transformations what Plato and Aristotle were to the story of things. It is with these two, and with the transformations they have worked and shrunk from, that the essays in this volume deal. Just as the traditional world could not begin until Aristotle came forth to confront Plato, so our contemporary world did not begin until Heidegger encountered Hegel. And so the present essays, like transforming thought itself, begin from that encounter.

The Encounter

This already presents a problem. Hegel and Heidegger are to be our guides to transforming thought; but their very ability to serve as such guides means that their own thinking is itself in perpetual transformation. Understood in this way, Hegel and Heidgger are wholly unwedded to any "positions" or "views." This is hardly unfortunate, given the nature of some of the standpoints which, from time to time, each embraced—Hegel's malfeasance tending toward the ridiculous, as in his dismissal of Africa as "the Spirit asleep"; Heidegger's toward the truly evil, as in his "Rectoral Address."[7] But the plausibility which Hegel and Heidegger gain when they are construed as offering a new kind of thinking, rather than a set of doctrines, is bought at a price. It means that their respective bodies of thought cannot be taken as two objects to be compared, contrasted, and finally evaluated. Their relationship is a dynamic one, in which self-transformations lead to mutual transformations and vice versa. It is to be construed on a variety of models.

One such model, espoused in different ways by Martin Donougho, Michel Haar, and Jacques Taminiaux, is to see Heidegger as prolonging themes broached by his *confrère* and predecessor, Hegel. For Donougho, this is a loose "resonating" in which Heidegger carries forward, with differences, the theme of art-as-collective-memory that Hegel began—a theme which resonates further into contemporary aesthetics, including Donougho's own views.

For Jacques Taminiaux, Heidegger's conscious critique of Hegelian views of aesthetics coexists in his thought with a restatement of those basic themes: in certain respects I will discuss later, Heidegger carries forward certain Hegelian views, while in others—and at the price of consistency with himself—he overcomes them. In particular, Taminiaux points out, Heidegger retains in his own history of art the periodicity that Hegel had already established: the famous sequence of "ancient, medieval, modern." And as Michel Haar observes, this (among other things) leads Heidegger to a point-for-point reversal of Hegel's view of history—of the history of art and of history generally. Thus, for example, the mass of received texts that Hegel transformed into the glorious story of Spirit's return to itself becomes for Heidegger a dismal unfolding of the forgetting of Being. Only in his concept of epochality does Heidegger actually go beyond Hegel to the point of asserting something which does not have a (negative) precedent in Hegel.

As Donougho, Haar, and Taminiaux make particularly evident, Heidegger's reception of Hegel transformed both of them. We may say that Hegel did not become a metaphysical theologian, in Heidegger's sense, until Heidegger crowned him one; and it was out of that coronation that Heidegger himself became what he was to be, namely the arch-subverter of the kind of metaphysics he had assigned to Hegel.

The reception of Hegel by Heidegger not only transforms them both, but is also capable of being itself transformed. This happens, to take one case, when their chronological order is bracketed: when Heidegger is viewed, not as someone who, with varying degrees and types of critical awareness, followed Hegel and thought about him, but as actually Hegel's contemporary. When Hegel and Heidegger are thus reconstructed as mutual contemporaries, the dynamism of their encounter remains: that encounter must take some such form as a dialogue, in which Hegel and Heidegger address and transform one another directly, or a contest, in which they encounter each other through some third thing (or person) for which they compete.

Heidegger himself, no doubt, was applying this contestatory model when he undertook to rescue Hölderlin, the friend of Hegel's youth, from German idealism. Kathleen Wright applies it to the thought of each on the *Antigone.* In Hegel's view of the play, Wright points out, its complex constellations of conflict all reduce to just one: the battle of the sexes. This Hegelian reading—forgotten by Heidegger—nonetheless holds and repels him in various ways; in effect, for Wright, Heidegger vies with Hegel for Antigone. Neither, for reasons to be discussed later, can capture her.

The contestatory model, with both gentlemen losing, is further applied by David Farrell Krell: like Antigone, the Hölderlin both tried to capture eluded both. For Hegel and Heidegger, as for all transforming thought (for reasons which will be seen), memory is essential to thought. Such essential memory—Hegelian *Erinnerung,* and Heideggerian *Andenken*—is, Krell notes, a matter of holding and retaining. For Hölderlin, such memory falsifies time. This is because what can be caught and kept—the "moment," for Hegel, or the "epoch," for Heidegger—must ultimately have a sort of unity. But for Hölderlin, the moment (to say nothing of the epoch) does not merely glide away irreplaceably, but actually explodes into a shower of intersecting (verbal) strategies and gestures;

memory is not so much a retaining and holding as the dislocation of all such attempts.

The contestatory model of their encounter thus pushes us, inevitably, beyond both Hegel and Heidegger—for both recurrently lose the contests we (or they) set up. In this respect, to retain and keep them is, as Hölderlin would expect, to lose them as well: memory is necessarily transformative. The same lesson applies if we adopt the "dialogical" model for their encounter. By bracketing the simple fact that Heidegger was born fifty-eight years after Hegel died, any attempt to reconstruct a "dialogue" between the two presumes that we must transform their encounter into something that it never really was. This is undertaken by Dominique Janicaud, who reconstructs an impossible Hegel-Heidegger dialogue which ranges across numerous topics basic to them both—including Being, truth, history, and the present age. In each case, Heidegger attempts to locate Hegel within one specific epoch, or "mittence," of Being—thus denying Hegel's claim to stand at the telos of the whole of history.

These attempts are met by Hegel's no less relentless efforts to locate dialectical contradictions in Heidegger's thought, and then to surmount them toward a truth beyond Heidegger. In their final *rapprochement*, as Janicaud orchestrates it, both thinkers converge on the view that ontology, the science of Being, necessarily becomes phenomenology, the science of appearance, and vice versa. The "phenomeno-ontology" thus set in motion converges in turn on *Selbstdarstellung*, the presentation of self; and that, in turn, is to be conceived as self-transformation, so that phenomeno-ontology is never finished and remains always open before us as a task.

It is perhaps already clear that reflection on Hegel and Heidegger is not merely a preliminary or propadeutic to transforming thought, but an ongoing part of it. This is partly because once one engages the path of such reflection, one is never finished: the two bodies of thought, Hegel's and Heidegger's, continually transform themselves as one reflects on them, and transform one's reflection itself. Moreover, it is impossible not to engage that path—not only because Hegel and Heidegger were among the first down it, but also because the concern of transforming thought with them is only part of its larger concern with history itself, and particularly with its own history. For just as science is, in the service of truth, directed upon the simultaneous copresence of state of affairs and proposition, of mirrored and mirror, so transforming thought is a form of memory, directed upon the past as being that which it must seek to transform. And the past in question can only be conceived as itself a series of transformations: as history.

Transformation as History

Thinking transforms transformations. The present is continually being transformed into the past, gaining definiteness, losing the possibility of ever being anything other than what-it-was-to-be: our essences are continually at our heels. The transformation of the present into the past kills the present but enlivens the past, for it enriches it with generically different content. This not merely characterizes but defines one aspect of the present as a felt phenomenon: it is the way certain stories are turning out, the extent to which certain transformations still underway have been completed. To move to a philosophical level of generality (as Heidegger and Hegel perhaps unwisely do) requires us to think *the* present as the culmination of *all* the transformations that have ever been: to think nothing less than the telos of history. The idea that history has a telos is thus not a metaphysical doctrine, but a tool of thought which has become transforming memory.

The telos of history is then a necessary theme of transforming thought, certainly of generalized transforming thought. But it has a problematic status, for (in addition to its possibly overgeneral formulation) it partakes of both the present and the past. The present is not a realm of completed transformations, for to be completed is to lose one's possibilities for change. To see a moment in time as *nothing more than* the telos of a previous transformation is to see it as something past and dead. To say that history has a telos, and that the present is that telos, is thus to say that the present already contains a moment that is entirely defined as how previous transformations turned out: it is to admit that the past is already gobbling up the present. The telos of history is thus always something about to become past, about to lose its possibilities, about to die.

To think transformation on a level of philosophical generality is then to think of *the* present; to think of it as the telos of history, and to think of it as something about to become past. As Dennis Schmidt points out, if Antigone acts out of solidarity with the dead, then we ourselves always act (if at all) in solidarity with the dying: with ourselves and each other. When such thinking is aware of itself, it must be as something which is not yet lost—but is about to be. Transforming thought is inescapably not merely memory but memorial. Such memorializing is an obvious dimension of the thinking we call "Hegel" and "Heidegger"; they dare, even, to mourn for God himself. They do this because of the structure of history and of their own thinking: transforming thinking transforms transformation; transformations are historical; history has a telos; and that telos is the death of the present. And yet, as Schmidt points out in his essay, "the reversal and overturning of history is something to which each wants to lay claim, out of which each claims to see through his own time to the deepest truths." Hegel and Heidegger see themselves, not simply as completing history, but as overthrowing it. And yet they see their own present as the outcome of what has gone before, as the telos of history. How can the overthrow of history be the telos of history?

David Kolb suggests three ways of viewing the telos of history: as completion, as exhaustion, and as the unblocking of circulation. The first two views are fixed respectively in Hegel's formula "absolute Spirit" and in Heidegger's term *Gestell*, for both terms signify results. Absolute Spirit is the completion of finite Spirit's journey of self-discovery and self-recovery, while the *Gestell* is the exhaustion of possibility brought about by the metaphysical forgetting of Being. And, as Janicaud points out, these two terms signify repectively, for Hegel and Heidegger, (almost) the entirety of the modern era: the present epoch is for both thinkers *nothing more than* the expression of a single principle, which means that it is nothing more than the way certain enterprises (Spirit's self-recovery, metaphysics) have turned out. It would seem that the present, for Hegel and Heidegger, is not merely being gobbled up by the past, but already part of it.

But Hegel and Heidegger, argues Kolb, cannot be read in just this way. For if history is to "end," then the epoch which ends it cannot simply fit into a predetermined space of possibilities (the way the standard sort of culmination of an enterprise is determined by the previous development of that enterprise). It must instead *define* a space of possibilities. This, for Kolb, is the fundamental power of Hegel's state: it is able to define our possibilities in a radically new way, through the rational development of intermediate social structures such as families, markets, corporations, and so on. For Heidegger, by contrast, the field of contemporary possibilities is opened up by the will to power, which expresses the direct opposite of Hegel's view of modernity: the lack of rational intermediate structures and their replacement by an unchecked proliferation of unstable ones. A truer telos of history, then—one to which Hegel and Heidegger point, but which can be reached only by transforming them—must incorporate what Kolb calls "repulsion," the pull away from any single telos toward an indefinite plurality of them. History becomes "a variety of unserious postmodern stories," each of which will end up with a different view of ourselves. The recognition of this repulsion is then the final unblocking of circulation, for it enables a commerce among various stories of history—one occluded by Hegel's and Heidegger's overly generalized, and in that respect still too traditionally philosophical, views.

It is to a similar transformation of the concept of the telos of history that Robert Bernasconi also thinks Hegel and Heidegger point us. They "point" us, not in what they say, but in how their texts suggest they are to be read. In particular, Hegel's *Phenomenology* can, on Hegel's own terms, be fully comprehended only in a double reading which oscillates between annulling time—seeing the various stages through which consciousness moves in the course of the book as moments of the Absolute—and instating it—seeing them as historical (or psychological) epochs in their own right. For Heidegger, the *Phenomenology* calls for a reading which is ultimately attentive to Being and its history, seeing the *Phenomenology* as the expression not of history itself in some absolute sense, but as merely one more *Ereignis*, one more mittence of Being.

But here Bernasconi moves decisively beyond Heidegger himself, as well as beyond Hegel. First, he effects their *rapprochement*: even absolute history, the giant Hegelian narrative, is merely (as Heidegger might have it) only one story among others. Bernasconi, however, relativizes Hegel's story, not to Being, but to politics. Hegel is wrong in dismissing non-Western peoples as, to coin a word, "historyless" (as Africa is dismissed), and in relegating them to early phases of our own story (as China and India are relegated). But Heidegger, on Bernasconi's reading, is no right-minded multiculturalist. His modern epoch is, for all its uniqueness and incommensurability as a mittence of Being, itself part of a giant narrative: it is conditioned by the whole history of metaphysics from the Greeks on, and that segregates it from the experience of what we might call "un-metaphysical" peoples. As with Hegel, Heidegger views history as exclusively a property of the Western peoples.

The *Phenomenology* thus permits both an Hegelian and a Heideggerian reading, and each reading founds a community. These two communities are as distinct from each other as Hegelian "oscillation" is from Heideggerian *Ereignis*. But both are nonetheless exclusive of "barbarians" (or perhaps, as Heidegger's Nazi adventures in the thirties indicate, inclusive only of these).

In thus opening history from the confinement imposed upon it by Hegel and Heidegger themselves, Bernasconi moves close to Kolb. Both accounts show us how Hegel's and Heidegger's terms—particularly the terms with which they think the telos of history—must be transformed in order for their own basic projects to be carried through. And we see—for the first time—that such transformation can come about only by considering Hegel and Heidegger *together*. Each offered his account of history, and of the present age as its telos, as the only adequate account. Neither could, on his own explicit terms anyway, accommodate the fact that equally plausible, yet very different, accounts can be given, even by other German philosophy professors—to say nothing of "barbarians." Or by certain German poets: for the lack of unity in the moment to which Krell and Hölderlin point is, among other things, the continual possibility of new stories.

The issue of repulsion at the telos of history, of the resultant proliferation of new histories—and thus of new pasts—also opens up issues concerning what I will call the "pace" of history, the basic way in which it moves, and the relation of both the pace and telos of history to its "inception." For both Hegel and Heidegger, as Michel Haar points out, history has no possibilities not contained in its inception; and we might gloss this rather startling insight by noting that it shows how true Hegel and Heidegger are to the historicality of thinking. For in order to be transformative, a thinking must be directed upon history; and in order to be historical, a transformation must be related to the transformations preceding it. Conceived at a certain (philosophical) level of generality, this relation to the preceding is a general relation to what we might call an "inceptive dimension" of history—whether or not we believe that there really was a recoverable temporal beginning to historical transformation. The inception of history, like its telos, is a tool rather than a doctrine: it directs us to the possibility of history only as transformation, and bars us from going beyond history as *transformans* to discover a pure beginning, an originary *transformatum*.

For Hegel, then, history has developed into Spirit's recovery of itself, a recovery which (as Bernasconi and Kolb have shown) is just the ability of the modern world to determine its own possibilities. This ability has been latent in the inceptive side of history all along. But it is not one which earlier stages of history in any sense offered us. What offers it to us is the modern state, and what earlier stages offered us was only the modern state. Each stage of history, in other words, leads only to what comes next. When it has produced that it is exhausted and has nothing more to give, so that for Hegel the inception of history is (by definition) something over and done. For Heidegger, by contrast, the inception of history is (as Haar points out) still before us: it contains possibilities which we have not yet realized.

These two attitudes toward the end of history are, though Haar does not say so, derived from two different views of history's pace. For Hegel, history proceeds via a series of dialectical steps in which each stage degenerates into contradictions that it cannot resolve without abandoning its own basic principles. To resolve the problem, history must move to a further stage, one based on different principles, and when it does this the original stage is definitively over: a return to it could offer us nothing more than the resurrection of a set of problems that have already been solved. Thus, on Hegelian terms the unblocking of circulation at the telos of history can only lead to further dialectical distancing from the inception of history, to an increasing affirmation of just how far we are distanced from the inception, to the triumph of mediation.

For Heidegger, the pace of history is a series of catastrophic leaps from one way of forgetting Being to another. And because forgetting Being means forgetting, or occluding, the true nature of history, to forget Being is also to forget the true nature of previous epochs—all of which, as Heidegger shows again and again in his readings of the history of philosophy, fairly brim with unexploited possibilities. For Heidegger, then, further thinking will be a return to and affirmation of our unmediated closeness to the inception, of our willingness and need for it to grant us fundamental possibilities. If, for Hegel, there is no return to the Greeks, for Heidegger there is. But we must return to the Greek world differently, for it will inevitably offer different possibilities to us than it did to the Greeks themselves.

Catastrophic leaps thus omit something, which challenges us always to return to them. Dialectical contradiction, by contrast, engenders definitive death. The very different attitudes of Hegel and Heidegger to the inception of history thus follow, as I have suggested, from their very different views of the pace of history. And it is no coincidence that the "pace" each thinker assigns to history is nothing other than the most basic gesture of his own thought: the way each handles transformation. Thus, Hegel sees history as radical but continuous change, proceeding, like his own system, via the generation and resolution of just one contradiction at a time. Heidegger's standard procedure, by contrast, is to return any thinker to the finitude of his or her own epoch (what Janicaud calls "retrocession"); and history for him is correspondingly a series of such epochs, with nothing beyond them but distinguishing discontinuity.

In reading the basic nature of history off from their own thought in this way, Hegel and Heidegger seem to follow a not very respectable precedent set by Aristotle. In his *Categories*, Aristotle derived the basic structure of sensory Being—that it consisted in independent, stable things (rather than, as Plato had it, a spatiotemporal chaos that "participated in" such things). He derived it from an account of predication: what most basically *is* is what is neither "said of" other things (and hence presides in the stablility of a substrate) nor "present in" them (and hence is, at least relatively, independent of other things). Aristotle is generally held, here, to be reading the basic nature of reality off from the basic nature of language. In fact he cannot be doing that, for such a project would presuppose that the nature of language is better known to us than the nature of things. But no one has ever seen or heard "language." We hear people call out, joke, murmur soothingly, ask questions, and quite often make statements. We hear them do it in English, German, Luo, or Chinese. But "language" is something we never encounter; and its structures, if they exist, are difficult to ascertain. They are surely not so familiar that we can with confidence read them into other domains, and that is not what Aristotle (who has no word for "language") is doing.

It is only with Aristotle that predication becomes the basic phenomenon of speech.[8] And it does this because it is the basic gesture of his own thinking, which aims to be descriptively accurate, even at the price of all else. It is no surprise that it was Aristotle who broke with philosophical tradition by writing prose, rather than poems (Parmenides) or aphorisms (Heracleitus), or by trading in the flirting, joking, and questioning of Platonic dialogue. And it is nothing other than this, his own basic gesture, that Aristotle reads out into the cosmos itself.

I mention Aristotle here only to capture his deeper contrast with Hegel and Heidegger. They take themselves to be transforming their "object domain," not stating truths about it. Reading their own basic gestures back into the nature of history does not claim to be the constitution of a set of facts about history—any more than do their views that history has a telos. Rather, it is for each thinker one step, the fateful step, in an attempted *transformation* of history. Thus, the "pace" of history is not something exhibited by the sequence of events that actually happened, but is merely one way of transformatively interpreting history so as to advance one or another of its important characteristics. Hegel seeks to construe history as, if not rational, construable as rational. Heidegger seeks to construe it as, at each step, inexhaustibly reconstruable.

That Hegel and Heidegger seek to transform history not only explains the importance of their view of its pace. It also shows us why, as Haar points out, history for both of them is in the first instance (and without apology) the history of thought. For if thought transforms transformations—if it is *that which* transforms transformations—then that which transforms the most, the *primum transformans*, is thought. And thought is with this the *primum transformabilum* as well: for if its nature is exhausted by the transformations it effects, then that "nature" itself is radically unfixed—and cannot resist being transformed. The history of thought itself is thus not only paradigmatic for transformation in general, but most amenable to transformation—more so than science, whose perception of its own intrinsic transformations constitutes a crisis, and unlike, as we will see, politics and to some degree nature. It is the history of thought—of philosophy—that offers itself as a peculiarly important "object" for transforming thought. Transforming thought is, because of this, self-referential and to some degree, as Bernasconi has pointed out, self-enclosed. It relates to other domains only through intermediaries.

But those intermediaries are important—not just to transforming thought, but to all those who live and act in its wake. For the transformations which are exhibited in the history of philosophy, understood as creative transformation rather than as successive refutation, are not wholly different from the kinds of transformation exhibited elsewhere. And the concepts which transforming thought transforms and mourns are not wholly different from concepts that operate outside philosophy. Indeed, it has since Plato been a truism that philosophical concepts are "philosophical" only because they are the most basic of concepts, and that their basic nature is shown in both their use to articulate broad stretches of our experience, as well as in the fact that concepts which articulate more specific domains are, in one sense or another, "built upon" philosophical ones. Any transformation in philosophical conceptuality, unless it is *by definition* trivial, will *by definition* have effects on how people in a broad variety of other domains understand thsmelves and each other.

Art as Transformation

One such intermediary is art. Art for Hegel was, as I have suggested contemporary science may be, trapped in its inability to satisfy the demand for absolute truth imposed on it by a culture without religion. The Hegelian artist could at most—and then only if her art was "great"—articulate the values and spirit of her own people and epoch. Hegel's proclamation of the death of art—his relegation of art to something merely particular, instead of universal—was in effect transformed, by Heidegger following Nietzsche, into art's resurrection. For absolute truth, in Hegel's view, had become the prerogative and burden of philosophy, which meant that art was stripped of the prerogative and relieved of the burden. The analogy with science is perhaps not so much with contemporary science, now beset by the philosophy to which it has given birth, but to science at the dawn of the modern age. Empirical science could get under way only after it had been relieved of the burden of referring natural phenomena to the will of God. So art, liberated from supernatural demands by Nietzsche, is for Heidegger free to flourish in its particular sphere. Once philosophy had relieved itself of the burden of truth as correspondence, leaving it (and its aporias) over to science, it was necessarily to art—as well as to its own history—that it turned for its paradigm of transformation.

This goes together with the suspicion, only natural in the war-torn Europe of the last couple of centuries, that art is a, perhaps the, most productive agent of social transformation. It may be no accident that history's greatest attempt to bring about social transformation on the basis of theory succeeded only in superimposing one static economy of concepts and practices on other, older ones—so that the moment Eastern Europe "freed" itself from communism, much of it would resume ancient traditions of fratricide and feudalistic patriarchy, both lodged comfortably within the remarkable matrix of an anti-Semitism without Jews. (It is perhaps no irony that while all this was going on Western civilization was in fact being creatively demolished by African-American music, bursting in repeatedly under the guises of the blues, rock 'n' roll, other rocks from acid to slam, and rap.)

Art's aspiration to absolute status had not often made use of the term "truth," which has traditionally stood to signify the timeless goal of thought. Rather, art's grasp on absoluteness was assigned to the rubric of "beauty," and it is from beauty that Hegel and Heidegger, in the first instance, liberate art. It is because they restore art to truth that, as Jacques Taminiaux points out, art can be central for them. But the truth to which art is restored is not the kind of supratemporal truth which had been denied to it, first of all by Plato. It is rather a transformative truth, temporal through and through: a truth which (in Gadamer's word) is an "event" rather than a property. For Taminiaux, this transformative truth is visible, for both Hegel and Heidegger, as a complex set of circularities.

Aesthetic circularity is proclaimed by Heidegger along two axes. The first is the reciprocity between the artist and the work of art. Is the artist an artist for any other reason than that she creates works of art? And—yet—are works of art anything other than what artists create? The second circularity (connected with the first in ways Taminiaux explores) takes shape from the reciprocity between the work of art, on the one hand, and art itself, on the other. Do we not understand art out of our understanding of artworks? And—yet—how could we recognize artworks except in virtue of our knowledge of what art itself is?

These interlocking circles are not, Taminiaux argues, foreign to Hegel. In the traditional concept, which gives rise to Heidegger's first circle, the artist is a self-enclosed individual subject. The work of art, however, is a physical "object" with an audience: it addresses, and must be understood by, a community. The first Heideggerian circle thus works out, for Taminiaux, to what Hegel, in the *Phenomenology*, calls "externalization," and applies to language. Before I utter a thought, it is mine alone, and its tiniest details are present within my subjectivity. Once I give it utterance, the meaning of my words is whatever my audience takes it to be; I lose the privilege of my possession. Yet my words do not, for Hegel, wholly cease in this to be mine. Indeed, I become theirs: I am identified in terms of them, as the person who uttered them; they circle back to reform and recreate my very self.[9]

Similarly for the other circle. Philosophy of art must derive the nature of art from the concept alone, strictly from the internal resources of the system. But the system must on its part do justice to the individual works of art that it seeks to comprehend, and every step in such comprehension can—should—enrich and transform the system.[10] Hence, the oscillation that Bernasconi located in the philosophical reading of Hegel is, for Taminiaux, transformed into a circle in art's truthfulness.

For both Hegel and Heidegger, then, art works a double transformation. First, it transforms the individual (artist) into the community, constituting the community (audience) it articulates and reconstituting the individual as, not an isolated subject, but a truly communitarian self. Second, art transforms itself through the work, and the work through itself. Since for Hegel and Heidegger the work of art presents truth, truth itself turns out to be a series of intersecting transformations of individual, community, work of art, and art.

But the heterogeneity of the Hegelian and Heideggerian circles must not, for Taminiaux, be overlooked. The Hegelian circles, he argues, consistently privilege the present: they circle in upon and constitute a larger, indeed all-embracing whole, which is ultimately the Absolute itself. The Heideggerian circles, as I noted earlier, for Taminiaux partly perpetuate and partly undo Hegelian categories. To take one example: art for Heidegger is, like art for Hegel, "great art"; yet as Taminiaux argues in detail, Heidegger transforms this Hegelian category in such a way that we can never be sure—and for ontological reasons—whether a given work of art is or is not "great." Heidegger's account of art is thus neither a univocal critique of Hegel nor a reversal. Rather, to adapt Bernasconi's word, it *oscillates* between instating, or perpetuating, Hegelian categories and annulling those categories by throwing their epochal nature into relief, showing them as gifts of Being (rather than as moments of the Absolute).

Another way of showing hidden proximities between Hegel and Heidegger is taken by Martin Donougho. Criticizing characterizations of Hegel as a philosopher of beauty and Heidegger as a philosopher of the sublime, Donougho argues that the sublime is in fact the defining cornerstone of Hegel's theory of art. For our impulse to the sublime is closely connected with our impulse to religion, and art's inability (for Hegel) to capture the sublime shows forth its defining difference from religion. Art can, then, be known to be restricted to beauty only from a standpoint which has already appreciated the sublime—and Donougho's Hegel, like Taminiaux's Heidegger, comes to contest the category of great art even as he instates it. For great art, in Hegel's view, was the art of classical Greece, and that standpoint not only failed to capture the sublime, but did not even recognize its importance. It follows that great art, unacquainted with the sublime, could not know itself as great art. Hence, the meaning of great art was always underdetermined. The artist, not understanding what art was, was unable to express her individuality fully, or to understand her own creative activity. Great art thus never existed—at least not *as* great art. The name "art" is a device by which we can remember something that never really was.

As both Taminiaux and Donougho point out, art—like philosophy for Bernasconi—has a community creating function in Hegel and Heidegger. As Donougho sums this up, for Hegel art recollects what a people was; for Heidegger, it reminds them of what they are called to be. In both cases, and with all the divergences I specified earlier in connection to Haar, art is a recovery of origins. Community, which is conditional upon shared origins, is thus constituted by a certain sort of memory, a memory which transforms in certain ways. It is in this social function of art that Sophocles's *Antigone* becomes exemplary. For here, precisely—and in a notable reversal to Aristotle's favorite play, *Oedipus the King*—the protagonist's solidarity with the community is achieved, not destroyed, by memory as the transforming recovery of origins.

Antigone achieves that solidarity, not merely by memorializing Polyneices, but by allowing her act of memory to be what Creon declares it must be: a political act, indeed one of suicidal rebellion. Her act thus becomes a sacrifice, one which Dennis Schmidt explores in its Hegelian and Heideggerian transformations. For Hegel, Schmidt argues, Antigone's sacrifice is, predictably, a reversal; for Heidegger, it is a "countermovement," one which does not pave the way for any larger reconciliation of family and state but which remains on its own level, significant in its own way.

Or, rather: for Heidegger (in *An Introduction to Metaphysics*), what is significant is not Antigone's death but Sophocles's play; and it is significant because it shows, for Heidegger, that the poetic language of tragedy has a pivotal role to play in the overcoming of metaphysics. Because the language which articulates the polis is seen to be that of a countermovement significant on its own unique level, politics itself bears upon and is borne by continual countermovements. Law itself cannot simply endure and prevail, but finds itself enmeshed in an unending series of aporias and contestations. But Antigone the person—the woman never discussed by Heidegger—shows, in the mere fact that he (and

Hegel) discusses her play, that an individual act can take on universal significance, can be something that everybody responds to. And this means that art presents us with possibilities, not only of contestation, but of community—possibilities that involve an essential sacrifice.

Heidegger's curious omission of Antigone from his reading is approached from a different angle by Kathleen Wright, who traces the different positions allotted to gender in Heidegger's successive readings of the play. Heidegger begins, in 1935, with what amounts to a reversal of the Hegelian reading. Where for Hegel the *Antigone* concretizes the supreme ethical opposition solely in terms of sexual difference, Heidegger attempts a transparently gender-neutral reading. In 1942, he tacitly reintroduces gender—but not in a Hegelian sense, as the supreme force governing Antigone's being and actions. Rather, Heidegger stresses Antigone's rejection, not only of Creon and the whole "fearsomely clever" (*deinon*) apparatus of male domination, but her sister Ismene as well. Neither faithfully feminine nor terrifyingly masculine, Antigone thus—on Heidegger's second reading—achieves, we may say, the neutrality simply presupposed in the first reading. Her action is governed by no law, gendered or other; she is prior to the ethos of the family as to the laws of the state. Her countermovement shines forth its meaning as do the stones of the Greek temple on John Sallis's reading, and in this Antigone becomes a paradigm of Heideggerian poetic dwelling itself: the pure creation of meaning out of struggle with world.

And in this, Wright notes, Heidegger's Antigone falls victim to a problem, not with herself, but with Heidegger: his long-remarked inability to produce anything resembling an adequate ethics or social philosophy. For the realm of poetic dwelling which Antigone comes to occupy is too far removed from anything specific—gender, law, and especially the technical hybris of the state—to be able even to criticize it.

Science—Politics—Nature

The history of interpretations and misinterpretations of Hegel and Heidegger—two almost coextensive domains—shows that their thought is particularly amenable to transforming interpretation. Indeed, like certain subatomic phenomena in quantum physics, the writings of Hegel and Heidegger can be said to have no meaning until they are interpreted: they function, to use a term I have introduced elsewhere, as "poetic elicitors."[11] I suggested above that history in general, and particularly the history of philosophy (as the prehistory of transforming thought), is susceptible of such treatment. But such is not the case for all domains: thought which sees itself as transforming transformations, rather than mirroring reality, seems likely to be of limited scope. The main effect of its introduction may be, in fact, to limit the claims of certain other types of thinking (such as induction and deduction) to be coextensive with reason itself. Among the many areas of traditional philosophical concern where transforming thought seems likely to encounter its limits, I will briefly discuss two: politics and nature.

It is, as Hegel knew, folly for a philosopher to approach the political realm as strictly a series of transformations, to be transformed in turn by one's own thought. This is shown by his tortured refusal, in the preface to the *Philosophy of Right*, to dictate to the state how it should be, or indeed to attempt anything other than the philosophical "comprehension" of its rational core. But even there, it is philosophy which, if it does not kill the modern state, ratifies its death, rendering that death public and thus transforming the state's demise—if not the state itself. For when Hegel refers to philosophy painting its "grey on grey," he is perhaps not thinking of the oil on canvas of a portrait. As he writes, "with grey on grey it [the state] cannot be rejuvenated."[12] But no portrait, except perhaps Dorian Grey's, ever claimed rejuvenative power. The brush in question is more that of a cosmetician, painting directly on the face of the state. For if portraits cannot rejuvenate their subjects, cosmetics claim little else. Hegelian political philosophy is possible, as nontransformative, only because the state cannot be transformed, because it is already dead. But even there, philosophy at least embalms.

That transformative thinking can attain no direct transformation of the political sphere is something that Heidegger, too, would learn. His own efforts, of course, involved gravitating to that political movement which, in the Germany of the thirties, promised the most radical transformation of all—a transformation that, even in 1933, explicitly included abandoning the entirety of our ancient heritage of ideas concerning freedom, justice, humanity, and common decency. Where Hegel had concluded that philosophy does not interfere with political processes but merely ratifies their demise, Heidegger's infamous "Rectoral Address" undertakes not merely to meditate upon the university, but to organize it by transforming its current transformations. Having articulated the central concept of his entire Nazi engagement—a semi-Nietzschean version of *Wissenschaft*—Heidegger then says: "Science in this sense must become the formative power of the corporate body of the German university."[13] This "must," of course, is grounded in nothing more than a philosophical megalomania that is saved from being genuine hybris only by its shallowness and pomposity. But it expresses a desire to transform political reality directly, for the German university is (again, by none other than Heidegger himself) set at the center of German society.

And all this "merely" transforms a transformation that is already under way:

> But we do not need to begin by awakening followers. The German student body is already on the march. *What* it is seeking is those leaders through whom it will raise its own determination to the status of a grounded, knowing truth, and posit it in the clarity of meaning-bestowing, effective word and work.[14]

The problem here, I take it, is not so much with the idea that thinking is to transform political realities as with the immediacy of the transformation that Heidegger proclaims, and with its specific content. I argued above that when transforming thought directs itself upon its own history, it can have effects on other domains as well, through intermediaries such as art and science. There is no reason why this should not hold for social and political realities. The problem is that the road to such transformation is too long to be overseen, least of all by the philosopher who sets out on it. The most that the philosopher can do is (1) not claim to see further down that road than she does, and (2) not advance transformations that are foreseeably evil in their effects.

More clearly than any other philosopher, Heidegger is guilty of both transgressions. As the passages I have cited from the "Rectoral Address" show, he seeks there an immediate transformation of the social sphere through philosophy, i.e., a transformation which he (as one of the "leaders" German youth is seeking) can oversee and guide. And the specific transformation he seeks—of intellectual life away from accommodation and consensus into *Kampf* and *Streit*—is obviously evil, even if it did not lead directly to Auschwitz and Lidice. The lesson is perhaps that while transforming thought has limited application in the sphere of politics, we must take care—here so near the outset of the enterprise—not to draw those limits too definitively. A further example is furnished by that realm which, it seems, is farthest removed from the spheres of transformation that transformative thought could hope to transform: nature itself.

For Hegel, the matter is clear. When he says that nature is "recalcitrant to the Concept," he means precisely that it is incapable of radical transformation. Natural laws and general truths will remain just what they are; indeed, the main contrast between the animal and the human species is precisely that the former does not change, but is passed uniformly to each new generation. It is only the human meaning of natural phenomena—their locus and function as centerpiece and occasion for various social practices—that can transform itself. But the line between "human practice" and "natural phenomenon" is not an entirely easy one. In his essay in this collection, John Sallis follows the Hegelian history of stone, for example, from its use in the pyramids to the soaring lightness of the Gothic cathedral, in which stone becomes a hymn to everything that stone is not: a paean, in particular, to the fight for heaven that soared above the entire Middle Ages. In each phase of that history, stone points toward pastness—by being incorporated into religion, for example, it points to the pastness of both nature and art—and to the future, as a visible promise of redemption.

Sallis transforms this Hegelian transformation of the historical transformations of stone by following it with Heidegger's even deeper transformation of the stones of the temple at Paestum. As Sallis shows, on Heidegger's account the stones shine forth the irrefragable darkness of their interiors, as they also shine forth the sky, the air, and natural surroundings. They are themselves preceded by nothing: not by nature, or by Spirit, or by truth itself. As we will see Heidegger's Antigone to be in Wright's reading, the stones of the temple are a pure opening of possibility, which transform *themselves* into nothing less than nature itself—even when, like the stones of the Jewish cemetary in Prague, they testify to an unrecoverable past and an unredeemable evil.

If totalizing claims on behalf of transforming thought are suspect, premature declaration of its limits may be even more so. Stone, on Sallis's account, is unable to resist the transformations of thought because the line between nature and Spirit, on the one hand, and between nature and Being, on the other, is a hard one to draw. And this highlights some ambiguities in my brief discussions of science and politics. For if science has lost all "essence" save for what is fixed for it by philosophy of science, who can deny that it has entered a period of radical and potentially fruitful transformation—one in which philosophy of science is already beginning to transform science itself? And if Hegel's attempt to "comprehend" the state without changing it was in fact grounded in the state's demise, which it turned out to ratify cosmetically, who is to say that thought cannot transform a situation in which politics is alive, one in which political realities are already transforming themselves, without falling into Heideggerian lunacies?

Transforming Thought

Back when everything was a thing, we thought we knew what thought was: it was our effort to respect the stability and independence of reality by representing it in an eternal mirror. But the mind, even collectively, is no mirror; to view it as such is to mistake the basketball court for the basketball game. Stability is not ultimate anywhere; even if things—some things—do not change, our knowledge of them does and will. The unchanging object cannot be empirically freed from our changing perceptions of it and becomes an ideal construct, going the way of Kantian noumena. It is transformation which threatens to confront us everywhere as basic.

With all this, the nature of thought has to change as well. Instead of mirroring reality, thought must transform itself into the transformation of transformations. I have suggested that the essays in this volume, among their wealth of topics and insights, can provide a series of indications of what the new thinking (and the new philosophy) will look like. By way of conclusion, I will summarize some of these.

First, thinking which transforms transformations operates on certain "things" in the world: on transformations already underway. Among the manifold transformations which are coming to present themselves always and everywhere, two types appear to be exemplary for such thinking. One is art, which provides the most effective and complete examples of transformation to be found anywhere, and is hence *exemplarily transformative.* The other is history, in particular the history of philosophy, which as a history of thought is itself allied to transforming thinking in ways that make it *exemplarily transformable.* The conjunction of history and art across the present essays is thus no accident, but part of the "logic" of transforming thought. As philosophy in the age of metaphysics directed itself primarily on the cosmos, and in modernity primarily upon the human mind and eventually language, so transforming thought directs itself primarily (but not exclusively) upon art and its own history.

If science is (and will continue to be) the study of things, it is art which—as its Greek name, *poiesis,* signifies—transforms. In art, as transforming thought takes it, the sensory (work of art) is transformed into conceptuality ("art" itself), individuals are transformed into communities, and communities are constituted and reconstituted. Part of the business of transforming thought is to aid these transformations in a variety of ways: to *highlight* their basic gestures (as Hegel and Heidegger highlight certain aspects of the *Antigone,* the temple stones, and their own readers); to *juxtapose* such gestures (as the present essays do with Hegelian *Aufhebung* and Heideggerian retrocession); to *expose* limits and unwarranted stabilities in each. In so doing, transforming thought brings us together with, through, and around art in an equal variety of ways.

The modern heir to *poiesis,* poetry, has not entirely lost the sense of its Greek name, and serves for Hegel and Heidegger—and for transforming thought—as exemplary art. And because Greek art has also not lost the breadth of scope suggested by its name, Greek poetry becomes also exemplary: Hegel, Heidegger, and the transformative world generally home in on the *Antigone* as a founding document.

The second exemplary field for transforming thought is history, the record of past transformations. But not, again, just any transformations: though Hegel and Heidegger take themselves to be talking about "history" in general, the history they deal with has already been understood to be the history of thought. For if transforming thought is simply human transformation which has become aware of itself, then thought is itself exemplary of transformation. Because its past transformations are the ones which have resulted in the set of transforming conceptualities that transforming thought today can bring to bear on anything, they are particularly amenable to further transformation by such thought. And so transforming thought directs itself upon its own history, even upon those aspects of its history that conceived of their own transformative power as nothing more than the critique of argument and the solution of problems.

The modes and standards for transforming thought are, as the essays show, diverse. In general, we can say that transforming thought cannot treat the transformations it transforms as "things" (the reason for my scare quote a few paragraphs back, as well as for these). Hegel and Heidegger—and Schmidt and Wright—do not see the *Antigone* as a thing to be reasoned about accurately or not—at least, not always. Though accuracy to the object has its place, *Antigone* is for them basically a set of transformations—in language, in narrative, in drama, in its audience, and so on—which predate Sophocles's play (based as it is on legend) and which are still going on. The transforming thought of all four thinkers seeks to play into and enhance these tranformations, spinning them into sometimes new directions.

Hegel's Antigone is not Sophocles's Antigone, or Heidegger's; but she is Antigone. Transforming thought not only does not treat its objects as inherently stable; it does not take itself to be independent of them. Antigone is, we may say, within Hegel, in that she is captured by his categories; but Hegel is no less within her, in that she helps define those categories and promptly escapes them, moving onward to new encounters and transformations. Hegel's *Phenomenology*, to use an example from the history of philosophy, similarly gains even temporary form only in being interpreted, and the shapes it takes depend on the interpreter. Transformative thinking, when directed upon its own history, is transformative reading, in which reader and writer not only collaborate to create the text anew, but actually blend into one another via a sort of intellectual addition of velocities.

Thus, to take a point from Janicaud, phenomenology—the most subjective and individualized of discourses—for Hegel and Heidegger transforms itself immediately (i.e., in being read) into ontology, the most objective and depersonalized. And in the reading of the *Phenomenology*, as Bernasconi points out, not only does the external material of Western intellectual history get appropriated and internalized by the reader, but the very process of appropriation reveals itself to be a sort of memory of one's own self.

Beginning from transformations already underway and not entirely separate from itself, transforming thought lacks fixed starting points. As I have noted, even the transformations it works are themselves transformations of earlier transformations it has undergone. It thus avoids, as Taminiaux points out for Heidegger and Hegel, the great Scylla and Charybdis of modern philosophy, rationalism and empiricism. It takes its "beginning," neither from sensory experience nor from intellectual certainty, but either from the transformation of each into the other (as in art) or from an indeterminate realm, such as the historical text, which hovers between both.

Transforming thought has no definite ending points, either. The exploration of Hegel and Heidegger as the two basic figures of the epoch of transformation has only just begun and will doubtless someday stop, but it will never reach any serious conclusion. For transforming thought will never be able to confute them (as Kant confuted a metaphysics based on Plato and Aristotle). Nor can it hope to reach a point at which it has learned all it can from them, because each lived body of thought is continually transforming itself to yield new insights. The same goes for the *Antigone*, or the Greek temple, or these essays.

The only overall goal that could be assigned transforming thought, and it is a thinly general one, is perhaps the development of communities. Certainly that is what both art and philosophy, we saw, do for Hegel and Heidegger, and it is the single most basic thread uniting everything that I have written here. For to join a community is to play oneself into a story already under way, to join and unite with a series of human transformations—often of just the kind that art and philosophy represent. Hence, transforming thought can only be an "essay"—not in the sense of a trial or attempt, but in the more ancient one of an *ex-actum*, a doing-out from something which leads not to sure knowledge and the solution of problems, but to communities beyond oneself.

Finally, transforming thought proceeds, at the moment, in two very different modes. In its Hegelian dispensation, such thought transforms transformations into dialectical reversals, presenting them as step-by-step transformations, however radical they may prove to be in the end. In its

Heideggerian acceptation, transforming thought operates retrocessively. It situates specific transformations within wider economies which are set in place, not via a series of step-by-step reversals but all (more or less) at once, in what Heidegger calls an *Augenblick.* The two modes complement one another in a larger project of community. Hegelian transformation provides a way to see the past as truly past, and our common distance from it as increasing; Heidegger shows how to find our way back to it, to see it as speaking directly to us rather than across intervening history, and as offering us new possibilities.

The larger project is one of transformation as temporalized interpretation, the fragile capture of the logos by time. In contrast to "presentistic" modes of thought, geared to truth and predication, Hegel and Heidegger teach that every logos has a *before*—the contradictions or problems that it solves—and an *after,* the unthought possibilities it conceals.

In responding to a logos, we join it: we make its past and future our own. The temporalized interpretations which transform thought thus set us *reflectively* between our past and our future. The problems and the possibilities of the words we hear and speak even as children open us up to communities underway and make us truly human. They situate individuals within communities, and communities within global horizons of problem and possibility (and only a globe has horizons!). They—the essays in this book, together with the Hegel and Heidegger those essays so multifariously transform and explore—are pathways out of the *impasse* of truth and into some of the most important tasks confronting today's thinkers, who seek to find their ways in worlds transforming.

1

Heidegger-Hegel: An Impossible "Dialogue"?

Dominique Janicaud
Translated by Nina Belmonte

In any approach to thinking the relationship of Heidegger's thought to that of Hegel, a certain series of texts inevitably present themselves. Already at Marburg, Heidegger devoted some seminars to Hegel (1925–26: *Hegel: Logik;* 1927: *Die Ontologie des Aristoteles und Hegels Logik,* not to mention two other seminars wherein Hegel was also most likely the subject). No doubt further manuscript notes exist, but volume 32 of the *Gesamtausgabe* offers only one somewhat later text: the lectures held at Freiburg in 1930–31 on *Hegels Phänomenologie des Geistes.* Indeed, this last volume, along with § 82 of *Sein und Zeit* and the *Grundprobleme der Phänomenologie* taught at Marbourg in 1927,[1] offer plenty of material for a paper. Still, I believe such a restriction to be undesirable, for reasons having to do with content.

In the first place, volume 32 is brief and incomplete, offering a commentary which almost exactly follows the opening sections of the *Phenomenology of Spirit.* It does not engage the debate with Hegel in its full scope—which will be developed and explicated masterfully by mostly later texts of Heidegger. Furthermore, in § 4 of this volume, Heidegger himself warns that: "The *Phenomenology* has nothing to do with a phenomenology of consciousness as currently understood in Husserl's sense—either in its theme or in the manner of its treatment, or above all in terms of its basic questioning and intention."[2]

Taking heed of Heidegger's warning, it is better to put aside for the moment—at the price of having to return to it later—this "false friend" phenomenology, in order to address directly the difficult question of the relationship of Heidegger's thinking to Hegel's philosophy.

This question has already been abundantly treated, first of all by Heidegger himself. Obviously, then, we must begin with the Heideggerian texts, though we need not necessarily restrict ourselves to them. Studies of the Heidegger-Hegel case have until now tended to be too limited to the question of whether Heidegger succeeded in "freeing" himself from Hegelian thought, as if the status of the latter were definitively settled and duly noted. Not only did Heidegger never treat Hegel as a "dead dog";[3] he made Hegel his partner in an open-ended "battle of the giants" concerning Being. There is a way then to take Heidegger at his word and give the floor to Hegel's thinking: a thinking still alive with thoughtful resource, defying the flux of time.

It is a matter now of attempting, across the years, a *dialogue.* Not, obviously, between two persons who can no longer speak, though not so chronologically far from one another (only fifty-eight years separate the death of Hegel from the birth of Heidegger). Rather, it would be a dialogue between two fundamental philosophical positions, two essential bodies of thought. At the beginning of his *Nietzsche,* Heidegger wrote that "the name of the thinker stands as the title for *the matter* of his thinking."[4] This holds equally for Hegel as it does for Heidegger himself.

All that remains before truly *beginning* is to set forth the question of dialogue and its rules. Everyone knows how difficult it is to organize and hold an authentic dialogue, and *a fortiori* a philosophical dialogue. It requires listening to the other, then replying, and developing a mutual understanding, *synousia,* as Heidegger himself indicated citing Plato's *Seventh Letter.*[5] In the present case, we have the advantage of possessing the opening of a dialogue with Hegel, proposed as such by Heidegger himself at the beginning of "The Onto-theo-logical Constitution of Metaphysics": "This seminar made an attempt to begin a conversation with Hegel [*ein Gespräch mit Hegel zu beginnen*]."[6] It is only logical to take up Heidegger's proposal and see how he sets the dialogue in motion. Following this, it will be necessary—lacking the power to give voice to Hegel himself in some fantastic "dialogue of the dead"—to reread certain Hegelian texts, watching for their agreement or disagreement. We will look in these texts for a kind of a thoughtful reply, wherein the same matter, *Sache,* is in question. Let us not anticipate the outcome of this dialogue, nor the evolution of its rules. There is always an element of drama in any essential exchange; let us keep the suspense.

And if the suspense is particularly intense, it is because the very possibility of the dialogue appears to be in danger—despite the "good intentions" displayed by Heidegger. How does one articulate a dialogue between philosophical positions so diametrically opposed regarding such issues as Being, time and history, truth, and philosophy itself? Being, for Hegel, is the most immediate and abstract of concepts; it is overcome in the beginning of the *Logic*. For Heidegger, on the contrary, it asserts itself as that which most merits thinking. For Hegel, time is only "the negative unity of self-externality"[7] and history proves to be the necessary process of Spirit's return to itself. For Heidegger, time is the transcendental horizon of the question of Being; and history reveals itself as the "free succession [*freie Gefolge*]" of destinal mittences, without any rational necessity. Hegelian truth is a speculative product; Heideggerian truth is disclosure, *Unverborgenheit*. Hegelian philosophy takes on the Fichtean ambition of constructing a science [*Wissenschaft*]. Heidegger, on the other hand, claims that philosophy must redescend "to the poverty of its provisional essence";[8] philosophy as metaphysics is estranged from the thinking (the truth) of Being.

This reminder allows us to reevaluate what is at stake. Heidegger issues an almost impossible challenge by his offer of "a dialogue with Hegel," an extremely difficult challenge to meet. This is further reason, and let us emphasize it, for taking Heidegger at his word and following, first of all, along the path he himself proposes. I will call this first phase that of "retrocession," a term which I will justify in what follows.

Retrocession

A dialogue is only possible in the first place if the partner is *recognized*. How is Hegel recognized by Heidegger? More radically than for any other philosopher, characteristics of bibliography, psychology, and style are eliminated: with the name, "Hegel," says Heidegger, we think of the culmination [*Vollendung*] of philosophy.[9] And since philosophy and metaphysics are synonyms, Hegel indeed represents the final achievement of Western metaphysics, that is, of the expression, full development, and exhaustion of its internal possibilities. However, there is a text in *Vorträge und Aufsätze* where Heidegger specifies that Hegel represents only the *beginning* of the completion, the most profound level being achieved later by Nietzsche.[10] How is this discrepancy to be resolved? Heidegger's *Nietzsche* gives us to understand that Hegel closes the epoch of modern philosophy (characterized by the tension between will and *cogitatio*) and that he is in this sense the *thematic completion* of metaphysics, a thematic completion that cannot be reversed. Nietzsche, by contrast, with his undertaking to overturn Platonism and all Platonic-Christian "values," prepares, with the aid of the will to power, a new age for the West, an age of globalized technology.

The term *Vollendung* being thus clarified (and not to be confused with a simple end or cessation [*Ende*] of philosophical activity), what are the conditions of the dialogue opened by Heidegger? At first glance, the "dialogue" proposed by "The Onto-theo-logical Constitution of Metaphysics" offers only a juxtaposition of points of view ("For Hegel . . . For us . . ."). This is so, particularly with regard to our third question ("What, then and now, is the character of this dialogue?"). Heidegger's response to this question is, in effect, that:

> For Hegel, the conversation with the earlier history of philosophy has the character of *Aufhebung*, that is, of the mediating concept in the sense of an absolute foundation.
>
> For us, the characture of the conversation with the history of thinking is no longer *Aufhebung*, but the step back [*der Schritt zurück*].[11]

Doesn't this set up something like the a quasifactual opposition which, while having the pedagogical merit of neatness, nevertheless is reduced to a simple contrast? Certainly it is not "dialectizable"—that is, recoupable by the Hegelian adversary—but neither does it appear to make any effort to *understand* the speculative dialectic, nor to discuss or refute it. Juxtaposition is not dialogue.

But this first impression is not enough; more subtly, Heidegger's attitude is responding to a genuine dialogical strategy, made possible by taking into consideration the matter of thinking [*die Sache des Denkens*]. "A conversation with a thinker can be concerned only with the matter of thinking."[12] Thus, *not only* does Heidegger make the effort to address what is at stake in Hegelian thought, and to characterize it most scrupulously ("For Hegel, the matter of thinking is: Thinking as such");[13] he formulates an *additional* requirement that seems to guarantee even more solidly an authentic dialogue. "Therefore, when we attempt a thinking conversation with Hegel, we must speak with him not just about the same matter [*Sache*], but about the same matter in the same way [*Weise*]."[14] Heidegger immediately specifies that the same is not the identical. But is this enough? What is this common *Weise*? This is defined a bit later as thinking the matter in question historically [*geschichtlich*].[15] Thus we have the same matter (thinking as such) and a common approach, this way of thinking Being in its history. But why *Geschichte* rather than any of the other essential points brought up previously (truth, philosophy)? Because to recognize that the Hegelian enterprise was a historical one is to uncover the dialogue that *Hegel himself carried on with the history of Western thought.* The dialogue *with* Hegel leads back to the dialogue *of* Hegel with philosophy's past.[16] This play of reference is the deployment of the sameness of a historicality [*Geschichtlichkeit*] that is metaphysics, at the heart of which and from out of which different approaches and gatherings of (steps back from) Being might be articulated.

Having thus clarified Heidegger's hermeneutical effort, we are better equipped to understand the *Schritt züruck,* the "step back" which Heidegger places in opposition to the Hegelian *Aufhebung.* This is not principally a retreat *away from* Hegel, but rather *into the essentials* of Hegel—into that which, at the core of his thinking, responds to the fundamental injunction of metaphysics regarding the modality of its historial completion. The point of this step back is not to abandon the site of Western metaphysics (the thinking of the truth of Being), but on the contrary to assume it, to reappropriate it in its essence [*Wesen*]: difference as such, unthought by metaphysics itself, though lodged in its very center.

Moreover, it should be noted that the spatial metaphorization, by which Heidegger puts into opposition a surpassing that overcomes [*die Aufhebung*] and a backward movement that redescends to the "provisional essence" [*der Schritt zurück*], does not allow him to fare any better than Hegel on his own turf (indeed, to surpass Hegel would still be Hegelian). It leads him, rather, to complete and to deepen the thinking of the Being of beings. "Retrocession" thus has the advantage of indicating simultaneously the stepping back and the restitution which reappropriates. The *Schritt zurück* does not think against *Aufhebung,* nor particularly *better* than it. Rather, the *Schritt zurück* restores to *Aufhebung* a depth of field which it surpassed from the beginning. Compelled toward finding the truth of beings, the dialectical-speculative movement cannot give attention to the ontological difference as such. It lives off of this difference, but excludes it from the very start, completing in this way the metaphysical forgetting of Being. In effect, in the "The Doctrine of Essence," difference as such falls back into absolute identity.[17] It appears impossible to tarry with it, to meditate on difference itself. By thinking the truth of Being as *process,* Hegel is perhaps impoverishing history, and must perhaps put epochality itself under the yoke of a universal method—which *levels* difference.[18]

In the second major part of the seminar on "The Onto-theo-logical Constitution of Metaphysics," Heidegger seems almost to forget Hegel, treating essentially the onto-theo-logical structure of metaphysics itself. However, so little does he in fact forget Hegel, that he utilizes the speculative proposition "The beginning is the result" to link Being as absolute *prius* (God) to the project of universal and categorical comprehension (ontology). Hegel's logic is thus reinterpreted as an *onto-theo-logic* in which the immanent *structure* of all metaphysics is unfolded. We find here the final act of retrocession: the appropriation of Hegel (and for Hegel) into the essence of metaphysics, which is realized in the comprehension of the speculative dialectic as the pinnacle of the onto-theo-logical structure. "Now we understand the name 'logic' in the essential sense which includes also the title used by Hegel."[19] Hegel is not forgotten. Quite the inverse; the Hegelian forgetting of the ontological site of difference is rememorialized [*remémoré*] in such a way that—through the mediation of *Geschichtlichkeit*—Hegel is rescued from an abstract and unthought eternity, from an excessively automatic process of "negation-sublation" on behalf of a retrocession of the enigmatic and destinal profundity of the unity of Western thought. Thus Heidegger has successfully accomplished (in a way which literally goes beyond understanding and its representations) the program which he set for himself at the beginning of the seminar in question. "But inasmuch as Hegel's thinking belongs to a period of history (this does not mean at all that it belongs to the past), we are attempting to think of Being, as Hegel thought of it, in the same manner, that is, to think of it historically [*geschichtlich*]."[20]

Beyond the fine "performance," we should applaud the profound coherence, the success of the initial project, the capture of his adversary in thought (him who Heidegger called his "opponent" [*Gegner*]) in the nets of a dialogue where, following in Hegel's footsteps, Heidegger *restores to Hegel* his own thinking, with a nondialectizable "supplement," an unreconcilable difference-in-sameness.

I have chosen "The Onto-theo-logical Constitution of Metaphysics" because its elliptical rigor and cogency seem exemplary. But the same retrocession is inscribed in other texts devoted to Hegel: the admirable "Hegels Begriff der Erfahrung," where the between-two [*dia*], on the basis of which the dialogue of natural consciousness with absolute knowledge operates, is clarified in terms of the more fundamental between-two, the *skepsis*, a look at the absoluteness of the absolute (which is *already* near to us).[21] Thinking the ontological *difference* restores the full dimension of this experience of the difference between the present and presence, which is the experience of consciousness or, by another name, the "phenomenology of Spirit." In "Hegel and the Greeks," the discussion of Hegel's interpretations of key words in Greek philosophy reveals the historial character of the dialogue Hegel opened with the founders of philosophy. The reversal of the Hegelian "not yet" reveals that the horizon of the "abstract universal" wherein Hegel believes he can contain Greek thought conceals precisely the unthought of *Aletheïa*. The "truth" of Greek philosophy does not reside, neither solely nor unilaterally, in its dialectical overcoming by absolute subjectivity, but in the essence of truth itself, immanent but unperceived in the Hegelian view which fixes Greece in the frame of its "beauty."[22]

One could comment at length on each of these essays. Rather, I will make one final, necessary point before "giving the floor" to Hegel. Essentially, this retrocession, so careful and attentive, to the site of the unthought in Hegelian philosophy has only been possible by virtue of a rupture, a fundamental rending effected in *Being and Time*,[23] the cutting edge of which is recalled at the end of the 1930–31 lectures on the *Phenomenology*:

> For *Hegel*, Being (infinity) is also the essence of time. For *us*, time is the original essence of Being. These are not theses which can be simply played against each other antithetically [*nicht einfach antithetisch gegeneinander ausspielbare Thesen*]. Rather the term *essence* [*Wesen*] says something fundamentally different each time, precisely because Being is understood differently.[24]

Thus, as early as the 1930s (it would seem, from the time of *Sein und Zeit*), Heidegger is formulating a fundamental thinking which is totally distinct [*grundverschieden*] from Hegel's and which, as a *thesis*, is (in Heidegger's expression) the exact opposite [*das Gegenteil*] of Hegelian thought.[25] However, the irreducibility of this radical difference is first of all *affirmed* with all the violence of which Heidegger is capable; only after and from out of this irreducibility is the reason for it made apparent and its understanding developed in the "retrocession" of the truth of Hegelian thought. This is clarified particularly in such texts as "The Anaximander Fragment" or the protocol of the seminar "On Time and Being." The two theses on Being, that of Hegel and that of Heidegger, are irreducible one to the other, irreconcilable (dialectically or otherwise) because they correspond to different epochal mittences [*Schickungen*]. Hegel completes the "illuminating withdrawing" of Being in its modern epoch; Heidegger reveals epochality itself in its indecision between technology and "the West."[26] On the other hand, the Hegelian absolute is an *Ereignis*, but when viewed with regard to *Ereignis as such*, is revealed to be "finite," no longer belonging to the history of Being and remaining open to other destinies, for the present unthinkable.[27]

Thus, in this play for "thoughtful recognition" there is something of a fight to the death in which Heidegger strikes first and right away reduces Hegel to silence by "telling" him, substantially (I am transposing a sentence from the protocol of the seminar "On Time and Being"): "Thus, for Hegel there is no *question* of Being [*Seinsfrage*], and no such question can even arise."[28] But it is precisely from out of a *Seinsfrage* that the historiality of the destinies of Being allows us to reposit the question of the *historicity of the forms of Being* and to situate the return to Hegelian metaphysics at the center of the greatest task—the "deflection" [*Verwindung*] of metaphysics as such.

Difference and sameness having thus been recalled, the logic of our project (which takes up that of the Heideggerian project and pushes it to its ultimate consequences) is now to let the Hegelian texts "speak" so that the dialogue might not be the work of only one of its participants, and so that all "good intentions" might be put to the test.

Contradiction

This moment is particularly delicate, given the dissymetry of the dialogue. One of the two protagonists—even if he is no longer with us—had the last word, at least chronologically. It is Heidegger who has "staged" the dialogue. This fact must be taken into account, but it is not an insurmountable obstacle if we remain aware of the following hermeneutical limits. It would be not only illegitimate, but superfluous, to imagine what Hegel *redivivus* would say of Heidegger; our only recourse can be to Hegel's texts. Let us see what their speculative reprisal permits us to think regarding the various points raised earlier.

First of all, as to the conditions of dialogue with another body of thought, the primary reference text—which Heidegger cites[29]—is evidently the passage from the *Science of Logic* on the refutation [*Widerlegung*] of Spinoza and Kant.[30] Its principal formulation is famous: "The genuine refutation must penetrate the opponent's stronghold and meet him on his own ground."[31] Hegel adds that we must recognize first of all Spinoza's view of substance as necessary in order—later—to raise it, from out of itself [*aus sich selbst*] to a higher point of view, that of the concept revealed as the true "realm of freedom." Given that Heidegger himself set the rules for his dialogue with Hegel precisely according to this Hegelian prescription, there is no disagreement here. And for this reason: Heidegger effectively begins with Hegel's *strength*, his "matter itself" [*Sache selbst*], to think thought as such and to think it in its essential relation to history (that is, *geschichtlich*).

Everything must be reexamined, however, with regard to what happens "later." Heidegger simultaneously applies the Hegelian program for refutation and is totally unfaithful to it. The reprisal reveals a betrayal, the one indissociable from the other. Heidegger indeed raises Hegelian metaphysics to its "truth" (its *Wesenraum*), but by means of a turn (completely unexpected from the Hegelian point of view) toward the unthought. "But only what has already been thought prepares what has not yet been thought, which enters ever anew into its abundance."[32] This recourse to a thinking which separates the "already thought" from the "unthought" can only appear, from an Hegelian point of view, as a *regression* into the abstract assumption that the provisional is ontologically richer than the development.

This formal agreement which turns into (fundamental) disagreement is equally obvious regarding history and historicity. *Geschichte* appears to be the privileged terrain of dialogue, but gets thinned out into an artificial middle term if development [*Geschehen*] is devalued to the advantage of the mittence, i.e., that which conditions and (in a sense) predetermines the development of the dialectic. Likewise, for the final position of completion [*Vollendung*] in Hegelian metaphysics.[33] The common use of the word *Vollendung* can only be a homonym which conceals a profound misunderstanding, given that the *Vollendung* of metaphysics, understood as the destinal limitation and exhaustion of its possibilities, is a concept that does not and cannot have any meaning in the Hegelian framework of presuppositions.

One could in this way develop the Hegelian critique of Heidegger, whether having to do with Being, truth, history, or the conception of philosophy. Such a critique is, furthermore, outlined by Heidegger himself when, in the protocol to the seminar "On Time and Being," he points out, playing noble, that from an Hegelian point of view, the existential analytic of *Being and Time* does not go beyond an abstract and indeterminate Being.[34] Nevertheless, if we are to take up the Hegelian game of refutation from Hegel's own point of view—in order to get the dialogue going again—we must not limit ourselves to restating Hegel's positions. Rather we must begin from that which gives the Heideggerian thesis its *force*, demonstrating its one-sidedness and then overcoming it on the basis of its own premises.

Heidegger's force is to be sought in the very place where the "dispute" with Hegel is played out: the place of thinking. At the beginning of the *Encyclopedia*, Hegel affirms that the rationality of the real is the presupposition of philosophy,[35] but he does not question what might happen to thinking *otherwise*. He is content to refute scepticism, though he recognizes its vertiginous character.[36] Likewise, there is a veritable abyssal *vacillation* revealed at the start of the *Logic*, which sets it in motion and never ceases to motivate it: thinking itself cannot determine itself; it founders in the bottomless pit of its own indeterminacy. Or again, the coming-to-be of Being-and-nothingness might be never ending; at each *Aufhebung* there is an evident risk of not making the leap, a risk that a given thesis will "fall" back into its antithesis, and vice versa, without reconciliation. That the field of play of the fundamental concepts of metaphysics—and in particular of Being itself—might be and should be sacrificed to the dynamic imperatives of the process of knowledge and the determination of effectiveness—this an Hegelian could admit without denying anything essential. But this would only be a concession; it would not constitute the beginning of a reversal which would put everything in question. Why would the latter be impossible? Because in refuting the Hegelian thesis that "The truth of *being* is *essence*" ["*Die Wahrheit des* Seins *ist das* Wesen"],[37] Heidegger can oppose to it only a quasitautological twist, "the truth of Being is Being itself" ["*Die Wahrheit des Seins ist das Sein selbst*"], or a reversal which has the appearance of a speculative proposition, but which carries out a fundamentally regressive approach. ("The essence of truth is the truth of essence.")

This regression to the "provisional" is condemned to abstraction by its separation of thinking (*der Gedanke* as the concretion of thinking's return upon itself) into the "already thought" and the "unthought." It is impossible rationally to justify this notion of the *unthought* upon which pivot the *Schritt zurück* and "retrocession" itself. In effect, if this unthought is not unthinkable (which Heidegger never claimed and which, furthermore, would be absurd), then it *can* be thought. But why wasn't it thought before; why isn't it thought now? Heidegger's only response can be that the unthought is such by virtue of the *Notwendigkeit* or the mittence [*Geschick*] of Being itself. But this response does not articulate an argument; it is a recalling to the destinal itself, in all its implacability. For there is indeed a destination, holding the possible in reserve, beyond the desires, actions or psychology of the authors. Hegel and Heidegger have no disagreement on that. However, whereas Hegel understands that which first appears rationally as the course of *fatum*, Heidegger disassociates understanding from the destinal. The initial character of the truth of Being, like its final stage or *eschaton*, is equally removed from every process of explication.[38]

Thus the disjunction of thinking into "already thought" and "unthought" has no justification other than the *presumption* of the epochality of Being, which cannot itself be justified but leads back to the concealment [*Verbergung*] itself of the truth of Being (or of the *Ereignis*). The move back from Being to time, effected in *Sein und Zeit*, is completed by the renunciation of all conceptualization in the face of the event [*Ereignis*]. The destinal can no longer *know* Being; it only *occurs* and its advent is, like the rose of Angelus Silesius, "without reason."

This critique of epochality thus turns out to be in favor of certain Hegelian positions. If Heidegger recognizes (by virtue of the epochality of Being) that "Hegel's thinking belongs to a period of history,"[39] and if, at the same time, he recognizes that this belonging does not reduce Hegel's thinking to a thing of the past,[40] and if, furthermore, the history of thinking is not a succession but a "free succession" [*freie Gefolge*], mustn't he also admit that *conceptuality* might still have a future? After all, given that the efficacy of the methodological and conceptual instruments of modernity is exercised more than ever in technoscience, it seems illogical to refuse to *Begreifen* (on the level of thinking) the field recognizably opened by its own effectivity.

Finally, and this general consequence is only a corollary: thinking Being cannot invalidate the legitimacy of thinking the Being of beings in its relationship with beings (in other words, the philosophical task of understanding beings in the light of their Being). A philosophy whose legitimacy and profundity are recognized can itself be, that is be alive, only as it continues to put its propositions to the test—and not as a dead body of doctrine. Heidegger can take distance from dialectical-speculative philosophy only by invoking an epochality whose fragility we have seen. In short, the system may be too certain of its results, but the path of the *unthought* surely exposes itself to excessive risks. Doesn't thinking, by ceaselessly preparing for an improbable event, give itself over to contingency and renounce being fully itself?

Nothing is more important for supporting and concluding Hegel's response to Heidegger than a return to the texts. Those Hegelian citations which are anti-Heideggerian *avant la lettre* should neither be neglected nor exaggerated. I will cite two, as reminders: "Wisdom never lies in secrets";[41] and "The Being of the universe, at first hidden and concealed, has no power which can offer resistance to the search for knowledge."[42] But the text which seems most worthy of our present attention is neither polemic (*avant la lettre*) nor punctilious. It is the fundamental text from the beginning of the "Doctrine of Essence" on the truth of Being,[43] which must have been the object of Heidegger's most scrupulous attention. After having written the famous phrases "The truth of Being is essence. Being is immediate," Hegel adds:

> In as much as wisdom desires to know the true, what being is in and for itself, it does not remain with the immediate and its determinations, but traverses it through and through with the presupposition that behind this being there is still something other than being itself, and that this behind and beneath is the truth of being.

This text summarizes the project and the very movement of philosophy; in this sense, it is irrefutable. In any case, Heidegger does not claim to refute it. Hegel can only *say* Being as immediacy on the supposition that we want to know the true. This supposition, sustained by the project of truth, is already a step (Hegel writes the word *Gang* a few lines later), a step which has already left pure Being, and has already discerned "something other than" Being. Knowledge which is movement, "the path of wisdom," is a "mediated knowledge"; it is no more inert in essence than Being remains in itself forever unknown. Essence only "begins" by grasping Being as other. Hegel writes that the move away from Being is its "preparatory path." But he immediately corrects himself: this move is rather "the path . . . of entry into the same" ["*den Weg . . . des Hineingehens in dasselbe*"]. It is indeed always a matter of Being, but in the knowing of it. This is why Hegel can "conclude" provisionally: "However, this step is the movement of Being itself."

That there can be no accession to the essential except through a movement which withdraws from pure or brute Being, separates itself from it and reveals it at the same time—this is what the *Phenomenology of Spirit* says, though in slightly different terms, and it is what philosophy *has been saying* since the Socratic-Platonic conquest of the *eidos*. There is no truth which is not grounded *kath' auto*, out of itself, and hence necessarily in a *Hintergrund*, a background. Knowledge of this, Hegel explains following Plato, is *Erinnerung*: interiorization and remembering, remembering as interiorization of Being itself. In this way, essence unfolds that which Being is "*zeitlos*," freed from time; essence is what Being has been, *id quod erat esse*. There is no *truth* of Being (of beings) in the proper sense, other than the metaphysical truth brought to full deployment by Hegel.

The Hegelian moment of our dialogue comes to this: a reaffirmation of the central and ineluctable necessity of metaphysics, and a rejection of the Heideggerian effort toward the *presumptive* (or toward semantic refining). To this extent, Heidegger cannot be said *to refuse* the Hegelian thesis on Being. He cannot refuse it, *insofar as it expresses the truth of metaphysics*. And isn't Heidegger far too sure of himself in placing his name alongside, and his thesis *against*, that of Hegel? Should the *thesis of philosophy* be placed on the same plain as the still uncertain and fragile questioning of it? Isn't this an artificial, rhetorical operation which courts disaster by making Hegel and Heidegger appear to be two subjectivities each presenting a "point of view"? Both agree that *die Sache der Philosophie*, the matter of philosophy, should not be reduced to a confrontation of "worldviews."

Thus the dissymetry of our dialogue is now reversed. Earlier, Heidegger seemed to have the last word; now Hegel speaks from the very center of philosophy, which has in its favor not only great age, but the entire apparatus of rationality: the mastery over things, the scientific conquest of the world, and the conceptual and argumentative means of making his "adversary" of the moment—whether he actually was one or not—appear marginal in the sense of expressing a mere opinion, a presumption. And Hegel has, in advance, diminished the importance of opinion with a play on words: "*Was ich meine, ist mein.*"[44] Has Heidegger succeeded, with an immense talent and an incredible capacity to fascinate, merely in valorizing his own "opinion"?

Conclusions and Conditions of Possibility of the Dialogue

I will not conclude by *taking sides* (which would not be worthy of the present debate), but by trying, rather, to draw certain lessons from this confrontation, and from our own efforts, regarding the importance of such a dialogue for philosophical thought.

First, I have not sought to "spare" Heidegger or Hegel; the "combat" has been harsh if not ruthless. Is it surprising then that it turns out to be a new *gigantomachy?* Heidegger's challenge has been taken up, though it evidently has not turned out to his exclusive "favor." But isn't this precisely the risk of the dialogue as we have undertaken it?

This leads to a second remark. The dialogue was at first believed to be impossible. Then, having admitted it was possible, it appeared to be mortgaged to Heidegger's (inevitably ambiguous) hermeneutic generosity. And finally, this dialogue was revealed to be suspended, undecided, still open.

Thirdly, then, it is necessary to take these remarks to greater depth regarding just what philosophical dialogue means for Hegel and for Heidegger.

The dialectical-speculative method lives on overcoming contradiction. Shouldn't Hegel then be the philosopher of dialogue *par excellence?* In fact, suspicious of all idle chatter, critical of the purely rhetorical aspects of Greek philosophy from the Sophists to Socrates and Plato—having himself written no dialogues and indeed considering this literary genre to be only irritating to moderns—Hegel posited strict conditions for elevating dialogue to the speculative level. Dialogue must effect a turning point [*Wendungspunkt*];[45] a self-determination of negativity. Otherwise, one is left with the "negatively dialectical," with misology.

With this in mind, how are we to evaluate the dialogue with Heidegger? We are forced to contend that it cannot be embedded within any specifically Hegelian determination; the concepts for thinking the confrontation *are missing* in Hegel. Heidegger understands dialogue differently, therefore his evaluation of it can only be different. The experience of thinking entails the risk of error: "He who thinks greatly, must err greatly." Consequently, Heidegger understands dialogue between essential thinkers as a sort of "loving struggle" wherein "simple adversaries" [*bloße Gegner*] become opponents [*Widersacher*].[46] His dialogues with Descartes, Plato, Kant, and Nietzsche provoke difficult and conflictual debates with their *unthought.*

This can also be seen in the dialogue with the Japanese: authentic dialogue, according to Heidegger, is a place of *danger.* Danger of misunderstanding and/or assimilation. Hegel is not, like Kuki, the other dressed in resplendent clothing. The danger is the inverse; it is in the "obviousness" of the mode of thinking of Western metaphysics. Perhaps Hegel, in his sovereignty, risks making all thinking which is "other" appear as "something indeterminate or ephemeral." Such is precisely the danger to which the Japanese oriental Dasein is exposed by "the European conceptual systems."[47] Heidegger's dialogue with Hegel permits the unfolding of a language and a way of thinking whose *contrast* with that of Hegel brings out, as clearly as possible, its questioning character: the conclusion of "The Onto-theo-logical Constitution of Metaphysics" is particularly questioning and cautious. An Hegelian would argue that the meditations on the *Überkommnis des Seins* and the *Austrag* are untranslatable into the language of the concept. But this would not stop him from admitting, and even (in principle) approving of a sentence from the closing paragraphs: "No one can know whether and when and where and how this step of thinking will develop into a proper (needed in appropriation) path and way and road-building."[48]

Finally, this text, and consequently the attempt at a dialogue with Hegel which constitutes its substance, concludes with the remark that: "That difficulty lies in language. Our Western languages are languages of metaphysical thinking, each in its own way."[49] The dialogue with the thinker of the concept, far from being caught up in the dialectical game (i.e., in the trap of a reversal which finds itself "recuperated" in a dialectical antithesis), and far from being put back to the level of the universal, lays bare the linguistic limits of all metaphysics. The destinal, then, is words weighted with immemorial significance. For Hegel, language is the product of thinking and not the inverse. Paradoxically, however, it is language which in the end, according to Heidegger, gives an unsuspected and unintended advantage to Hegel the metaphysician, even if he never claims it. This "advantage," in spite of everything, and particularly in spite of the difficulty of certain texts, lies in the comprehension and security achieved by the reign of "completed metaphysics." It comes back to this: by Heidegger's own admission, Hegel's epoch is not over, even if "essential thinking" has the "right" (that is the enriching possibility) to push forward recognition of "things other."

If the dialogue has unfolded amidst this divergence from its own nature, it is—it bears repeating—thanks to the immense efforts of Heidegger to recognize the stature of one whom he calls "the only thinker of the West who has thoughtfully experienced the history of thinking."[50] We have understood this effort as "retrocession." But perhaps it is not too late to make room for a doubt expressed by Michel Haar:[51] Isn't Heidegger's thought forever tied to a Hegelian heritage?[52] Isn't there a Hegelianism of the history of Being? From this perspective, Heidegger would be close to Hegel in the following three principal ways: (1) faithful thinking is the interiorized memory of the essential past [*das Gewesene*]; (2) the succession of epochs of Being obeys an inflexible and quasicumulative necessity; and, finally, (3) the eschatology of the history of Being suggests "the idea of a final gathering . . . of the whole historical process in a final configuration."[53]

Though it is not possible to discuss Michel Haar's paper here in the detail it deserves, let us at least indicate certain "sensitive points" which will help us to conclude.

It is true that Heidegger and Hegel come closest to each other regarding the question of the history of Being, in that Heidegger assumes a connection between the epochality of Being and that of history.[54] We must not forget, however, that Hegel, for his part, is not a thinker of history for its own sake, but only as the return of Spirit to itself and as a function of its eternity: "But philosophy is not meant to be a narration of happenings but a cognition of what is *true* in them."[55] As for Heidegger, we must remain aware that each approach to Hegel is also a distancing from him, since—as Michel Haar recognizes—"Heidegger accepts neither the dialectic of Spirit, nor the rationality of the real, nor the teleology of knowledge."[56] It is not, therefore, simply because Heidegger has displaced certain Hegelian concepts that one might go so far as to charge him with a "re-editing—perhaps more prudent—of Hegelian idealism."[57]

If Heidegger is a "Hegelian," it is not in the place where one would most expect it; it is less in his general conception of the history of Being than in his understanding of the *present epoch.* There is a revealing moment in volume 32 of the *Gesamtausgabe* where, in order to explain the limitations of Hegelian metaphysics, Heidegger takes up the concept of *Weltgeist,* in its own right, and acknowledges its "power."[58]

More generally, he characterizes the present epoch again and again as an epoch of global technology; it is as if the epoch of technicity were united around its principle—*Gestell*—in such a way that, to the very end, it can be only the expression of that principle according to some implacable necessity. Heidegger perhaps credits too much to the essence of modern technology—in any case, more than a prudently phenomenological inquiry would allow.[59]

But the most secret point of proximity to Hegel (in spite of all the differences discussed above and not withstanding the tension of a fundamental divergence) perhaps lies hidden in the friction with regard to phenomenology. If we go back to the sentence cited at the beginning of this essay, wherein Heidegger warns his students against any reconciliation of Hegel's phenomenology with that of Husserl, we must note one very important omission: it is not a question of phenomenology in the sense of Heidegger's own fundamental ontology. In another passage from the seminar, Heidegger states that:

> In Hegel's conception of the phenomenology of spirit, on the contrary, spirit is not the *object* of a phenomenology. Here "phenomenology" is by no means a title for an investigation of or a science *about* something like Spirit. Rather, phenomenology is not one way among many, but *the* manner in which spirit itself exists. The phenomenology of Spirit is *das eigentliche und ganze Auftreten des Geistes* (the genuine and total coming-out of spirit).[60]

Far from objectifying Spirit and placing it as if at a distance from itself alongside other objects, Hegelian phenomenology is "the science of the experience of consciousness" (at least in its first major part) and is itself implicated in this experience. It should be understood, says Heidegger, as *die Selbstdarstellung der Vernunft*, the self-presentation of reason.[61]

Upon reflection, we find that this word, *Selbstdarstellung*, says everything. Everything, that is, which concerns the very conditions of possibility of the Heidegger-Hegel dialogue. *Darstellung* signifies the showing [*monstration*] of the phenomenon which the *Phenomenology of Spirit* does not deduce, but *shows* in the immanence of a consciousness which detaches itself from its aims in order to understand them. Phenomenology is the "presentation of phenomenal knowledge," as Heidegger says in "Hegels Begriff der Erfahrung."[62] Not only does this showing have something to do with the idea of phenomenology as such, but it also corresponds to the spirit of the "phenomenological method" presented in § 7 of *Being and Time.* We find there, almost word for word, the same terms being used to characterize the *Heideggerian method* which Heidegger will later use to oppose Hegelian phenomenology to its Husserlian homonym: "The expression 'phenomenology' signifies primarily a *methodological conception* [*Methodenbegriff*]. This expression does not characterize the *what* [*Was*] of the objects of philosophical research as subject matter, but rather the *how* [*Wie*] of that research."[63]

One might say, however, that the "phenomenon" is radically different in the two cases. For Hegel, it is rational knowledge progressively revealing itself; for Heidegger it is Dasein. Certainly. But let us look at it again, more closely, from the point of view first of the definition of phenomenon, and then of its "content." What is it to be a phenomenon, for Hegel? Heidegger answers this in his course on the *Phenomenology of Spirit:*

> To be a phenomenon [*Phänomensein*], to appear [*Erscheinen*] means coming forward [*auftreten*] in such a way that something shows itself which is other than what previously showed itself, in such a way that what comes forward does so *in opposition to* what previously appeared, and what previously appeared is reduced to *mere illusion* [*Schein*].[64]

And what is it to be a phenomenon for the Heidegger of *Being and Time*? The phenomenon is, according to § 7A, the "showing-itself-in-itself [*das Sich-an-ihm-selbst-zeigen*]," as simultaneously distinguished from illusion [*Schein*] and from appearance [*Erscheinung*], a relationship of reference at the heart of the being. "Appearance" and "illusion" are diversely founded in the phenomenon, for Heidegger. The phenomenon is thus, on both sides, this differentiating showing (or better still, this "becoming other" in relation to self)[65] from out of which the "thing itself" unfolds.

Hence we come to this "thing itself," this content, the *Selbst* of *Selbstdarstellung*. Isn't this a matter, for Hegel—passing by way of consciousness, then self-consciousness, and reason—of the *Absolute?* And isn't it, for Heidegger, a quite different matter of the *Selbst* of the self-understanding of Dasein, which unfolds the hermeneutic circularity of its being to the point of gathering Being itself in its fundamental difference? But then again things are even more complex. While distrusting all abusive or hasty comparisons, we should nevertheless pay attention to the thesis, constantly affirmed by Heidegger in the 1930 lectures as well as in "Hegels Begriff der Erfahrung," that the *Phenomenology* (and for that matter, the *Logic*) gathers the Being of beings. Absolute knowledge is "onto-theology," as Heidegger affirms already in § 10 of his lectures, thirty years before the conference on "The Onto-theo-logical Constitution of Metaphysics."[66] But what is fundamentally at issue in *Being and Time*, at the heart of Dasein's questioning of itself? The answer, from the first page on, is that: "It is a matter of posing anew *the question of the meaning of Being.*" And as early as the second page, Hegel is mentioned: "What these two thinkers (Plato and Aristotle) understood has survived, at the price of various alterations and 'retouchings,' all the way to the *Logic* of Hegel."

We are indeed dealing with the Same, the question of Being and, in a *way*, with a method which allows itself to be totally transformed and implicated by this "very thing": Being. In other words, we are dealing with ontology, that great and only ontology which meets the challenge of the Greeks. And this ontology is phenomenological, in *Being and Time* as well as in the *Phenomenology*, in that it is the "science of the experience of consciousness."

Now we can better understand the extraordinary impression of intimacy (at once thoughtful and critical) left by a reading of "Hegels Begriff der Erfahrung," revealing in the introduction to the *Phenomenology* the "twofold *dia* of the twofold *legesthai*," the play of ontological difference in the dialectic of consciousness.[67] Conversely, the ontological reading of Hegelian phenomenology can be intersected by a reading of *Being and Time* which is phenomenological in the Hegelian sense. Even if no dialectical progression is to be found there, the critique of everydayness [*quotidienneté*] and of the "one" is indeed a critique of "natural consciousness and its certitudes. Though Being, like the Absolute, is already near to us in its ontological precomprehension, still its truth must be thematized in care and assumed in resoluteness. *Seinkönnen* is not given any more immediately than it is in Hegelian *Phenomenology*; it is by a *diakrinein*, departing from its immediate phenomenality in order to attain its phenomenality as such, that Dasein like dialectical consciousness makes its true way, its true openness of vision in order to conquer what is most proper to it.

Thus, the dialogue with Hegel is understood in the conditions of its possibility as a dialogue with a fundamental possible of ontology, as a self-presentation of the truth of Being, announcing that which—following a "turning"—will be called the *Verwindung*, the "deflection" of metaphysics. It is the first step toward the returning-home of metaphysics in its unthought essence.

Appropriation (which simultaneously outlines the "thing itself" and the dialogue which presents it) is the Ariadne's thread which allows us to follow the continuity of the Heideggerian path in its fidelity to the great metaphysical tradition of which Hegel is the modern completion. Speculative circularity is taken up again and deepened in hermeneutical circularity.

It is on this terrain of a phenomenology of rationality, furthermore, that the question of Being is connected—in a state of contiguity—with a self-explication of rational appropriation, still to be discovered and meditated upon. Whether Being is finite or infinite, whether the Concept is the power of time or the inverse,[68] their appropriation is won: it is a path, an experience. That is why, having once deconstructed phenomenology as eidetic, phenomenology as a thinking which interrogates the phenomenon and its phenomenality is always a task.

2

The History of Being and Its Hegelian Model

Michel Haar
Translated by Reginald Lilly

"At first sight one hardly knows how to deny that there is a striking proximity and similarity between Heidegger and Hegel"—such at least is the widely circulated impression in France reported by Jean Beaufret in a remark at the seminar *On Time and Being!*[1] Nevertheless, instead of raising the correlations and analogies that he finds "evident" and discussing them, Beaufret hastens to insist on the impossibility of any comparison, an impossibility which, according to him, is due to the fact that there is no such thing as a "Heideggerian philosophy"! Since the points of divergence with Hegel are obvious inasmuch as there is neither dialectic nor the rationality of the real in the thought of Being, it may be useful, for once, to ask if the correlations between the history of Being and the Hegelian history of Spirit arise only from a vague resemblance or from a more profound complicity. No doubt the history of Being does not correspond to the logical development of a rational Idea. No doubt it is governed by a principle of *discontinuity* (epochs arise "suddenly") and by *errancy*, whose origin is impenetrable to reason (sending, the *Geschick*, the destiny of Being) and is linked to the complementarity of disclosure and withdrawal. Nevertheless, an initial, apparent similarity between them seems to be situated at the level of the thought of a destiny. It is not man, as great as he may be; it is not the thinker that decides, it is the "matter itself," Spirit or Being, which at the base of history has always already decided for him. As metaphysical and perfectly blind to the ontological difference as it may be, is not the Hegelian approach to the past of *thought* recognized, in certain regards, as necessary and *exemplary?*

When Heidegger hails Hegel, "the only thinker in the West who had a thinking experience of the history of thought,"[2] such praise, which is accentuated by the extreme valorization of the expression "experience of thought" in the Heideggerian context, sufficiently indicates that there is merit, if not to Hegelianism in general, at least to Hegel's history of philosophy. It is even explicitly stated elsewhere that Hegel "was right": "When Hegel thinks about the nature of his thought he does so through a dialogue with the history of previous thought. He was the first who could and had to think thus."[3] But why was Hegel right? How was he the first not to separate his thinking from a dialogue with the history of previous thought? For instance, neither Aristotle nor Leibniz dissociated the essence of their thinking from such a dialogue. Might the novel and outstanding merit of Hegel stem from the fact that when considering the previous history of thought he makes it appear as an organic totality and not simply as the thought of some one or other great predecessor? Does he not also identify history with the "sublation" of the past?

What Heidegger admires above all in Hegel is the discovery of the convertibility of Being and history as "the essential having-been" (*das Gewesenes*), as the gathering and recollection of a having-been that continues to last. For Heidegger, who abandoned the primacy of the future at the same time as he abandoned the primacy of Dasein, Being is the essential past: *das Gewesene.* The phrase "The History of Being is Being itself and nothing but this"[4] seems to take up again, in reverse, the great principle of Hegel: *Wesen ist was gewesen ist.* When he distinguishes the historical from the historiographical (*Geschichte* and *Historie*), to what extent is Heidegger taking up again the Hegelian distinction between history, which concerns the inner and essential progress of Spirit, and purely exterior and anecdotal history? To what extent does the use of this distinction not perpetuate, in the thought of Being, the metaphysical difference between the transcendental-necessary and the empirical-contingent? Does not all Heidegger's understanding of history, by disparaging forgetfulness and insisting on the task of remembering, reveal a perpetuation not only of Hegelianism but even of Platonism?

Nevertheless the Hegelian structure may be even more profound: if it is true that for Heidegger reason is not what governs history, neither is it chance or blind destiny. The series of the epochs of Being obeys an inflexible and coherent necessity which, he writes, "is like a law and logic."[5] What constitutes the "logic" of history in Heidegger?

In short, what at first urges bringing Hegel and Heidegger together is the thought of "eschatology," the idea of a final gathering (perhaps of a sort of synthesis) of the whole historical process in a final configuration. For Heidegger it is a question of thinking history as "the dialogue of the dusk with the dawn."[6] But then is not eschatology the equivalent of absolute knowledge insofar as each epoch finally finds its sense with respect to the totality of the process? Yet this point of greatest proximity is also, paradoxically it seems, the point of greatest remove inasmuch as the Heideggerian totality rests on the abyss of the ungrounded, and inasmuch as the Greek dawn is not the only commencement possible. Besides the Greek dawn there is indeed "a new dawn" that offers the possibility of an end of history that is radically different from that of Hegel insofar as for Heidegger it is not a recommencement but a totally different, unprecedented, absolutely new commencement.

The Primacy of the Past as *Gewesen*

True history is not the ephemeral, the anecdotal, the perishable, the finished, but what has-been, lasting till the present and harboring the future: "What is historical [*historisches*] which means, the past as such [*Vergangenes als solches*] is no more, it is dead. . . . In the History [*Geschichte*] of thought, what is at issue is thought itself. . . . Everything is preserved. The History [*Geschichte*] of philosophy busies itself with the past, but equally with the present."[7] For Hegel, this past which is preserved is the eternity of the shapes of Spirit. History, in a decidedly Platonic manner, is nothing but the presentation in time of the shapes of Spirit such as they exist in themselves. The Platonism of such an opposition between the immutable and the changing is dialectically overcome, which means preserved notably in the form of the difference between the Idea in itself—the *Logic*—and its manifestation in time—the *Phenomenology*. History possesses at one and the same time a preeminent value in that it is the Absolute itself, and a subordinate value in that it is only the instrument of the manifestation of the eternal Spirit, which has always existed in itself. "History," Hegel writes, "is the *representation* [*Vorstellung*] of Spirit as it comes into its own"[8] (emphasis added). Inasmuch as for Heidegger truth or Being does not preexist its appearance (for Being is not something in itself), what sort of nature does this essential past have such that it produces history as "that which abides"? It goes without saying that if it is opposed to a past that simply slips away and disappears (*Vergangenes*), it is above all because it is capable of a future: "the essential having-been [*Gewesendes*] abides in coming."[9] Having-been as such transcends the dimension of the pure past: it is neither the past that has disappeared, slipped away (as the root

Gang in *Vergangenheit* indicates), nor the isolated present by itself, nor of course is it only the future. Having shown at the end of his essay on Rilke in *Holzwege* that the spurious eternity is *Verganglichtkeit* raised to a *nunc stans*, "to the emptiness of a moment without duration," Heidegger suggests that the true eternity is *das Gewesenes*, that which, having been, has not ceased to be.[10] Indeed, contrary to Hegel, *das Gewesene* is not the product or result of history but an absolutely inaugural anteriority. What controls all history, as Heidegger emphasizes in a number of texts—particularly in *Erläuterungen zu Hölderlins Dichtung*—what summons the future is the exigency of the inaugural, the *Anfang:* the first *Gewesenes*, the first essential having-been, the first grasp of Being, exerts a destiny-like influence over the whole tradition; such is the force of the Greek *aletheia.* "The inaugural never passes away, it is never something past."[11] Genuine history is the future of an essential and inaugural past. Inaugural *Gewesenes* is interpreted as the source of history.

The definition of history as *Geschick*, destiny in the sense of *Schickung*, destination, the sending of Being, is simply the recognition of the omnipotence of this inaugural past. History is not only what is already there, but it is what is already accomplished in the destiny of the commencement. In "Principles of Thought," Heidegger again takes up into his account the words of the Book of Ecclesiastes, the truth of which Hegel had also shown: "nothing new under the sun." "There is nothing new," Heidegger comments, "except what is old in the inexhaustible power of metamorphosis of the inaugural; this phrase touches on the essence of History. History is the advent of what does not cease to be. Namely, what has already unfolded its essence, and nothing but that, is what comes to us."[12] The realm of destinal necessity exerts itself here with a rigor more implacable than rational necessity in Hegel, and in a more frightening way because it is blind, unfathomable. As in Hegel, history is completed not only at its end but at its commencement, in that it governs all that arises from its development. Being is thought of less as difference than as identity deploying itself. Nothing happens that hasn't already been originally gathered in the essence of Being: "What is is what comes about. What comes about already came about. That doesn't mean finished. What already came about is what is uniquely gathered in the essence of Being; it is the essence of having-been [*Ge-Wesen*]."[13] This preformation of history in the inauguration of Being explains the enigmatic phrase at the end of the afterword to "Was ist Metaphysik?": "Every *Geschick* of beings is inaugurally already accomplished in being."[14] *Geschick*, the destiny of Being, "contains" in advance the totality of history's possibilities. This strict self-closure of history, which excludes everything outside of it, everything other, is this not some new variety of Hegelianism?

It seems as if Heidegger had revived the Hölderlinian theme of the omnipotence of the commencement in order to radicalize it in a Hegelian sense. Instead of "As you commenced, so shall you remain" (*The Rhine*), Heidegger's phrase would go: "As you commenced, so you will develop yourself" or "so you developed." The commencement persists throughout the entire history of Being. If the Greeks have such importance for us, it is because the essence of modern technology is simply the development of the Greek question about the Being of beings. If the commencement did not preserve what has been (*das Gewesene*), which means the gathering of what continues to last, then the Being of beings would not dominate our epoch from out of the essence of modern technology. But in reality the commencement does not develop. One must not confuse commencement and starting point. A starting point disappears in what it produces. The commencement abides unalterable, unchanged in all the sequences arising from it. Here there is a somewhat Hegelian aspect to Heidegger: the commencement has always already fallen into oblivion, has always already been left behind like the pure indeterminate being of Hegel's *Logic*, but remains sheltered within the entire process. "The inaugural never disappears."[15] The essential past as *das Gewesene* governs the future as would an immutable destiny, and not simply as would a first term in a series of transformations. It is clear that the later Heidegger renounced making the future the fundamental dimension both of time and history. Thus one can read in *Unterwegs zur Sprache*, "What we ordinarily call the future is the *Gewesenes* that comes to encounter us," and in *Erläuterungen zu Hölderlins Dichtung*, "Everything to come has its advent in the While of the uniqueness of what has-been [*in der Weile der Einzigkeit des Gewesenen*]."[16]

To this privileged position of *das Gewesene* there corresponds, in Heidegger, a persistent defining of thought as "recollective thinking" (*Andenken*) or remembrance (*Gedächtnis* or *Erinnerung*), which, despite the distance between dialectic and the thought of the ontological difference, calls to mind an affinity in the understanding of what one could call the commemorative essence of thought. The essence of thought is retrospection. Recollective thinking from the first *looks back* (thus only the "step back" is capable of grasping the essence of metaphysics): thinking gets its light from this inaugural and essential past.

> Presuming that commemorative thinking [*Andenken*] thinks ahead, then thinking-back cannot think something merely by-gone (*Vergangenes*), about which one can only say it is irrevocable. Thinking upon [*Denken an*] what is coming necessarily amounts to thinking what has-been [*das

> *Gewesene*], and with that expression, in contradistinction to the merely by-gone [*das Vergangene*], we mean that which from then on essentially is.[17]

The first chapters of the second part of *What Is Called Thinking?* define this commemorative essence of thinking by showing that acknowledgment, thankfulness, and self-collection belong to thinking: thinking has the character of a "holding back," a remaining near to . . . To think is to preserve what on its own gives itself to thinking to be retrieved: "We call the gathering of recollective thinking around what offers itself to thinking: Memory."[18] But this memory does not depend on the human faculty of remembering. A nonoblivious thinking is simply one that responds to what on its own has already been gathered, preserved in Being. Here we come upon another analogy with Hegel. *Erinnerung,* calling to mind the history of Being, is not the result of man's efforts, but it is done by Being. In the phrase "the *Erinnerung* of Being" "Being" plays the role of a grammatical subject which communicates *Erinnerung* to thinking: "*Erinnerung* helps thinking to be reminded of the truth of Being."[19] Just as Spirit makes use of man in order to realize itself in time and to know itself, so Being grants to man the role of a witness summoned to make an appearance in court. The only liberty thus left to man would be the refusal to testify, not so much out of revolt as out of distraction or blindness. In any case, man is not the one that effects the reversal from out of the oblivion of Being into a caring about a recollective thinking of its history. It is only by thought that man can recognize the necessity, everywhere at work, of a destiny (*Geschick*) about which he can do nothing.

Is There a Heideggerian System of History?

The history of Being possesses a systematic coherence in its development. It possesses unity and totality: "The unity of the One shows itself throughout the history of Being in configurations that are sometimes different, configurations whose difference proceeds from the mutation of the essence of aletheia, of the concealing disclosedness."[20] It possesses its own necessity[21] and, in the irresistible and irreversible character of its unfolding through to an end, it has a strong teleological structure. Indeed, just as in Hegel the progression is governed by the realization of Absolute Spirit, in Heidegger it is governed by the *telos,* which is constituted by the completion of metaphysics. Just as in Hegel's *Phenomenology* consciousness is defined at every moment by the "not yet" of the moments to come and of the final stage, so it is the itinerary to the perfection of

Being as will, the maturation of the "will to will," that orders, gathers, and calls, so to speak, the previous moments back to itself. Thus Heidegger writes regarding the difference between Hegelian metaphysics and the metaphysics of the will to power (still to come): "This possibility was not yet possible. . . . The will has not yet appeared as the will to will in the reality which it has itself prepared. This is why metaphysics has not yet been completed in the metaphysics of spirit."[22] The "motor" of history is therefore not this final totalization itself. It is true that metaphysics tends toward the constellation that forms the essence of technology, a constellation inasmuch as it gathers and sets to work all the past metaphysical principles (like the principle of reason which transforms itself into cybernetics) that are preserved and actualized in the present.

But what propels history, what permits taking into account the mutations of the essence of truth, is the *increasing oblivion* of the commencement, of the inaugural essence of truth as *aletheia.* It is in this sense that one can again speak of an *inversion of Hegelianism:* the Hegelian becoming of truth becomes the progressive establishment of the reign of errancy, the development of nihilism. The withdrawal of Being hides to the point of leaving nothing; even that of oblivion effaces itself. History is not the progress of consciousness toward self-transparency, or the absolute movement, but is the gradual loss of the sense of presence as clearing and withdrawal. The "evil telos" that orients history is the complete obscuring of the meaning of Being. "The history of Being is the history of the *increasing* oblivion of Being."[23]

Although the history of Being may be divided into epochs, as can *Weltgeschichte,* there is no possible comparison between the Hegelian sense of an epoch as a moment in an evolutionary process conceived on the model of a biological increase (thus the Greeks are the adolescents of the Spirit) and the Heideggerian sense of an epoch as *epoché,* which means the *abeyance,* the holding back, the withdrawal of Being. For Heidegger there is no global rationality ruling the succession of epochs; this is why he can say that their succession is a "free succession," *eine freie Folge.* It is without doubt free in regard to a dialectical necessity that would permit the deduction of the epochs one from the other, but not in regard to the destiny of the oblivion of Being. Each epoch echoes the secret of the dispensation that is compared to "a unique source (from which) arise diverse streamlets which feed into a river."[24] Heidegger is also led to recognize another necessity, or to put it more precisely, "something which is like a necessity, which is like a law and a logic."[25] This law, which is precisely that of the increasing oblivion, is articulated in the same passage of the seminar *On Time and Being:*

> Between the epochal metamorphoses of Being and the withdrawal one can perceive a relation which nevertheless has nothing to do with a relation of causality. One can say that the further away one is from the dawn of Western thinking and from *aletheia*, the greater is the oblivion into which it falls, the clearer is the manner in which knowledge and consciousness break into the open, and the manner in which Being thus withdraws.[26]

The rule which presides over the succession of epochs and over the linking of the mutations of the essence of truth is, such as one can extract it from this law, apparently completely vague in its generality: the withdrawal of *aletheia* frees (or makes possible?) Being as *energeia;* the withdrawal of *energeia* in its turn frees *actualitas;* the withdrawal of *actualitas* frees truth as *certitude*, certitude comes down to self-justification, which becomes the will to self-justification, etc. This rule implies that the commencement, the grand pre-Socratic commencement, is not, as the Hegelian commencement, the most abstract and impoverished moment but rather the moment which is relatively the fullest and richest. Yet the very idea that the commencement could have been an absolute plenitude without any lack or reserve seems contrary to all of Heidegger's thought. But does the commencement belong to that which "actually" took place? As we know, Heidegger distinguishes the commencement, the inauguration (*Anfang*), from the beginning or outset (*Beginn*): the commencement itself is never given, it is obscured in the outset.[27] But then what is the status of the commencement? Heidegger has vacillated on the subject of the outset of the history of metaphysics which is either with Plato or Anaximander; the status of the commencement is enigmatic. Indeed, either the pre-Socratic commencement "places itself" outside of history, in which case it presents itself as the manifestation of the essence of *aletheia* in all its purity, and hence as a fullness anterior to history and in a certain manner nonhistorically underlying the entire development—which dangerously resembles the "in itself" of Hegel's Spirit!—or the commencement is eclipsed at the very start of Western thought, insofar as this outset is the oblivion of the commencement, an oblivion which "happens" from the commencement on—but then would not the hidden essence of the so-called initial truth become mythical, supratemporal, or a sort of retrospective crepuscular fiction?

Whatever it may be, the "logic" of the history of Being orients itself according to a double series of relations.

Relations to the commencement. Which means all the mutations of the essence of truth (*energeia, actualitas, certitudo,* will) according to a growing oblivion.[28]

Relations to the end. Among these, the notion of preparation works to unify the historical development and to explain the passage from one epoch to another.

Descartes prepared the metaphysics of the will to power (he already posits it, but *nur unwissentlich,* only unconsciously). Leibniz prepared the basis for the completion of the epoch of modernity.[29] Completed metaphysics (Hegel and Nietzsche) constitutes the preparation for the reign of technology. What is the meaning of this preparation? Is it a kind of condition of possibility? Sometimes Heidegger suggests that a figure of truth makes possible a subsequent truth. Or is it only a prefiguration of it? Another logico-historical notion close to preparation is that of the incubation: the principle of reason is in some sense lying dormant in the Greek and Christian epochs but already is active before having the power to bring itself irresistibly to bear once it has been stated. Another logical necessity: the tendency in the history of Being toward the unification of metaphysical positions that make completion possible.[30] There is even a logic of transitions: just as the Hegelian *Übergang* is characterized by the decomposition of a preceding world, so the plurivocity of the senses of Being at the end of an epoch is the symptom of a transition: "The equivocal character of the essence of reality (multiple signification) is the symptom of an authentic transition."[31] It is the call to a decision, not the one by Descartes, but by Being through Descartes. The history of Being, says Heidegger, has nothing to do with the psychology of philosophers!

The relations to the commencement spread themselves out over two parallel planes of the history of Being: (1) The plane, most generally, of the epochs, which means the major modes of the withdrawal of Being; Heidegger distinguishes four major epochs of Being: Greek, Christian-medieval, modernity, and planetary;[32] for Hegel there are instead four "worlds": the oriental, the Greek, the Roman, the German. (2) The more specific plane of the mutations of the essence of truth: thus the Greek epoch experiences not only the mutation of *aletheia* into *ousia*—presence—but also the passage of *aletheia* to *homoiosis* (*adaequation*). The mutations of *energeia* into *actualitas,* of *ousia* into *substantia,* of *hypokeimenon* into *subjectum* simultaneously occur within the Christian-medieval epoch along with the concept of *ens creatum.* At each moment it is the essence of truth which determines these mutations according to what Heidegger calls "a hidden necessity in its origin"[33] (the destiny of oblivion). But the logic of the obscuring of the inaugural Greek understanding is on a par with another logic which is not contradictory: a cumulative logic of metaphysical propositions. Thus once Being became *actualitas, Wirklichkeit,* effectiveness, the efficacity of making as manufacturing, Being remains fixed throughout the modern epoch and the planetary epoch, where this sense is reinforced. *Actualitas* is a structure of completion, which means, one of the constituents of the constellation of the will to will. Heidegger writes, "inasmuch as it is reality, Being is a substructure which makes possible diverse fundamental positions."

These mutations of the essence of truth remain inaccessible to metaphysics, just as its own essence, which equally has a power of necessity, remains foreign to it. Example: in completely conforming to metaphysics Nietzsche "must" think the *essentia* and *existentia:* or "must" think the foundation.[34] It is in his cumulative logic (the "concrescence" which preserves the past stages in the depth of the present) that Heidegger here clearly comes close to Hegel, even if he distinguishes himself from Hegel when he asserts that completion is not at all a perfection, a finishing off. But this distinction is just a way of attributing to the completion a value that is the inverse of what Hegel would have recognized it as having.

"Eschatology," or the Logic of Completion

It is in the concept of the eschatology of Being[35] that the Heideggerian thought of history is most in accord with Absolute Knowledge and, in another sense, that from which it is most divergent.

The very idea of an end of history is Hegelian. Heidegger does not hide from it: "We think the eschatology of Being is the sense that corresponds to the one in which the *Phenomenology of Spirit* must be thought in order to respond to the history of Being."[36] And he adds that the *Phenomenology* constitutes a "phase" of the eschatology of Being. Phenomenology is an eschatology not thought through to the end: "the history of Being is the true *Weltgeschichte.*"[37]

But what sort of end is it? What eschatology means here is that "the history of Being terminates":[38] in the last epoch, that of technology, a gathering (logos) of the final (*eschaton*) sending of Being takes place. The present of technology takes up again and totalizes the entirety of what essentially has-been, all of *das Gewesene.* While signifying this last recollecting of Being, eschatology also signifies the departure of Being, the separation from Being or the farewell to Being (*Abscheid*). As the epoch of *Gestell,* eschatology has a double face, "a Janus-head."[39] On the one hand it prolongs the Hegelian project of totalization which is that of metaphysics as a whole: the will to appropriate, to possess, is applied here to Western history. The oblivion of Being is reversed into memory. For the thinking of Being, the "turn" consists in coming back into possession of itself. But is not the memory of the history of metaphysics a new metaphysics precisely to the extent that the project of overcoming metaphysics ultimately requires its acceptance (*Verwindung*), its appropriation (*Aneignung*), its interiorization (*Erinnerung*), an operation of interminable digestion? Is it not a question, as Heidegger says (and precisely in regard to Hegel), "of speaking of the same matter in the same manner"?[40]

But, on the other hand, Heidegger completely abandons the Hegelian model when he says that the history of Being has ended and that it is necessary "to leave metaphysics to itself."[41] Metaphysics is well and truly dismissed. It is necessary to leave even the thought of Being, to cross out Being (to write it under erasure), because "the history of Being is the history of metaphysics, and nothing else." *Ereignis* is not a new name for Being. With the awakening to *Ereignis,* Heidegger says, the oblivion of Being "overcomes itself": "*die Seinsvergessenheit 'hebt' sich 'auf.'* "[42] This placing of "*Aufhebung*" between quotation marks is at the very least surprising! All the more as Heidegger adds: "Now the veiling does not veil itself anymore; on the contrary it is to this veiling that the attention of thought applies itself"! Since veiling makes up an integral part of the essence of truth, or oblivion an integral part of the manifestation of Being, it is necessary to conclude (the "abandonment" or "crossing out" of Being would confirm it) that the question of Being is itself what would turn out to be dismissed.

Yet such a conclusion contradicts the majority of the texts of Heidegger where Being is described as the missed mark, the goal not yet reached by thinking: "Being is the unique goal not yet established by essential thinking provided that such a thinking is inaugural and in the other commencement it is necessary for it to precede even poetry in the sense of poetic imagination."[43]

It also contradicts the recurrent theme of the unthought: what may be thought is the unthought of metaphysics. What is the use of thinking the not yet thought, since in any case it is not from the not yet thought that thinking can wait for the upsurge of the "other commencement"? Is it in order to restore an improbable totality of Being?

Despite these uncertainties, eschatology makes the indeterminable possibility of an "other commencement" appear: "the most distant goal of thinking . . . is situated at an infinite distance from our epoch; it belongs to the historical distance of an other history."[44] Despite the precariousness of this "other history," one cannot maintain that it enters into the Hegelian model. One might say that the possibility which is opened by the thought of eschatology is an empty possibility, a pure fiction, a non-sense. One might ask: Can there be a thought which prepares this nothing which is totally other? Which waits without knowing what it is waiting for, which has in view its own impossibility? Why not, if it is true that Dasein can anticipate its own death as the possibility of impossibility? Why couldn't the West anticipate its limit? Nevertheless, the true encumbrance that presses on the thought of the "other history" is what Heidegger calls "the danger." The true danger is that technology "insists" and persists quasi-indefinitely. The end of the planetary epoch can have the slowness of what Heidegger calls a *Verendung*, an "expiration that lasts." "This expiration lasts longer than the history accomplished by metaphysics up till now."[45] In simpler terms this means that more than twenty-five centuries of technology await mankind! But the supreme danger is that there may never be a new commencement: it is the "threat of the possibility that to man may be refused the return to a more original disclosure and hence the promise of the experience of a more inaugural truth."[46] There also remains the possibility that this "other thinking" may exist, but stay unseen, unnoticed, perhaps unable to break through. Heidegger compares the fate perhaps reserved for his thinking to that of the poetry of Hölderlin, which during more than a century remained misunderstood and yet waited for a true audience and understanding.

Heidegger's thought of history leads, like Hegel's, to a justification not only of the history of thought but also of empirical history. Here again we have an inversion: the Hegelian satisfaction in the face of rationality turns into a quasifatalistic resignation in the face of the progress of errancy. For Heidegger it is useless to become indignant in the face of the "*Führers*" just as it is useless to fight the destruction of earth with technological means, for the basic structures of reality are not determined by human action and cannot be changed by it.

To the question "What should we do, then?" Heidegger gives a clear but somewhat deceiving answer: *wir sollen nichts tun, sondern warten*, "we should do nothing, but wait."[47] The eventual overcoming of technology does not depend on man's will. But it belongs just as much to man to be attentive to the hidden metaphysical essence of technology as it belongs to him to accompany it in some way through to its "expiration." The "completion of metaphysics," says Heidegger, "certainly depends on a historical decision."[48] What does this mean? Not that man may be capable of deciding that there may or may not be a completion, but that he decides to respond or correspond to this completion by thinking. As it is said in *Holzwege:* "Are we the late ones that we are?"[49] For Dasein "Being" means having-to-be. We have to assume the role Being prescribes to us. And it is in this acceptance that our poverty-stricken freedom can find both its measure and its strength.

3

Circulation and Constitution at the End of History

David Kolb

Hegel's claims about the end of history seem bold and disturbingly specific. Could he really have believed that the institutional forms he discerned in the Europe of his day were the last word in society and politics? Many argue that developments since Hegel's time have undermined any claim that the particular political and economic structures he describes are the final and necessary mediations of social unity. Others, liberals or postmoderns, do speak about what amounts to an end of history today, but they are satisfied with far less detail than Hegel; usually they restrict themselves to general commendations of capitalism and representative democracy. But their real difference from Hegel concerns more than generality; it concerns the necessity Hegel sees for definite intermediate structures in thought and society. This necessity also puts Hegel at odds with Heidegger's comments about the end of metaphysics and the final technological society.

Speaking of his own time, Hegel says:

> The realm of fact has discarded its barbarity and unrighteous caprice, while the realm of truth has abandoned the world of beyond and its arbitrary force, so that the true reconciliation, which discloses the state as the image and actuality of reason, has become objective. In the state, self-consciousness finds in an organic development the actuality of its substantive knowing and willing; in religion, it finds the feeling and representation of this its own truth as an ideal essentiality; while in

> philosophic science, it finds the free comprehension and knowledge of this truth as one and the same in its mutually complementary manifestations, i.e. in the state, in nature, and in the ideal world. (*PR*, § 360)[1]

This citation is one of many expressing a satisfaction with the present that suggests Hegel believed history had in some sense been completed. But in what sense? In a weak interpretation the passage could be expressing satisfaction with a present that has completed the process of overcoming some long-standing dualisms, but without ruling out the emergence of new fundamental tensions and dualities. In a strong interpretation, Hegel would be saying that at least on certain levels a definitive turning had been achieved. Ours is not merely the latest but in some ways the final stage of history. This does not mean that historical events will cease. But the stage on which the dramas of peoples and nations and economies will play their roles is now fully displayed and fully furnished, and no radically new institutional structures are to be expected.

It is the strong interpretation that interests me in this essay. While the weaker interpretation reduces to a dialectical variant of the Enlightenment belief in progress, the strong claim challenges us to think more deeply about the relation between modern times and social possibility in general. It has contemporary relevance as well, since certain problems that emerge in considering Hegel's thesis challenge today's fashionable views that maintain their own versions of the end of history. These problems impugn both the triumphalists of the American way of life and the grave diggers of metaphysics.

Ends for History

Presumably, if we were at the end of history we would relate to our possibilities for action in a changed way. The obvious approach to thinking such a change is as *the completion of a teleology*. At least on the large scale of political and social structures, a set of potentialities would have achieved its full actualization. This would happen in a structure that as part of its completion leaves possibilities open for individual and group action on lower levels of generality. Such a description fits Hegel, and the Aristotelian overtones are appropriate. The final stage has its own definite structure with its own institutional identity, which for Hegel is a version of the liberal, capitalist state. Some recent proclaimers of the end of history, notably Francis Fukuyama, agree that representative democracy and capitalism are the final social forms.[2]

A different image for the end of history is as *the exhaustion of possibilities.* We find this in Heidegger and some of his descendants. Our age would complete the trajectory of Western metaphysical culture and exhaust its potential. Without a radical break, which we cannot bring about on our own, anything "new" that develops would remain within the now closed orbit of possibilities marked by the general flow of our age. That flow can be either regretted (with Heidegger) or celebrated (with many postmodernists).

This will be clearer if we consider a third image of the end, as *an unblocking of circulation.* Barriers would have been removed that restricted the movement of something whose flow creates society. This unblocking can be seen optimistically; in Marx the end of history is an opening rather than a closure, because old restrictions are being removed that have blocked the circulation of communal self-affirmation and resources.[3] But the unbinding of circulation can also be thought in a bleaker way. For Heidegger, our final epoch of metaphysics has no one particular institutional form, but the possibilities open to us are all of a kind. They are all within the sweep of a circulation that makes them its way-stations and undercuts all resistance to the movement of surfaces and usage.

Hegel's "end of history," like those of Heidegger and Marx, can be described as the unbinding of a circulation. In it, the movement of mutual recognition and/as Spirit's self-comprehension finally overcomes otherness and completes the circle of Spirit's becoming. But Hegel thinks this final stage under the sign of Aristotelian actuality whereas Heidegger and others think it as Nietzsche's eternal return of the same.

All these theories distinguish two levels. On the general level a final stage has been reached; the lower level remains a sphere of relatively free variation. It may appear that Hegel only differs from later theories in that Hegel's higher level is more elaborate; he dictates more institutional structures and leaves less room for social variety. I argue below that there is much more going on than a disagreement over levels of generality. At stake are different ways of thinking about how social possibilities are established and connected.

Views that proclaim or imply an end of history today tend to be unstable. They slip and slide in four directions. The first direction is back to the general Enlightenment narrative of progress in which history has no final stage but does exhibit a steady direction toward an ideal of liberation. This view has lately become a familiar target for attacks from both right and left. Under such attack the Enlightenment narrative tends to slide in the other directions.

The next direction is away from global claims. You merely tell a local story which appraises current institutions and finds them good when measured along some pragmatic axis of evaluation. An example would be Richard Rorty's discussions of the effectiveness of current values and institutions.[4] He gives us a local story of Western development, with a positive judgment but no claimed necessity. This is a down-to-earth position but it lacks the drama many contemporaries find in claims about the finality of technological or media society. And since Rorty's kind of story remains internal to our own local narratives, it leaves room for competing external and internal stories. This is not a problem for Rorty, but it bothers Hegelians and Heideggerians who seek more necessity in their analyses of current society.

The third direction is back toward fuller Hegelian claims for necessity and detail in the end of history. Interpreters find themselves arguing with Hegel about just what institutions would be required to properly mediate the various aspects and partial unities that make up political and social community. They end up defending some updated version of Hegel's constitutional and economic arrangements. Positions of this kind can be found, for example, in the writings of Richard Winfield or Klaus Hartmann. This direction leads into rough argumentative terrain because of the difficulty of locating the line between necessary structures and contingent detail.

The fourth slide is the most fateful. For the reality of and the discussions about civil society have not stood still since Hegel's day. The fourth slide is toward Heidegger, Adorno, and postmoderns such as Baudrillard, Lyotard, and some aspects of Foucault. Though these thinkers have their own disputes, they stand together in affirming a perverse finality for the present age. Heidegger's essays on technology, in particular, picture a world where the destiny of metaphysics has been completed. In a manner that would be repugnant to the Plato who nonetheless was its ancestor, our time fulfills the goal of bringing all beings into the certainty of grounded presence. With the long-prepared death of God and his substitutes, no foundational being remains withdrawn from the leveling movement.

In the age of technology every being stands revealed as material for ordering and use, but there is no controlling center to which these uses all refer. Even the apparent domination of the world by human subjectivity has given way to the engineering of subjects themselves, producing whatever types are most useful for the flow of will and power. That larger circulation has no closure or goal beyond its own increased efficiency and velocity. The will to power is the will to will.

In discussing Hegel I will be speaking much about intermediate structures. For Heidegger, by contrast, today's world brings the flattening of human reality and the dedifferentiation of modes of being. Individual beings are confronted directly by the naked imperatives of use, and individual subjects face directly the anonymous forces of impersonal bureaucracy and efficacy. Whatever intermediate structures remain in our world have lost their power to mediate individuals into an articulated totality.

If Heidegger proclaims the end of our particular Western history, the newer postmodern stories go further. By moving Heidegger's discussions into economic and semiotic registers, Baudrillard arrives at the description of a final age that absorbs all fixed identity into the circulation of capital and floating signifiers. This story deepens the interchangeability and replaceability that characterized particulars in Hegel's civil society. Institutional structures themselves become indifferently replaceable within a movement that overcomes them in the name of a circulation that lies beneath any stability. In order to get some perspective on these claims about the end of history, I will concentrate on Hegel's theory, bringing in Heidegger along the way, and returning later to the postmodern theories.

Ends in Hegel

The end of history involves the larger question of closure in Hegel's system. When Hegel's thought is taken as a whole it is difficult to determine to what degree he did endorse finality and closure. I have argued elsewhere that his system is indeed meant to be final on a certain level of categorial generality.[5] The keys to this closure are to be found in Hegel's treatment of the categories of thought in his logic. In this essay, then, I will look to his logic to find the categories that would be needed to describe a strong end of history. I will be asking how Hegel would describe the relation between a final historical situation and the field of possibilities that surrounds it. That is, I will investigate what kind of thing an end of history would have to be, rather than examining what precise institutional details Hegel argues for in his *Philosophy of Right.*

What are the categories Hegel claims are needed if we are to think a closure in social and political structures? He has thought deeply about closure and what it would demand and so has, I will argue, very stringent but convincing criteria for what would count as a strong end of history. One major problem he sees and works to overcome is what he calls "repulsion," which undermines weaker claims about an end. Looking at that problem, I will argue that contemporary thinkers who proclaim an end of history cannot meet the criteria Hegel establishes for closure. Since I doubt whether Hegel himself can meet those criteria, the results will dispute *any* claim about such an end.

At a strong end of history certain kinds of social change could only be conceived as regression. This is a daunting claim because it legislates about future possibility. How would we ever be in a position to establish such a sweeping claim? A universal preference (say, for liberal democracy) cannot prove a strong end of history; people have had different widespread preferences in the past. The proclamation of the end demands some necessity beyond an empirical survey.

Generally the strong claims have a Kantian base: we have come to know something about the conditions of the possibility of social institutions, and those conditions both open a field of possibilities and show its limits. Knowing those limits we can sketch out the final stage which comes when we can self-consciously create institutions that express those conditions fully and nakedly.[6] Hegel elaborates that Kantian base in his logic, which develops from Kant's inquiry into categories and conditions of possibility but is much more concretely concerned with what it means for something to be determinate and definite, and how things relate to their possibilities. Hegel shows that this happens in many different ways. There are many ways for a being to be determinate: as simple qualitative presence, as measured quantity, as realization of essence, as a thing with properties, as formed matter, and so on. These are not for Hegel reducible to one another, and they all have their own various relations to possible other determinations.

The end of history is a stage of history distinct from others. We can then ask how we are to think its difference from other past or imagined possible stages. If we think the final stage as one among many, simply present with its own definitions and structures, it will be an example of what Hegel calls Dasein, the category of determinate being. Any entity or system described this way is thought of as occupying one determinate location within a space of possible qualities. It is blue rather than red or black, democratic rather than monarchical or oligarchical. Its identity is bounded by the things it is not, just as they are bounded by it. There is nothing in its qualitative identity that makes it special or final. If the end of history were to be thought using this notion of determinate identity, there would have to be some extrinsic reason or measure that nominated this rather than another as the final stage. Its finality would be contingent, since there are many different external standards that could be brought to bear.

The end of history, however, must be more than some situation that for extrinsic reasons happens to terminate society's wandering through various structures drawn from a larger pool of possible structures.[7] It should also be more than the culmination of one local narrative inserted amid a space of other possible narratives. It should have some necessity and should dominate the field of alternatives. To think the end of history as truly final, then, we must think of it as relating internally to earlier stages and rival narratives—perhaps by encompassing the field of historical possibilities, perhaps by relating to other stages of history as deficient or primitive forms of itself, or perhaps by subsuming rival narratives into itself.[8]

The obvious candidate for thinking the end of history in this way is Hegel's category of the good or true infinite, which occurs conveniently in the logic at just this point. In a sense this does provide his answer, since its general move is to a self-enclosed totality. However in its first appearance the good infinite is not sufficiently developed. Many people (including Heidegger in his lectures on the *Phenomenology of Spirit*) read Hegel as if the crucial moves are made early in his works and then explicated in the long continuations. Because Hegel's works are so long, it is pedagogically easier to declare that crucial moves are made at the beginnings, but this can be very misleading: in comparison with their later developments, the early versions of the crucial moves remain themselves abstract and too immediate. At its first appearance in the logic the category of the infinite itself remains too impoverished. As it reappears during the continuation of the logic it acquires more content (becomes more "concrete," in Hegel's terms) until the appropriate categories are reached at the end of the logic.[9]

The good infinite is often presented as the result of a transition from the notion of an endless linear infinite series to a notion of circular infinite self-relation. However, the bad infinite is not so much a linear series as an indefinite oscillation. "Something becomes an other; this other is itself something; therefore it likewise becomes another, and so on ad infinitum" (*E*, § 93). We do not yet have an infinite progress but only a directionless wandering through the space of possible quality-states. This arises from combining the demand for unity with a type of identity that is not equal to that demand because the unity it offers is negatively defined (i.e., its identity is bounded by the things it is not). When the unity is affirmed, its constitutive relation to others is also affirmed, and so the unity cannot be final and self-enclosed. As long as determination is thought as limitation and relation to otherness, there can be no real closure.

For example, Aristotle's famous discussion in the *Politics* of the forms of government classifies different types and ranks them, but Aristotle makes no claims about any necessary order in which the different forms occur. Over time, a given city can move from democracy to monarchy to tyranny to democracy to oligarchy without there being any overall pattern or culminating stage. In Aristotle's case the space of possible social forms is relatively small, and history wanders about within it. Particular transitions or revolutions may have their own goals, but there is no overall goal. There is a best form of government, but there is no unified historical process leading to the realization of that form. History overall is not an entity that realizes a potentiality. More recent theories may make the space of possible social forms quite large, or even indefinitely large, but they keep the unordered wandering through possible forms.

Hegel's subsequent treatments of the infinite enrich the notion, but not enough for use in thinking an end of history. In the discussion of quantity we find an ordered infinite series, but one without a goal.[10] In the section on measure this becomes a series that can be thought as maximizing some quality.[11] That treatment could allow us to think history as a directed process of growth that increases a measure such as population or resources. But since it is in the nature of measured change that there can always be more of it, this model too cannot provide a concept that describes an end.[12] It is only in the third major part of the logic, the "logic of the concept," that categories will be available that combine totality, self-relation, and a key change in the relation of particular states to the field of possibilities within which they find their identity.[13] Hegel thinks that fully self-enclosed unity (such as must characterize the end of history) will find its identity in *defining* a space of possibilities rather than in *belonging* to one. Such self-relation will demand a mediated unity with its own intermediate articulation of the field of possibilities.

Repulsion

Before continuing to those final categories, however, I need to clarify the challenge that they must overcome. I have been claiming that the various treatments of the good infinite do not give us a notion of self-enclosed unity adequate to thinking an end of history. Hegel acknowledges this in his first discussion of the good infinite. While in the notes to that first discussion he anticipates much that he will develop later, the actual text of the transition moves only to the category of "being-for-self," which lacks the kind of closure we need. This lack shows up in its affliction by what Hegel calls *repulsion.*[14]

Repulsion is an Hegelian expression of the problem of competing multiple unities and plural stories. Repulsion is the categorical implication whereby the attempt to think a self-enclosed unit demands that the unit be thought as amid a multiplicity of such units, each indifferent to the other yet necessarily implied by them. The possibility of the unit is also, then, the possibility of other such independent units. Hence, a "being-for-self" is thought as independent of any constitutive relation to others. But just because of this independence from context, such a unit can be thought only as one of an indifferent multitude of such units. In its independence and its isolating closure on itself such a unit has no ability to define and control the space of possibility it inhabits. Its categorial structure provides no way to think uniqueness, for this would demand some constitutive relation between the unit and the field of possibilities. So, the category allowing the thought of one such unit demands the thought of a possible indefinite number of them.

Hegel's repulsion bears an uncanny resemblance to Heidegger's discussion of identity and difference, and to that deconstructive dissemination that denies any unity its attempted closure.[15] Repulsion works to multiply closure rather than fracture it, but that multiplication denies the self-sufficiency of the attempted closure precisely by asserting it.

Evading repulsion is crucial to the end of history. The basic proposal was to think the end of history after the model of the good infinite that affirms an enclosed being-for-self instead of an aimless alternation of different social forms drawn from some larger pool of possible forms. But self-enclosed, "good infinite" unities suffer repulsion. Thought as self-enclosed, the end of history will be thought as one among a number of externally related histories within a larger space of possible stories.

Repulsion raises the specter of a multitude of different stories unifying the "same" events of our history. There would be no reason why these stories should all end at the same time. Moreover, repulsion threatens to dissipate the universal end into a multitude of unrelated local ends. Our history and the Martians? What about European history and Chinese history? American and Canadian history? Massachusetts and Rhode Island? Boston and Cambridge? There would be no categorial reason why the many histories could not be ever more finely distinct. Nor need they be simultaneous, nor structurally alike. It would be an empirical question whether the end of history was widely shared or not—and how would that empirical question be settled? Such local teleologies would lack any universal significance. If by chance they showed many local paths leading to a similar goal, this coincidence would be only external. At this point repulsion would have shattered not only Hegel's end of history but also the kind of unity claimed for Heidegger's history of Being and age of technology.

Hegel wishes to find categories that evade repulsion by internalizing it. Everything hangs on the success or failure of that maneuver. This requires, in turn, a rigorous essentialism, to control which descriptions of events and which groups of events fit into legitimate stories. If such essentialism is not externally enforced, as in Augustine's *City of God*, then it will likely depend on an attempt such as Hegel's—or Heidegger's—to define the conditions that make any story possible. It is crucial that the final self-closure be able to control the field of possible stories. If it cannot successfully station itself above that field and legislate its contours, then the closure will suffer repulsion. Unless we can accept something like a full Hegelian closure—and we cannot—all doctrines of the end of history, weak or strong, Hegelian or Heideggerian or postmodern, suffer a repulsive dissipation.

Ends That Work

So we return to the question: What is the status of the field of possibilities within which the end of history is located? To what extent does the end of history constitute and overarch that field rather than being located within it?

What Hegel needs is a conception of identity and unity that avoids repulsion both for the particular content and for the overall unity. Such categories are offered in the logic of the concept. There, the basic ontological unities are conceptualized first as the universal which particularizes itself, then as objective systems which include their determinate members, then finally as cognitive, volitional, and "absolute" wholes that include a field of possible subordinate determinations within their dialectical identity. These categories transform plurality into self-mediated totality.

Of course, to invoke these names is not to establish the corresponding categories as the only legitimate and necessary ways of thinking totality and closure. Other "end of history" theories tend not to accept Hegel's elaborate categories. But at this point we can see better the reasons why Hegel feels such categories would be needed. Whether or not Hegel succeeds, his worries about less than perfect closure still apply to other theories of the end of history.

It is in the logic of the concept that we find the categories that provide Hegel's conceptual resources for thinking a strong end to history. Here the particularity of historical stages is treated in a new way.[16] In this sphere, a limit is not a *Schranke* or a reference outside to other possibilities that have been excluded (*WL* 12, 36/604). "The concept . . . is determinate and possesses its determinateness in this true way, namely, that it differentiates itself within itself and is the unity of these fixed and determinate differences" (*WL* 12, 91/665).

In the logic of the concept, the universal unity is self-related in and through its spreading out into particularization. The key, Hegel thinks, is to realize that while the identity of this or that particular content is in relation to other actual and possible particular contents, the whole field of possible determinations obtains because it is constituted in the self-positing of the universal unity. That unity comes about through the establishment of a space of possibilities and not as one item within such a space. The ultimate implications of this must lead to the overarching "Absolute Idea," since the various universals must themselves be related in a similar way to some overarching unity which finds itself through positing the possibilities of their multiplication. This is the ultimate block to repulsion. But if that full closure is weakened, repulsion will attack all its unities.

In the logic of the concept the bad infinite makes important final appearances in the discussions of the formal universal and the formal syllogism (*WL* 12, 98/673). Earlier bad infinites were rooted in the constantly recurring negative *otherness* that defines any identity. Now, bad infinity occurs as the endless *substitution* of one positive particular for another within a mediated universal unity. The higher identity is defined as the inclusive whole, self-determining because it defines the space of possible determinate particulars. However, in the "formal" universal and syllogism the bad infinite enters because the unity is still too unstructured; it is a form that can receive arbitrary content. The space of possible particulars is too abruptly juxtaposed to the unity. There are no necessary intermediate articulations of the field of possibilities into groups and classes that resist indiscriminate substitution. As a result, any particular contents will do to realize the universal, and none are final; they are interchangeable and infinitely substitutable for one another.

For example, almost any contract, any monetary transaction, any arbitrary social role can count for membership in a modern "civil society." The circulation of identity and need in that society depends on endless substitution. In Hegel's view such unity is both too much and too little. Too much because the universal unity is too close to the particular content, baptizing each of them with the same meaning. Too little because the universal unity provides no necessary structures to articulate the field of possibilities, and so allows endless substitution of one content for another. The formal universal in civil society substitutes plurality for totality (*WL* 12, 75/648). This description also fits the open flow of power and use in Heidegger's *Gestell* and its descendants.

In order to have a truly final universal unity, what kind of connection does there have to be between that unity and the determinate content it is to unify? Hegel criticizes his contemporaries for declaring philosophical unities that are too formal, as he reads Schelling's Absolute or the electric polarities of romantic *Naturphilosophie.* These unities can encompass all particular content but they make no distinctions; they can be attached indifferently to any state of affairs. The total unity stands indifferently next to the content, and does not incorporate the content into meaningful intermediate structures.

Intermediate Structure

Hegel claims that the basic insight needed at this point was provided by Kant. The prime example of a universal unity is the "I" or ego, which maintains its identity precisely in and through differentiating and uniting the diversity of time and experience through the structure of the Kantian categories.

> Differentiation must be regarded as an equally essential moment of the concept. Kant has introduced this consideration by the extremely important thought that there are synthetic judgments a priori. This original synthesis of apperception is one of the most profound principles for speculative development; it contains the beginning of a true apprehension of the nature of the concept and is completely opposed to that empty identity or abstract universality which is not within itself a synthesis. (*WL* 12, 22/589)

Pure blank unity is not enough. There is no sheer presence of the "I" to itself. Nor is the "I" merely juxtaposed to the varied particular content of experience, as Hume sought it. Rather, the unity of the ego is maintained across and through the diversity introduced by the necessary synthetic a priori truths. The categories and the principles that express them allow for the structuring of experience in such a way that it can be unified under the self-conscious ego. The unity of experience is not that of an other-related multitude facing a blank ego-unity. Categories and principles give necessary structure to the whole, and the relation goes both ways: the necessary structure makes possible the unity of experience, and the structure is itself necessary because of its role in that unity.

The categories are the necessary intermediate structures that allow the unity and the diversity of experience. They define the dimensions that *open* the field of possibilities used to understand things: causal relations, temporal relations, sameness, inherence, and so on. These structures define what it is to be an experience and an object of experience. They are not themselves determined as one kind of object within a field of possibilities. Nor are they selections from some wider field of possible categories. If they were, the transcendental question would recur, demanding an account of the larger field of possibilities. This is why Kant can write a "metaphysics" of morals or nature and claim to have proven necessary conclusions.

For Hegel the ego is a prime example of a self-differentiating universal unity that includes necessary intermediate structures.[17] But there are other such unities as well, including some which overarch individual self-consciousness. The unity of these other universals also demands that they have nonarbitrary intermediate structures akin to Kant's categories. These intermediate structures cannot be thought using the other-related categories of being or essence. The only adequate self-conception of such unity is as containing within itself the categories that are the parameters for fields of possible particulars. The universal thus opens fields of possibility rather than belonging to them.

Hegel tries to develop his version of Kant's categories from the controversial beginning point of the logic in pure thought alone, asking what it takes to effectively think content and determination. The resulting categories are arranged in the complex series of inclusions and oppositions that make up the logic. The necessity of the categories is shown in their self-development from the indefinite beginning to the all-encompassing final category. This development is not a history, but a tissue of relations of more abstract and more concrete categories (in Hegel's special sense of "abstract" and "concrete"). The sequence encompasses the contradictions and resolutions that occur in earlier categories. Its final member contains the earlier ones as impoverished versions of its own richness and complexity.

The different levels of these categories provide Hegel's means for thinking nature and history on a variety of levels suited to the varied content of experience. Most importantly for our topic, the final categories provide Hegel's way of thinking temporal development. The final stage in a temporal development embodies in itself not only the field of possibilities for its current particular content, but also the earlier stages of its own history, now seen as past anticipations and subordinate current components of the final unity. Thus the end of history is an end in a much fuller sense than would be intended by Kant's Enlightenment notions of progress, or by current Enlightenment-style praises for liberal democratic institutions.

As a way for thinking closure, this Kantian-Hegelian program provides for a bilevel treatment of detail. In both Kant and Hegel, the program presupposes a level of purely contingent data that enters into structures it cannot on its own supply. This avoids the problem of deducing Krug's pen and provides a way for combining closure and openness. In Kant, some general truths will be synthetic a priori and others will be empirical generalizations unified by the categories. In Hegel, some determinations will be necessitated by the overall unity while others will be contingent and free. Thus the end of history can occur on one level of generality while leaving us free to act within its parameters on other levels.[18] As in Kant so in Hegel this is in practice a very difficult, perhaps impossible, line to draw.

State and Civil Society at the End of History

While the end of history requires both unifying categorial structure and free particular content, Hegel does not believe that the structures of civil society (the free market and a minimal state) provide sufficient categorial structure. I have argued elsewhere that Hegel believes that the transition from formal to more structured universality applies to the relation between these two institutional forms.[19] The inner necessity of the universal unity of the state must be expressed by more elaborate structures that have internal connections with the concept of intersubjective community rather than with the formal rationality of the market.

If this is the case, then the end of history cannot be an apotheosis of civil society. That would be to claim that a species of formal universality was enough. Civil society is almost all contingency, caprice, opinion, and the outer necessity of the market and the system of needs. There is not enough of the mediating intermediate structure that creates self-enclosed unity. In civil society, the parameters that open the space of social possibilities are set by arbitrary will (contract), nature (basic bodily structure and needs), and contingency (the indefinite multiplication of needs in the market). The space of possibilities so constituted has no internal shape; it provides for almost unlimited circulation and substitution. But without any internal dimensionality and differentiation, the space of possibilities remains open and uncontrolled; no final narrative can be told about it except the story of more and more freedom and commodities, a story that achieves no final actuality.

This is why the recent stories of the finality of civil society tend to fall back into the Enlightenment two-stage narrative: for a long time circulation and substitution (and so freedom) were limited in many ways, but now the limits are being removed so that circulation and substitution and freedom are open to continual increase. As a result, civil society stands ambiguously in the present debates; it is sometimes a particular set of institutions, and sometimes a kind of social metastructure for generating institutions characterized by substitution and circulation. The formal universality of this social metastructure may remain stable but its contents are constituted by repulsion, the combination of particular sufficiency and mutual indifference. We can recognize in that joining of empty universality and arbitrary content the lineaments of Heidegger's technological world and its postmodern descendants (such as Baudrillard's world of surfaces and network relays).

For Hegel this cannot be enough. The space of social possibilities needs more internal structure so that individuals and groups can achieve a social identity integrated into a whole of social possibility, rather than slipping and sliding through the almost featureless circulation opened by civil society. In Hegel's jargon, there must be structures that more fully mediate and give equal weight to the moments of universality, particularity, and individuality. Civil society over-emphasizes particularity at the expense of the other two moments. This is shown, Hegel claims, by the self-transcending tendencies he sees in civil society, tendencies that reveal the necessary inherence of civil society within a wider community with more elaborate intermediate structures. The *Philosophy of Right* discusses those structures in detail. The elaborately interrelated institutions of Hegel's government involve a citizenry differentiated into economic and occupational groups where natural inclination meets a rational representative structure unfolded within the concept of a self-constituted community.

Thus at the end of history we have, for Hegel, a rational constitution encompassing while profiting from the dynamic of civil society. Ordinary events will not cease, of course, because these structures function precisely by encouraging and unifying a whole mass of contingent desires, actions, and events. Nor does this mean that every nation will be the same, for the rational constitution is still fairly general. The French and the English will not "do" it the same way, for they have different histories and different national spirits that emphasize different values. But overall the modern world will tend toward worldwide economic relations and one general type of political institutions.

Hegel claims that we have reached a time of self-comprehensive rational closure, where the necessary intermediate structures are in principle available. Of course he sees that many serious problems remain to be addressed, but they are to be handled within those structures, or else they are signs of the inadequacy of any institutional structure to bear the full weight of the logical Idea.[20]

Yet Hegel also questions the adequacy of any given institutional structures. We are familiar with his image of the owl of Minerva bringing understanding only when a form of life has grown old. In the logic of the concept he also writes: "The highest maturity [*Reife*] and the highest stage which anything can attain is that in which its downfall [*Untergang*] begins" (*WL* 12, 42/611). This quotation is somewhat out of context, but Hegel is indeed asking whether any particular finite arrangement can really express the full dynamism of the universal unity.[21] After all, that unity maintains itself in part by demonstrating its independence from any one determinate state of affairs (though not from all).

The most straightforward application of this passage is that the rational state as a type endures while particular states grow and decay. For Hegel political universality is not the ultimate unity. The rational state is the end of world history in the sense that it exemplifies a set of institutions that mediate all the aspects of social unity. This state is a type, not a particular nation. Any individual nation and people has its downfall. If the story of social and institutional development has a relatively harmonious ending for Hegel, the overall story of national development remains tragic. No particular national identity will last forever, and international relations find no final institutional structure in a world state such as Kant envisioned. There is no end of history on that level, though Hegel expects conflicts to be somewhat muted by the increasing rationality of the inner constitution of states. Our final self-conscious reconciliation will not be found in the removal of tension and negativity from history but rather in the more contemplative arenas of art, religion, and philosophy. So Hegel can consistently maintain that nations have reached a rationally satisfying institutional structure, without claiming that the play of nations in world history is over.[22]

All this suggests that one might agree with Hegel about the need for what the *Philosophy of Right* discusses as the transition from the atomism of morality (*Moralität*) to the intersubjective structure of ethical community (*Sittlichkeit*), but at the same time try to show the necessity of a different set of institutional structures than those Hegel discusses. Or one might try to argue that while the transition to ethical community demands *some* institutional structures, the particular structures in any given community are a matter of contingent detail.

Hegel would not be happy with such positions. They leave the unity of ethical community only a formal unity to be specified by contingently available institutions. This puts us back with a determinate form of society inserted within an empirically given field of possibilities. Only a weak end of history is possible at that point, namely the metaclaim that we have realized the final truth that social mediation is necessary though the form of that mediation is contingent. For Hegel this would leave the final self-relation too general. Logically, it would be subject to repulsion. Practically, it would undermine the detailed systematic necessity Hegel thinks we need in order to resolve the lived dichotomies of the modern world. He would reiterate his general arguments for the transition from formal to substantive universality, and his particular arguments for the transition from civil society to the state. It is just these topics that are emerging in current discussions that imply the end of history.

Postmodern Ends

When Heidegger speaks of the trajectory of Western civilization having completed itself in *das Gestell* of technological society, he is not thinking of any Hegelian unity. There is still a Kantian impetus, however, because the closure Heidegger speaks of is also due to something that must be thought as opening a field of possibilities rather than as one item within a given field. The event that grants the meaning of Being to our era opens the ways actions and individuals will understand themselves. It is not itself a happening within some larger space of determinate possibilities.

However, the pedigree of Heidegger's *Gestell* is not simply Kantian. Besides the link to Kant's categories and to the self-relation achieved by Kant's rational will, there is Nietzsche questioning the necessity of a unified epistemological or political subject. Nietzsche converts the Kantian and Hegelian self-return into a wandering circulation of will and power. Nietzsche's self-affirming but never self-present will is what is reappropriated in Heidegger's *Gestell*, then reworked by others.

In Heidegger as in Hegel there is a fundamental "motion" that opens fields of possibility rather than being an item or a trajectory within such a field. But for Heidegger that motion is not the self-distancing-and-return circulation of Hegel's Spirit. Temporalization in Heidegger is not a self-unity but a distension and binding and separating that is prior to any unity. It is an opening that allows for goals, movements, and closure without itself being any thing of that sort.

In Hegel the circulation of Spirit's self-affirmation establishes its own space and its own stations. Spirit establishes those stations by unfolding itself into a necessary set of intermediate structures. These structures open the distances and articulations that make social life possible. The achieved necessity and transparency of these intermediate structures mark the end of history.

However, in Heidegger and his successors it is precisely the *lack* of necessary intermediate structures that marks the end of history. Once we have found that all such structures are only stopping places in *Gestell*'s flow of use and will (or of capital or power or signifiers), then we have achieved the final stage. No institutional or value change will move us from this place where all institutions and values exist only as nodes or temporary stations that are always already being passed by. Rather than being mediated by necessary intermediate articulations, this universal goal-less circulation is *directly* in touch with particular possibilities and actualities. The overall flow imposes no structures or limits but is always there beforehand, disturbing all unities. There is no depth of structure, so the possibilities are all the same. Particular structures remain and are multiplied ad infinitum. We cannot do without them, but they lose their finality, their weight, their necessity. There are some necessary structures found by Heidegger's analyses (such as his discussions of temporality and the fourfold), but they remain extraordinarily general and reach across epochs and eras. They are not themselves determinate structures of a particular epoch and they do not unfold into necessary intermediate structures.

From the perspective of the Hegelian problematic as I have been expounding it, Heidegger and his postmodern successors tell stories of the end of history that look like a retreat to formal universality, with all the problems Hegel sees in such formal unities. There is indeed something about these stories that resembles the romantic *Naturphilosophie* that Hegel criticized so sharply. Like the followers of Schelling, Heidegger and the others go about putting the same labels on everything. The Schellingian tells us that both love and magnetism are embodiments of an absolute polarity, and now we are told how the Beatles and the Internet both exemplify the technological age and its undermining circulations.

Such formal universality simply asserts its own dominance. It tells us we now understand the movement that makes institutions and values possible We have reached the end of history because we have moved from societies where the basic circulation was bounded (or unrecognized), to a final stage where it overreaches all structures. No matter how ironic its stance, this final story must itself override (undercut, corrupt) all others, yet without making the detailed Hegelian attempt to mediate other stories into a final identity. Intermediate stories are untold. This Heideggerian story may seem more appropriate to our troubled times. But its formal totalization does forbid the detailed analysis that might find crevices and tensions in our world that could lead to change. To that extent Heidegger's story of the history of Being and its end wars against the more deconstructive aspects of his own thought.

There is another problem as well. Heidegger's story of the history of Being and the technological age avoids Hegel's self-closure and its necessary intermediate structures that try to generate and enclose possibility. But as a result Heidegger's story is liable to repulsion. And this has happened. Heidegger's has multiplied into a variety of postmodern stories that lack the seriousness and weight Heidegger hoped would counteract our reduction to functioning units within the technological age. In these other stories circulation is unbound still further so that we become Nietzsche's last men, without the depth of memory and the piety of thought so important to both Hegel and Heidegger.

In Hegel's theory historical becoming and the earlier forms of the state are *aufgehoben* into the present structures. The system breaks the immediacy of present social structures; we achieve a kind of double vision that both remembers past institutions and values as they once were when they were dominant, and sees them as they are now, differentiated subordinate functions within a greater whole.

In contrast, Heidegger's final technological age erases earlier modes of being into undifferentiated availability and presence. Yet Heidegger allows for a more active memory, since part of what the thinker can still do in our era is retrieve past possibilities. In Hegel the retrieval is already performed, and telling Spirit's story of its past completes our present identity. Whereas in Heidegger retrieving the past offers some limited hope of expanding or at least challenging what we have become.[23]

The difference between the two thinkers concerns the past as possibility. In Hegel our historical origins contained possibilities that have been presently realized. The past cannot be interrogated further since it contains no undeveloped possibilities. Our destiny is now, and it enfolds the past. History is differentiation, not retrieve. That differentiation binds circulation into necessary patterns, and repulsion has been contained. For Heidegger our historical origins open space in a circulation that cannot be overseen. The appeal to our origins is to a history that cannot be capsulized, to a distention of possibility that does not reduce to a present field of alternatives no matter how dialectically interwoven. The past may yet surprise our present identity.

But it is this more "deconstructive" aspect of Heidegger that is challenged by his somewhat Hegelian story of the history of Being and the technological age.[24] Repulsion has multiplied that story into a host of variants clamoring for just the finality that the more deconstructive Heidegger wants to reject. Perhaps we should go further with that repulsion and renounce the attempt to announce a privileged description of our situation or to tell a single overarching story about it. Repulsion undermines the seductive hope of becoming either the universal overseer or the universal underminer.

That renunciation might lead to a nonfinal way of talking about history and modernity. To hear it we could attend to some aspects of Hegel, to Heidegger's *Identity and Difference*, and to some of his deconstructive descendants. The best of these do not proclaim the end, for they avoid total stories. Hegel's repulsion challenged the singularity of any self-enclosed units that did not themselves control their field of possibilities. Repulsion now challenges the stability of any fixed or enclosed set of possibilities. This splinters both the weak and strong stories of the end of history. It dissipates such claims not into rival total stories, but into contentious threads that do not make either allness or totality. At best there may be some general and very formal truths about our situation, but these would be operative in any story, so there would be no final story of some structure or circulation that would definitively embody our endless venturing.[25]

4

"We Philosophers": *Barbaros mēdeis eisitō*

Robert Bernasconi

I

There is a moment in Heidegger's 1930–31 lecture course, *Hegel's Phenomenology of Spirit,* in which he addresses his audience directly on the subject of reading Hegel. Following a brief discussion of the structure of the *Phenomenology* from which Heidegger concludes "we can begin to understand the work only if we have already reached its end," the teacher separates himself from his students: "In this lecture course I presuppose such a first reading of the entire work. If such a reading has not taken place or does not take place in the next few weeks, there is no sense in sitting here: You cheat not only me but yourselves." (*GA* 32, 52; *HPS,* 36). Although Heidegger does not discuss in any detail, either in the lecture course or elsewhere, the second half of the *Phenomenology of Spirit,* there is never any question—as there might be for some of Hegel's other commentators whose remarks are confined to the early portions of the book—that Heidegger has passed beyond a first reading. But what does it mean to read a book, not with understanding, but as a prelude to understanding it? It is as if there could only ever be a rereading, because a first reading, if possible at all, is not yet a reading. Of course, at one level the demand does not sound so unusual. Many books cannot be fully appreciated except on rereading and, more profoundly, the fact that the meaning of a narrative is for the most part understood as being gathered in its end or conclusion argues that its coherence is established only retrospectively, which would mean only on second reading. The problem is exacerbated because of the notorious difficulty of the *Phenomenology*, its alleged unreadability. The initial task therefore, and it is not unique to Hegel, is to generate the first reading. However, the first reading of the *Phenomenology* is anything but a formality, as Heidegger himself concedes without exploring the possibility that this might constitute an impasse for the first-time reader: "However, the first reading is not a guarantee that with the second reading we really [*wirklich*] understand the work. Perhaps the first reading must be frequently repeated, which is only to say that the first reading is utterly indispensable." The first reading as a reading without understanding is now characterized as a reading without "really understanding" and its success measured simply insofar as one succeeds in passing from it to a second reading.

Heidegger does not show a great deal of interest in this first reading that he assumes his students have already managed on their own as a condition of attendance. He does not help them meet this requirement or indicate how they might begin reading. Even worse, ten years later in *Hegel's Concept of Experience* Heidegger explicitly precludes the suggestion that the *Phenomenology* provides the route "from prephilosophic representation to philosophy" (HBE, 134; *HCE*, 58).[1]

> With its first step if not before then, the presentation dismisses natural consciousness as that consciousness which in its very character remains wholly incapable of following the presentation. The presentation of phenomenal knowledge is not a path that natural consciousness can tread. (HBE, 132; *HCE*, 52–53)

This seems to leave the students high and dry. Heidegger is concerned to generate a philosophical reading of the *Phenomenology*, but his remarks make it highly unclear what a first (not yet philosophical) reading would be like. Not just the *Phenomenology* but every *philosophical* work requires two readings, the first nonphilosophical, the second philosophical. This is because one must be familiar with the whole work before one can begin to read it philosophically. The problem unique to Hegel, however, the reason why "an understanding of the end is plainly indispensable" in his case, is, as Heidegger explains in the 1930–31 lecture course, that an understanding of Hegel's basic intention and inquiry begins and must begin with absolute knowing (*GA* 32, 53; *HPS*, 37). However, the attaining of absolute knowing seems to be rather more than one can legitimately assign to a first, not yet philosophical, reading of the text.

There are problems also with Heidegger's characterization of the second reading. This is because the reading that Heidegger gives is rather more than just a reading of the *Phenomenology* in the light of Hegel's own conception of the book's structure, which is what Heidegger's description of the first reading might lead one to expect. Both in the lecture course and even more markedly in *Hegel's Concept of Experience,* Heidegger's reading follows the model of a "dialogue between thinkers," which was never a matter of discovering the intentions of previous thinkers, but was rather concerned with what those thinkers left unthought. To anticipate what follows, this leads to a situation whereby what Heidegger means when he claims that the *Phenomenology* can be understood only on a "second reading" differs markedly from what Hegel means by a similar claim. Or, rather, an ambiguity develops within what Heidegger understands by the second reading, an ambiguity between, on the one hand, the second reading that Hegel himself prescribes and which Heidegger characterizes as a dialogue between natural consciousness and absolute knowing (HBE, 186; *HCE,* 146), and, on the other hand, Heidegger's own dialogue with Hegel. This ambiguity can be located in Heidegger's treatment of the "we" and the "for us" as Hegel employs them in the *Phenomenology.*

In the second section of this essay, I attempt to clarify the question of the two readings as Hegel himself addresses it in the *Phenomenology of Spirit,* particularly in the preface and introduction. In the third section, I pursue the same question with specific reference to Hegel's "we" and to the final chapter of the *Phenomenology,* which is where one must turn to clarify what is meant by "absolute knowing." In the final section I investigate Heidegger's attempt to assimilate the two readings which structure the *Phenomenology* to his own schema. However, it will be found that Heidegger's appropriation of Hegel's "we" cannot simply be understood as a distortion of the *Phenomenology.* Heidegger does not simply rob Hegel of his "we." Heidegger embraces Hegel's "we" because he finds there the basis of a community which, while not exactly Hegel's community, nevertheless embraces Hegel, among others. This community is established under the title: philosophy. Hence my title: *We philosophers.* But this title not only gathers; it excludes. It excludes not only in the name of philosophy, but also in the name of Greece, for the identity of philosophy as Greek or Western will also prove to be at issue. Hence my subtitle: *barbaros mēdeis eisitō* or "Let no barbarian (non-Greek) enter here."

II

The *Phenomenology of Spirit* for the first-time reader is what life is said to be in the famous aphorism: "just one damned thing after another." Shapes of consciousness are given in quick succession, but they follow one from another in a sequence apparently without rhyme or reason. Hegel himself admits this when at various points in the introduction he contrasts, on the one hand, the "succession" (*Reihe*) of shapes (*Gestalten*) or experiences (e.g., *PG*, 56; *PS*, 50), which are presented only "by chance and externally" (*PG*, 61; *PS*, 55), with, on the other hand, the "necessity of a progression" (*PG*, 56; *PS*, 50). The difference is the difference between a first and a second reading. But how is "the succession of experiences through which consciousness passes (*die Reihe der Erfahrungen des Bewusstseins*) raised into a scientific progression" (*PG*, 61; *PS*, 55)? How does one pass from the first to the second reading? Hegel addresses this question in terms of a discussion of *Wissenschaft.*

Hegel acknowledges that "an exposition of how knowledge makes its appearance" may seem "not to be Science" (*PG*, 55; *PS*, 49). This provides the possibility that the *Phenomenology*, understood as "the path of the natural consciousness which presses forward to true knowledge," "the way of the Soul which journeys through the succession [*Reihe*] of its own configurations" (*PG*, 55; *PS*, 49), can be regarded as an introduction to the system of science. However, this interpretation is at best one-sided or incomplete. When Heidegger in *Hegel's Concept of Experience* strenuously rejected the widespread view of the *Phenomenology* as "the description of a journey which will lead everyday consciousness to a scientific knowledge of philosophy" (HBE, 131; *HCE*, 51), he did so from the standpoint of what I am calling the second reading. As I have already indicated, I will later raise questions as to how Heidegger understands this second reading. Hegel himself is somewhat more nuanced in his rejection of this characterization of the book.

So, for example, the text from the introduction that serves as the basis of Heidegger's discussion actually reads: "the succession of configurations which consciousness goes through along this road is, in reality, the detailed history of the education [*Bildung*] of consciousness to the standpoint of Science" (*PG*, 56; *PS*, 50). It is not that Hegel does not undertake to educate natural consciousness by leading it through a succession of shapes, so much as that in the course of being led consciousness discovers that in fact the path is that of the history of the education of consciousness. As a history that consciousness has already undergone, the history of the education of consciousness already belongs to it. It is not something *external* to consciousness that has to be *learned*, but something *interior* to it, a history that need only be *remembered.* This, as Hegel shows in the section of chapter 6 entitled "*Bildung,*" is something *Bildung* itself refuses to acknowledge. Hegel says that *Bildung* takes the world which it has produced as something alien, so that in setting about the task of "conforming to actuality" it affirms its self-alienation (*PG*,

268; *PS*, 299). In this way *Bildung* thinks of itself as internalizing facts or theories external to it, when it would better understand itself as taking possession in a way that allows it to have at its disposal what already belongs to its formation and so in another sense is already inherent to it. The history of the *Bildung* of consciousness can be written only when *Bildung* has proven to be other than what it thinks itself to be. The description of the *Phenomenology* in terms of *Bildung* gives way to one in terms of *Erinnerung* or remembrance.[2] To emphasize the contrast between the externality of the former and the interiority of the latter Hegel near the end of chapter 8 writes *Erinnerung* as *Er-Innerung* (*PG*, 433; *PS*, 492).[3]

Hegel also addresses this issue in the preface and he does so in terms of a distinction between the particular individual and what he calls, in a striking turn of phrase, the universal individual, *das allgemeine Individuum* (*PG*, 24; *PS*, 16). The notion of the universal individual, which is explicated in the second edition as self-conscious Spirit and in the first edition as the world Spirit, allows the issue to be discussed with greater precision. In the particular individual one shape or concrete form of consciousness predominates. Previous forms belong to the particular individual only as a trace (*Spur*). They are available to remembrance (*Erinnerung*) where they still appear as something external, but they also belong to the universal Spirit as the substance of the individual. This provides another way of approaching the idea of education: "the task of leading the individual from his *uneducated* standpoint to knowledge had to be taken in its universal sense and the universal individual, the self-conscious Spirit, had to be considered in its *education*." Hegel's point is that although the individual *as particular* may not yet have made the past his or her own, the fact that the individual *as universal* has already shared in that past makes passing through the contents of the *educational* stages of the universal Spirit easier. It is because the universal Spirit already belongs to the individual as his or her substance that what absorbed the greatest minds centuries ago is now an exercise for schoolchildren. What appears to the particular individual to be the internalization of the external is, from the standpoint of universal Spirit, the raising of substance to self-consciousness. In other words, it is the becoming and reflection into itself of the universal Spirit. This redefines the task that the *Phenomenology* must perform. It is less a novel voyage of discovery than a taking possession of what one already is in one's substance as a universal individual (*PG*, 25–26; *PS*, 17). Although for each reader as particular individual, reading the *Phenomenology of Spirit* is a question of taking possession of material which appears external but which in fact is not, from the point of view of the universal individual, it is a question of accumulated substance Being brought to self-consciousness.

In the course of reading the *Phenomenology* therefore a shift takes place in how the text operates, which is why Hegel finds himself obliged to correct the provisional characterizations of the text that he offers in the preface and introduction. So it is only when Hegel has had the opportunity to explain his notions of *Bildung* and of *Erinnerung* that it becomes clear why it is so important to him to distinguish the education of consciousness, which the *Phenomenology* does not undertake, from the history of that education that it recalls. Similarly, in the preface the reader is told that he or she has a genuine right to demand of the science a ladder to raise him or her "to the absolute standpoint," but, when Hegel revised the *Phenomenology* for a second edition shortly before his death, he departed from the metaphor and added a phrase that more accurately describes what takes place: science shows the individual this standpoint within himself or herself (*PG*, 23; *PS*, 14–15). That is to say, there is a sense in which as heirs to the tradition every potential reader of the *Phenomenology* has already read the book before picking it up. Or, more precisely, the history of the education of consciousness is inscribed in the substance of each potential reader. In that sense every actual reading of the book discovers itself to be a rereading of it. The first reading passes to the second reading at the point where one recognizes the book as a record, a reminder, of one's own history qua universal individual; or, in Hegel's own terms, it is the reminder of a history in which existence has already been transformed into the in-itself, and which is now in its turn elevated to self-consciousness through the recollection of that history.

However, reading the *Phenomenology* in this way does not yet meet Hegel's intention. It does not yet establish the scientific status of the work, its necessity. There is no doubt that Hegel thought of the *Phenomenology* as belonging to the system of science. When Hegel first presented the book that we now know simply as *Phänomenologie des Geistes*, it appeared under the title *System der Wissenschaft—Erster Theil: die Phänomenologie des Geistes.*[4] As preparation for science, as introduction to science, it was and needed to be already scientific. Hegel said so explicitly in the introduction: "the way to Science is itself already Science" (*PG*, 61; *PS*, 56).[5] Furthermore, the original edition carried an internal title page between the preface and the introduction, which was originally to have read *Erster Theil: Wissenschaft der Erfahrung des Bewusstseyns*, but which at the last moment was changed to read: 1. *Wissenschaft der Phänomenologie des Geistes.*[6] The *Phenomenology* was understood by Hegel as intrinsic to the system of science, and not as extrinsic, standing outside, offering a ladder to the system. Hegel suggests that the scientific status of the work can be established in two ways, following an internal and an external necessity. The internal necessity belongs to the very nature of the science and so can only be explained by the presentation of philosophy itself. One shows the possibility of a system of science by providing a system of science. The external necessity lies in a demonstration that "the time has come for the elevation of philosophy to Science" (*PG*, 11; *PS*, 3–4). Hitherto a history of the education of consciousness would have appeared to be a mere aggregate of unscientific, unsystematic information (*PG*, 9; *PS*, 1). The resolution of the question of the passage from arbitrary sequence to necessary progression has, according to Hegel, only become possible in his own time. The possibility of a second reading only arises now. It is sometimes supposed that the *Phenomenology*, which presented itself as the first part of the science, was restricted to a demonstration of this external necessity. Hence the moments it presented appeared in time. The subsequent part or parts of the system of science, which were to comprise a logic, philosophy of nature, and philosophy of Spirit, would as the scientific system itself provide the demonstration of the inner necessity. This would render the *Phenomenology* somehow external to the system. And yet Hegel says that the external necessity is the same as the internal necessity, albeit in that shape in which time represents the existence of the moments of science (*PG*, 11; *PS*, 3).

This is why the image of a ladder by which the reader can be raised "to the absolute standpoint" is misleading. If the scientific character of philosophy is to be secured, then any ladder or introduction to the science must itself be scientific. "The beginning of philosophy presupposes or demands that consciousness finds itself in this element" (*PG*, 22; *PS*, 14), that is to say, the element of science, which is that of "pure self-recognition in absolute otherness." But were consciousness already in this element there would be no need for a ladder. If natural consciousness and science or absolute knowing are thought of as opposed, as they seem to be by virtue of their contrary demands, each insisting that the other come to meet it on its own terms, this would exclude consciousness from science, irretrievably. It seems that just as consciousness makes a demand on science to provide an introduction to it, so science must presuppose that consciousness is already with it. "Science on its part requires that self-consciousness should have raised itself into this aether in order to be able to live—and [actually] to live—with Science and in Science" (*PG*, 23; *PS*, 14).

The problem also emerges in an advertisement for the book, which we can speculate was almost certainly written by Hegel himself on the grounds that it first appeared in June 1807 in a newspaper of which he was then the editor. The advertisement for the *Phenomenology* reads in part: "It considers the preparation for Science from a point of view, which makes it a new, an interesting, and the first science of philosophy" (*PG*, 446). The formulation is striking because it emphasizes the crucial ambiguity noted earlier: the preparation for science is the first science. The first science? "First" in the sense of succession, the introductory science; "first" in the sense of preeminence, the science which makes science possible; or "first" in the historical sense, the first time philosophy has attained the level of science? To a certain extent all of these. The advertisement also enjoins the question of the two readings of the *Phenomenology:* "The wealth of the appearances of the Spirit, which at first glance [*dem ersten Blicke*] seems chaotic, is brought into a scientific order which presents them according to their necessity in which the imperfect ones dissolve and pass over into higher ones which constitute their next truth. Their final truth they find at first [*zunächst*] in religion, then [*dann*] in science as the result of the whole" (*PG*, 446). Hegel grants here quite clearly that it is only on second glance or on a second reading that the *Phenomenology* ceases to be chaotic and shows its necessity. And the *Phenomenology* emerges as the first science when the reader passes from the first—the initial—final truth, religion, to the second final truth which is located in the book's final chapter, "Absolute Knowing." It is not a passage or transition like any other in the book. It is made simply in the course of recognizing the identity of Spirit in its own world and Spirit in religion (*PG*, 364–65; *PS*, 412), or, to say the same thing differently, giving to the content that religion couched in the form of figurative thinking (*Vorstellung*) the form of absolute Spirit, as it was attained at the end of the chapter on Spirit (*PG*, 427; *PS*, 485).[7]

It is to the final chapter then that one must turn in order to address the bind in which Hegel seems to find himself: How can the *Phenomenology of Spirit* maintain its double position as both exterior to the system, preparing for it, and an integral part of it, specifically its first part? If the book is already science from the outset, does it not come too late to provide the student with an introduction to the science? On the other hand, if "the detailed history of the *Bildung* of consciousness" (*PG*, 56; *PS*, 50) is to show its necessity, and not just display a succession of shapes of consciousness, then must it not already be science? I shall also now finally introduce the small word on which every reading of the *Phenomenology* that is not a first reading hangs, the word "we."

III

In the introduction to the *Phenomenology of Spirit* Hegel says that raising the succession of experiences of consciousness into a scientific progression is "our contribution" (*PG*, 61; *PS*, 55). What is the nature of this contribution? How is the apparent arbitrariness of the sequence of shapes supposed to give way to a necessary progression? And who are we who make this contribution? Who is the "we," the "for us," references to whom litter the *Phenomenology?*

The necessity of the succession is accessible only to "us." Hegel introduces this issue in the introduction in terms of his concept of experience, which in turn provides the focus of Heidegger's essay *Hegel's Concept of Experience.* At the time that Hegel wrote the introduction to the *Phenomenology* the book was, as I have already mentioned and as Heidegger emphasizes, to have been called *Science of the Experience of Consciousness* and this formulation dominates the introduction. The crucial sentence runs "This dialectical movement which consciousness exercises on itself and which affects both its knowledge and its object, *inasmuch as the new true object issues from it,* is precisely what is called *experience.*" As Heidegger notes, Hegel refers the notion of dialectical movement to experience and not the other way round (HBE, 169; *HCE*, 119). Whereas consciousness itself is simply aware of mere change, Hegel's word experience refers to the movement which gives rise to a new object for consciousness. So far as natural consciousness is concerned, this second object simply arises "by chance and externally." But, according to Hegel, we recognize how the new object arises out of the relation of consciousness with the old object through "a reversal of consciousness," whereby we must talk not just of a new object, but equally of a new form of consciousness (*PG*, 61; *PS*, 55). Recognizing this is our contribution and "it is not known to the consciousness that we are observing." Otherwise said, attaining the second reading is accomplished when one ceases to follow the sequence of shapes of consciousness and instead adopts the standpoint of the "we."

Hegel does not say explicitly who we are and surprisingly few commentators have addressed the question, given its clear importance; those that have, have not succeeded in reaching agreement. In 1970 Dove catalogued the leading contenders in his article "Hegel's Phenomenological Method" and noted that among the few commentators who broached the question, Heidegger was the only one who considered the issue at any length.[8] Dove himself suggested that the "we" applies to any consciousness that has discovered that it is Spirit, which takes place initially with "the 'I' that is 'we' and the 'We' that is 'I' " at the advent of self-consciousness in chapter 4 (*PG*, 108; *PS*, 110).[9] Werner Marx identified the "we" with the phenomenologist without saying very clearly who the phenomenologist was.[10] More recently, Joseph Flay argued that the decisive point occurs at chapter 5 when the standpoint of reason is attained, although he acknowledges another second but separate "we," which applies to "all those who have traversed the *Phenomenology*" in its entirety.[11] The most detailed study of the question, Parry's *Hegel's Phenomenology of the "We,"* concluded that the only point at which the "we" appears to be identical with the shape of Spirit under investigation is in the chapter "Absolute Knowing" and that "the activity of an absolute knowing was undertaken by the 'we' throughout the course of the *Phenomenology*."[12] In what follows I shall accept an interpretation of the "we" in terms of absolute knowing and so I shall turn now to the chapter of the same name in order to clarify how it can be understood.[13]

By the time Hegel reaches the chapter "Absolute Knowing" he is able to say more clearly than he could in the introduction what is meant by "our contribution." At the beginning of "Absolute Knowing" Hegel distinguishes between science, knowing as the pure comprehension of the object, and this same knowing in its becoming. In terms of this becoming, each shape of consciousness as such can also, from another angle, be thought in terms of "a number of such shapes which we bring together" resolved into their moments (*PG*, 423; *PS*, 480). "Our contribution" is that "we" gather the individual moments (*PG*, 427; *PS*, 485). It emerges that when Hegel said that we see the new object arising out of the old, he meant not just that we see how what serves as the essence or standard for one shape of consciousness becomes the object for the next, but also and more decisively that "we" see the previous shapes of consciousness as moments of each new shape. Hegel comments on this at various crucial stages throughout the *Phenomenology*. At the beginning of chapter 4, the essences of the previous forms of consciousness examined in the first three chapters are found to be "no longer essences, but . . . moments of self-consciousness" (*PG*, 104; *PS*, 105). At the beginning of the final section of the chapter on reason, it is said that the previous shapes are developed solely within itself as transparent moments (*PG*, 215; *PS*, 237). Similarly, at the beginning of the chapter on Spirit, it is said that the previous shapes of consciousness are abstractions of it, which result from Spirit analyzing itself distinguishing its moments (*PG*, 239; *PS*, 264). And, at the beginning of the chapter on religion, the shapes of the totality of Spirit, which display themselves in sequence and thus as time, are contrasted with the moments which have no existence in separation from one another (*PG*, 365; *PS*, 413). What I have provisionally been calling the second reading (and which is in one sense the first real reading, as the so-called first reading is a reading without understanding awaiting the discovery that a first reading is preinscribed in the memory of the reader) divides between, on the one hand, a reading of the *Phenomenology* in terms of shapes and time and, on the other hand, a reading in terms of moments and the annulment of time. It is better thought of, therefore, as a double reading. As such it is not the combination of two readings separated sequentiality, such that the first gives way to the second. Furthermore, even if the double reading is not the journey by which natural consciousness passes to true knowledge, it is nevertheless a journey and one in which the reader's expectations can be disrupted in the course of reading.[14] One such expectation is the conviction that the *Phenomenology* is simply the record of history as a narrative, the history of the education of consciousness.

Even though Hegel insists in the final chapter, as he did in the preface, that "Science does not appear in time and in actuality before Spirit has attained to this consciousness about itself" (*PG*, 428; *PS*, 486), he adds that "Spirit . . . appears in time just so long as it has not grasped its pure concept, i.e. has not annulled time" (*PG*, 429; *PS*, 487). The time of the science is therefore a no-time, the time of the suspension of time. At the point where the *Phenomenology* is able to show the necessity of the history it records, it gives up the pretence of being primarily a history. "We" who first give coherence to the story renounce it as a story. For as a story or a history it is still a narrative which as such belongs to *Vorstellung*—to figurative thinking—and has not yet made the transition from chapter 7 to chapter 8, the transition to the science. It is not a transition away from the *Phenomenology* to a science situated elsewhere as a separate part of the system. It is rather, or also, a transition to absolute knowing, knowing in terms of the concept, which is also a shape of Spirit, albeit the last shape: Spirit that knows itself in the shape of Spirit (*PG*, 427; *PS*, 485). There is a passage at the end of the *Phenomenology* which is often taken to be referring to the *Phenomenology*'s relation to the *Science of Logic* as a timeless logic, but which on closer examination can be seen to be concerned with making the transition to the second reading as a double reading of the *Phenomenology*. The first limb of this double reading, which is already a step beyond the first reading that sees only chaos, is in terms of "the specific shapes of consciousness." The corresponding second limb (within the double reading) is in terms of "the specific concepts and their organic self-grounded movement" (*PG*, 432; *PS*, 491). As introduction to the science each moment is the difference of knowledge and truth, and the movement in which their difference is sublated (*aufgehoben*). As already science it is not a question of the difference and its *Aufhebung*. Rather it is the immediate unity of the objective form of truth and of the knowing self.

With the annulment of time and the passage from linearity, each of the individual moments "exhibits in principle the life of Spirit in its entirety" (*PG*, 427; *PS*, 485). For conceptual knowing it is not a question of a series of shapes of consciousness which finally attain the element of science, that is to say, culminate in self-recognition in absolute otherness as the final stage. Self-recognition can retrospectively be seen to have operated at each stage. Each of the "slow-moving succession of Spirits" is endowed with "all the riches of Spirit" (*PG*, 433; *PS*, 492). However, the reading in terms of moments does not dispense with the reading in terms of the necessary progression of shapes of consciousness: "science contains within itself this necessity of externalizing the form of the concept, and it contains the passage of the concept into *consciousness*" (*PG*, 432; *PS*, 491). Hegel also says something similar early in the preface: "The actuality of this simple whole consists in the various shapes which have become its moments, and will now develop and take shape afresh, this time in their new element, in their newly acquired meaning" (*PG*, 15; *PS*, 7). The so-called first reading, as a reading without understanding, sees only the mere succession of shapes, and is displaced by a double reading, one limb of which recognizes these shapes in the necessity of their progression by virtue of the other limb of the double reading which operates, not in terms of shapes of consciousness, but of moments.

Hegel's own clearest statement of the double reading of the *Phenomenology* can be found fittingly in the closing sentences of the very last paragraph (*PG*, 433–34; *PS*, 493). The preservation of the succession of Spirits appearing in the shape of contingency is said to be history. This is the chaos of history as it appears at first glance, preserved nevertheless as the substance of the "I." The chaos and preservation together embrace both aspects of the first reading that seems to close off the *Phenomenology* before opening it up. Hegel contrasts this with what I have presented as the first limb of a double reading, this history seen in terms of its conceptualized (*begriffne*) organization, however, where it emerges as "the Science of appearing knowledge." As science, what would remain would only be the organization of the moments, the structures that govern the whole. But Hegel resists construing such a science as the result, whereby history would be sacrificed. Instead he writes, "Both together, conceptualized history [*die begriffne Geschichte*], form the remembrance and the Calvary of absolute Spirit, the actuality, truth and certainty of the throne, without which it would be lifeless and alone." The phrase "Calvary of absolute Spirit" is a reference to chapter 7 and concludes the survey of the book which occupied the previous couple of paragraphs. Within the context of this survey, this calvary prepares the passage from *Vorstellung* to *Begriff* as it corresponds to the passage from *Bildung* as externalization to *Erinnerung*. Hence the juxtaposition of calvary and *Erinnerung* in the sentence just cited.

History and concept, the two together, neither sacrificed to the other, nor the two dissolved in a unity, but in Hegel's phrase "both together" (*beide zusammen*) allowing the continuing oscillation between the two, that marks a double reading. Were the concept uppermost, the *Phenomenology* would simply give way to the *Science of Logic* and the *Phenomenology* would lose its place in the system. Were history uppermost, the *Phenomenology* would be read simply as the necessity of its progression without the reading in which time is suspended and Spirit grasped in its concept also being acknowledged. It is because Hegel sustains "both together" that he is able to maintain ambiguous answers not just to the question of whether the book is an introduction to the science or already science proper, but also to the question of whether the *Phenomenology* gives way to the *Science of Logic* or whether in some sense it is already the *Logic*.[15]

IV

Heidegger presents his interpretation of Hegel's "we" in *Hegel's Concept of Experience* in the limited context of a reading of the introduction. In the 1930–31 lecture course, Heidegger treats the first three chapters and the opening of the fourth. The first question is whether this interpretation would survive a reading of the final chapter, which is where the heart of Hegel's interpretation is inevitably located, as Heidegger himself concedes: an understanding of the work begins with absolute knowing.

Heidegger's interpretation of the "we" in the 1930–31 lecture course emphasizes the role that the "we" plays in the dynamic of reading. Initially Heidegger seems to offer a clear identification of the "we": "the 'we' refers to those who already from the outset know *absolutely*" (*GA* 32, 66; *HPS*, 47). And again, "'We' are those who know in terms of the science of absolute knowledge" (*GA* 32, 67; *HPS*, 48). Subsequently, the interpretation seems to become somewhat less clear. Heidegger notes that in the early chapters of the book "we" must serve as proxy for consciousness to bring it forward, but that this is given up as consciousness returns into absolute knowing from out of consciousness's self-alienation (*GA* 32, 188–89; *HPS*, 131).[16] But in the course of focusing on the "we" as serving proxy for consciousness, the identification of the "we" with absolute knowing becomes uncertain. How otherwise could Heidegger say that absolute knowing "takes *our place*; it actively fills our position now; and there is no longer anything which we for our part could or should be proxy for" (*GA* 32, 188; *HPS*, 131)? To say in chapter 8 not only that "We ourselves, the 'we,' are brought to our true selfhood," but also that there is thereby some loss of the "we," emphasizes the role of the "we" in the *Phenomenology* as history at the expense of the "we" in the *Phenomenology* as science.[17] It is perhaps to forget that in the chapter on absolute knowing the "we" is most prominent in its task of bringing together the individual moments that had originally exhibited themselves in shapes of consciousness, such that those moments now come to take the form of absolute knowing, itself a shape of consciousness, for which each moment in principle exhibits the life of Spirit as a whole (*PG*, 427; *PS*, 485). In *Hegel's Concept of Experience* Heidegger similarly can be found emphasizing one limb of the double reading at the expense of the other (by focusing on the moment when history becomes science), but there his philosophical purpose in doing so is clearer.

Although in *Hegel's Concept of Experience* Heidegger explicitly poses the question "Who is meant by 'we'?" (HBE, 173; *HCE*, 126), he does not repeat the answer that he gave in the 1930–31 course. He does say that our essence consists in our being in the parousia of the Absolute (HBE, 175; *HCE*, 130): "our contribution" is the inversion of consciousness that allows for the parousia of the Absolute. There is a kinship between "we the observers" and the absoluteness of the Absolute that arises from the fact that it belongs to our essence to be part of the *parousia* of the Absolute. This suggests that Heidegger would again have interpreted the "we" in terms of absolute knowing, had he addressed his own question directly in Hegel's terms. However, what one finds is a definition of the "we" that is couched in unmistakably Heideggerian language: " 'We' are those who skeptically pay heed to the Being of beings, and thus pay it authentic respect" (HBE, 188; *HCE*, 149). Heidegger's rewriting of Hegel's "we" radically alters the *Phenomenology* because it inscribes within it a concern for the question of Being. In other words, Heidegger's reinscription of the "we" transforms the sense in which the *Phenomenology* relates to history and indeed the meaning of the history to which it relates.

This can be most easily shown by turning to the conclusion of *Hegel's Concept of Experience* where Heidegger moves beyond the introduction to the *Phenomenology* to a reading of the sentence cited earlier from the book's closing paragraph: "Both together, conceptualized history, form the remembrance and the Calvary of absolute Spirit, the actuality, truth and certainty of the throne, without which it would be lifeless and alone." Heidegger interprets the "both together" not in terms of a doubling of the text, as I have done, but in terms of the "unifying unity" (HBE, 188; *HCE*, 148) that is the hallmark of Heidegger's encounter with Hegel elsewhere also (*ID*, 69; *IaD*, 71). According to Heidegger, the "both together" is a reference to the two terms of the dialogue that governs the *Phenomenology*—natural consciousness and absolute knowing (HBE, 186; *HCE*, 146). In the chapter "Absolute Knowing," the dialogue comes to a halt because of a loss of one of the partners. Absolute knowing is "the presentation of the appearance of the Spirit as it exists" (HBE, 186; *HCE*, 146), and the chapter that treats it is the consummation of the dialogue between natural consciousness and absolute knowing at the point where "consciousness itself dies its own death, the death into which it is rapt by the force of the Absolute" (HBE, 186; *HCE*, 146). This is how Heidegger understands the reference to calvary. In "the consummation of the dialogue" there is an "it is finished." What is finished is natural consciousness in its historical essence: the history of its appearing shapes (HBE, 188; *HCE*, 148). But at the very point where it seems that Heidegger has abandoned the *Phenomenology* as history and reduced it to its conceptual organization, he reintroduces a reading of the *Phenomenology* in terms of history. At the very point where Heidegger appears to lose sight of Hegel's double reading of the *Phenomenology*, he produces his own version of a double reading of the *Phenomenology* through the "we" now understood as "those who skeptically pay specific heed to the Being of beings."[18] That is to say Heidegger introduces the history of Being into the *Phenomenology* through the "we," to produce his own double reading.

Heidegger does more than locate Hegel within the history of Being, as he does when he interprets Hegel's concept of experience in terms of "subjectness" (HBE, 169–70; *HCE*, 119). The history of Being speaks through and in the *Phenomenology*. This is what allows Heidegger to say that "the strange word 'experience' . . . has come due" (HBE, 166; *HCE*, 114). Hegel's word *Erfahrung* is read as saying "Being" (HBE, 116; *HCE*, 113–14). It is by reading the *Phenomenology* in terms of the history of Being that Heidegger opens up his double reading of the text. The *Phenomenology of Spirit* is, as it is for Hegel, science, but it is for Heidegger also ontology, where the history of Being "conceals itself from us behind the term 'ontology' " (HBE, 163; *HCE*, 108). Furthermore, by reading Hegel in terms of Being Heidegger addresses the question of how a first reading of the *Phenomenology* is possible, a question which the lectures from the academic session 1930–31 left unanswered. In *Hegel's Concept of Experience* it emerges that the problem of the introduction into philosophy as science parallels that of the introduction to Being: "There is for man no introduction to the Being of beings because man's nature, his life led in the escort of Being, is itself that escort" (HBE, 189; *HCE*, 150).[19] In other words, "we are already in the parousia," just as we have already read the *Phenomenology* insofar as it is inscribed in us. In *Being and Time*, Heidegger formulated it in terms of the pre-ontological and in *Hegel's Concept of Experience* he takes the unusual step of returning to this vocabulary. At a certain point in the course of his reading of Hegel's introduction, Heidegger translates the dialogue between natural consciousness and absolute knowledge into a dialogue between pre-ontological ontic consciousness and ontological consciousness or philosophy (HBE, 161–64; *HCE*, 105–9). By means of this translation Heidegger finds in the pre-ontological an answer to the question of the first reading of the *Phenomenology*, and thereby explains how he was able to dismiss so quickly the possibility of reading the *Phenomenology* as a ladder. Heidegger's reading of the *Phenomenology*, or rather his double reading and his negotiation of the problem of a first reading, differs markedly from that outlined by Hegel, but nevertheless follows its structure closely.

Said differently, Heidegger's interpretation of the "we" extends and transforms Hegel's "we" to form a new community or kinship. It remains only to examine this new kinship that is gathered around the notion of history, specifically the history of Western metaphysics as Greek philosophy and its heritage. The privileging of Greece found in Heidegger is also characteristic of Hegel, even if, as I shall show, it was not quite the same in Hegel. These differences are not easily marked, nor does Heidegger always mark them in the ways one would expect him to. The history of Being is not another history of philosophy and the relation between the history of Being and Greece is less easily drawn than is the relation of the history of Western metaphysics to Greece. Nevertheless, there is no denying the fact that Heidegger himself sometimes fails to underline these points. This is especially true for Heidegger's various discussions of Hegel, where Heidegger, in the very act of differentiating his dialogue with the history of philosophy, never fails also, sometimes in spite of himself, to show their proximity. This is because in large measure Heidegger cannot enter into a dialogue with the history of philosophy as such without focusing on Hegel, who in such a context can never be reduced to the status one philosopher among others: "For Hegel was the first to think the philosophy of the Greeks as a whole and to think this whole philosophically" (HG, 256).

The kinship Heidegger forges between himself and Hegel is most marked in *Hegel's Concept of Experience.*[20] Nowhere in "The Onto-theological Constitution of Metaphysics" does Heidegger say "we" and include Hegel, as he does in *Hegel's Concept of Experience.*[21] But although in "The Onto-theo-logical Constitution of Metaphysics" Heidegger almost invariably means only himself when he says "we," he does also speak of "our Western languages" (*ID*, 72; *IaD*, 73). Heidegger says "we" and means "us (Europeans)."[22] What Heidegger says with the "we" in *Hegel's Concept of Experience* in particular is not just "we philosophers," but more precisely "we Greek philosophers." If Heidegger does not spell it out explicitly, it is only because it would be for him a pleonasm. Heidegger makes the point expressly in *What Is Philosophy?* in explaining that the phrase

"Western European philosophy" is a "tautology": "The statement that philosophy is in its essence Greek says the same as that the West and Europe, and only they, are in their innermost historical development originally 'philosophical.' "[23] The consequence is important. Although Heidegger and Hegel are a pair when it comes to thinking the history of philosophy—they constitute the pair who think the history of philosophy philosophically—Heidegger's "we" is not to be understood as solely that of a couple, but as embracing all those who philosophize as Greeks, that is to say, as heirs of the Greeks.

By reconstituting the "we" as "we Greek philosophers" and by rewriting natural consciousness as pre-ontological ontic consciousness, Heidegger narrows the focus of the *Phenomenology*. He confines it to philosophy; more precisely, to Western philosophy. This is already apparent in the 1930–31 lecture course where Heidegger says: "Only when we see the Hegelian problematic in terms of the whole of Western philosophy . . . do we have the basis for really understanding Hegel" (*GA* 32, 183; *HPS*, 126) The reference of Hegel to "the whole of Western philosophy" from its beginning in Greece to its completion thus emerges as another presupposition for really understanding Hegel. So long as this presupposition is not met, one reads Hegel without understanding and one listens to Heidegger himself without purpose: one cheats oneself. Or, perhaps, this is not another presupposition. Perhaps it amounts to the same presupposition, as is indicated by the fact that, in the same context in which Heidegger introduced the question of the preconditions for reading Hegel, he identified "the history of the manifestation of beings as a whole" as the presupposition of philosophy (*GA* 32, 53; *HPS*, 37). For both Hegel and Heidegger, therefore, one must already be educated to gain admission to the classroom. It is as if there was a sign over the entrance that read: philosophers only. No non-Greek, no *barbaros*, may enter here.[24] Otherwise you cheat not only Hegel and Heidegger, but yourself.

In this way Heidegger effectively restricts the impossible reading which is already inscribed in the reader as universal individual to the tradition of Western philosophy. This is in part a function of the selectivity of Heidegger's reading that omits chapter 6, where Hegel broaches the history of Spirit, and chapter 7, which deals with the history of religion. The consequence is particularly striking in the latter case as the chapter on religion does not begin with Greece but extends further back to include what might tentatively be identified as discussions of in turn the Jewish, Indian, and Egyptian religions.[25] An examination of the *Encyclopaedia* and the Berlin Lectures shows that it is only in the case of philosophy that Greece is presented as providing the beginning. For

Hegel it is only of philosophy, and not of history, art or religion, that the question "With what must its history begin?" warrants the answer Greece (*V* 6, 196; *I*, 173).[26] The Indians and Persians, among others, are introduced by Hegel into his history of philosophy only to challenge the place given to them in previous histories. This is particularly true of the Egyptians (*V* 6, 67; *I*, 30), who had only recently been denied the place in the history of Greek philosophy that the Greeks themselves had accorded them.[27] Whatever precedes Greek philosophy is, according to Hegel, to be judged as merely preparatory. One speaks of it only out of erudition. By contrast, "the educated man" feels at home when one speaks of Greece, and this is especially true, according to Hegel, if that person is German.[28] Such a person feels even more at home with Descartes, because he marks the beginning of modern European philosophy, or, as Hegel also likes to say, Germanic (*germanisch*) philosophy (*V* 6, 135). By focusing exclusively on philosophy in his reading of the *Phenomenology*, Heidegger limits its scope and limits what it means to the reader to have read it. He thereby also focuses on what in Hegel is most identified with Greece.

Nor was the emphasis on Greece unmotivated in terms of the present. Both Hegel and Heidegger agreed that the Germans had a special relation to the Greeks that no other peoples shared. Heidegger is more pronounced in this conviction because he was persuaded of the "special inner relationship" between the Greek and German languages.[29] For both Hegel and Heidegger, there were only two kinds of philosophy: the Greek and the Germanic. The other candidate, Roman philosophy, was a symbol of decline. Furthermore, for Hegel, as for Heidegger, albeit in quite different ways, the privileging of Greek philosophy historically is a privileging of German philosophy for their own times. Rosenkranz characterized Hegel as the national philosopher of the Germans and not without basis.[30] No doubt Heidegger would have wanted that title for himself, albeit it would have meant something else in the politically charged atmosphere of the 1930s. In any event, for Heidegger, German philosophy was not modern philosophy, as it was for Hegel, but the possibility of another beginning in relation to the first beginning that happened in Greece. Heidegger was always clear that what was at stake under the title "Hegel and the Greeks" was not just a conception of the beginning, but also at the same time what it meant that Hegel's understanding that the system of science marked a completion (*Vollendung*) (*ID*, 66; *IaD*, 67. *HG*, 255, 260–61). Here too, therefore, Heidegger's reinscription of the "we" makes a difference to the thrust of the work, but both Hegel and Heidegger shared and located in the "we" a certain idea of Greece, not least a certain idea of the absolute purity and unconditionality of Greece that was foreign to the Greeks, but that helped give definition to the German people.[31]

The question of the alleged universality of the Hegelian philosophy is a familiar one, but it perhaps receives greater definition within the present context because it is here addressed in terms of one's access to that philosophy qua science through the first reading of the *Phenomenology*, a reading that must be inscribed in the reader in advance. Different peoples have different memories, and Hegel sets out a route to the science that is identified with the Germany of his time and the remembrance of the history that culminates in it. Hegel's *Phenomenology* is on his own terms a closed book for anyone who has not shared in or inherited the history that the book relates. This marks the finitude of Hegel's thought even if it is not clear whether he would have acknowledged it or how he might have thought to circumvent it. It can always be said that there is a sense in which all cultures and peoples are conceived by Hegel as sharing in the life of Spirit insofar as they are each manifestations of Spirit that also seem as steps in a single process.[32] However, this would seem to apply at best only to historical cultures and not to those deemed by Hegel to be "unhistorical."[33] Furthermore, it would still only be true of the European, even a certain kind of European, that Spirit finds its culmination in him or her (though Hegel would probably not say "her"),[34] such that that person would be able to read the *Phenomenology* by virtue of it being preinscribed in the reader in advance. Only by becoming "European" would anyone else be able also to attain this status.

By contrast with Hegel, Heidegger presents his thought as a thinking of finitude, and the finitude of thought as he thought it is germane in this context. For example, Heidegger would ask his Japanese students why they did not attend to their own tradition, rather than pursue the latest developments in European philosophy.[35] The answer of the Japanese philosopher in "A Dialogue on Language" was that modern technicization and industrialization left no alternative but an encounter with European philosophy. That Heidegger himself establishes a connection between Western metaphysics and technology, such that there comes to be a question as to whether the dominance of technology does not in fact expand the boundaries of "the West" so conceived, does not render Western metaphysics any less particular or finite. It does make all the more pressing the question of the survival of those traditions of thought that do not look to Greece for their identity, just as it renders questionable the tendency of the philosophers of "Greece" to dismiss out of hand alternative ways of thinking, alternative ways of identifying what counts as philosophy, for example, within the institutional framework of the university.

There is a great deal at stake therefore in saying that a precondition for reading the *Phenomenology* is that the student—Hegel would say "the uneducated"—is already *substantially* educated. It means that such a person must have already been inscribed in the culture whose history Hegel records for the possibility to arise that after multiple first readings they perhaps pass to a second reading. But the corollary is that a person who was in Hegel's terms "uneducated" would be excluded from making this passage. Any attempt such a person might make to read the *Phenomenology* would be cheating. No amount of attention to the text of the *Phenomenology* could of itself make good the lack. Heidegger is at least as severe as Hegel in setting the prerequisites for reading the *Phenomenology*, and I have not tried to resolve finally the question of which of them was more exclusive, but only to indicate the way in which the restrictions they imposed were intimately related to their different conceptions of the double reading of the *Phenomenology*. This is because it was there that they located the sense of who "we" are. "We" are Greeks. Greeks and, because of their kinship with the Greeks, Germans. One must know Greek in advance and one must in a certain sense already be Greek. The acceptance of the privilege of Greece as a precondition for entering a philosophy class is relatively new. It was quite unknown to the Greeks but it is today widely assumed. And yet, however widespread, Hegel and Heidegger are among the very few that have argued the privileging of Greek philosophy philosophically. It is in terms of this question and the violence it sustains to the *barbaroi*, the others of the Greeks, that I believe that the phrase "we philosophers" must be interrogated, not just when "we" read it in Hegel and Heidegger, but whenever "we" appeal to it ourselves, particularly if "we" are teachers cheating our students.[36]

5

Ruins and Roses: Hegel and Heidegger on Sacrifice, Mourning, and Memory

Dennis J. Schmidt

I

". . . to know one's limits is to know *how to sacrifice one's self*" (*PG*, 807), or so says Hegel at least in the penultimate paragraph, the last passage (in the proper sense of the word) of the *Phenomenology of Spirit.* But of course one does not have to wait for that paragraph to find sacrifice at work in the *Phenomenology:* there are over two dozen moments in which sacrifice animates and defines the movement of Spirit. The "labor of the negative" (*PG*, 19) is the path of repeated sacrifice. Nonetheless, it is a path of return and redemption, the movement of reconciliation in which "the wounds of Spirit heal and leave no scars behind" (*PG*, 669). It is a path that, as the roots of the word sacrifice (*sacer/facere*) remind us, repeatedly sanctifies itself. That is why Hegel has no difficulties when he describes history both as a "theodicy" (*VPG*, 540) and as an "altar" and "slaughterbench" on which sacrifices are made to freedom (*VPG*, 33). But such redeemable sacrifice comes only with a special knowledge, namely the knowledge of one's limits: "*to know one's limits* is to know how to sacrifice one's self." Sacrifice bears witness to the truth of one's knowledge of one's limits, and it is to be thought as the reasonable act of a reasonable knowledge. Even more: of the most important form of knowledge, since Spirit lives by running up to its limits and transgressing them, and from time to time at least that means by sacrificing itself.

It should go without saying that the whole of Hegelian thought, not just one nor even many passages, takes itself to be the elaboration of precisely such a knowledge of limits—of, in fact, a knowledge of an epochal limit, an end, a certain consummation, of history. The claim is well known, even if only one side of its Janus-face is typically portrayed, the radiant side namely of Hegel's claim to mark the completion of history, the redemption of every promise of history still in abeyance. The hybristic sense of that claim, the arrogant side of Hegel's understanding of "*Vollendung*," never gets overlooked. In part Hegel's own rhetorical excesses are culpable—one thinks for instance of his promise in one of the deferred, false-starts of the *Logic* to deliver "the thought of God before creation" (*WL*, 31). But there is another, darker, side to this effort to write out of the logic of the limit of history, and it is precisely that dimension of Hegelian thought that I want to highlight today; namely, the acknowledgment that Hegel's thought marks a certain *exhaustion* of possibilities, and it knows itself as in a peculiarly impossible situation. This is the sense of the limits of history that leads Hegel to characterize his age as one in which "Spirit has not only lost its essential life; [but] is also conscious of this loss and of the finitude that is its own content" (*PG*, 7), and to confess that "by the little which now satisfies Spirit, we can measure the extent of its loss" (*PG*, 8). In the end, when we speak of the knowledge of limits with Hegel we must remember that this knowledge only comes with an essential loss, and that the measure of that absolute knowledge to which Hegel lays claim is found in the full depth, the absoluteness, of that loss. Only once Spirit has reached the point at which it truly confronts its own death, the impossibility of further loss, only once it confronts and wins recognition from that which Hegel refers to as the "absolute master" (*PG*, 194, cf. also 455), only then does it find itself readied to recognize itself and its own truth. The trials of Spirit are, in Hegel's own words, "trial by death" (*PG*, 188) and "the life of Spirit is not the life that shrinks from death and keeps itself untouched by devastation, but rather the life that endures it and maintains itself within death" (*PG*, 32).

Hegel's claim is that his era is one in which Spirit has come full circle back to itself so that it now has before it its own past, and when it surveys that past it sees, in the final words of the *Phenomenology*, "[its own] memory and Golgotha [*Schädelstätte*]" (*PG*, 808).[1] At this juncture of history, privileged by being the exhaustion of possibilities that is at this completion of history, the task of Spirit, its final trial, is to confront its memory and deaths—to grieve its losses to completion. But for that to happen we must be ready as well to recognize that the essential contours of thinking as we have inherited it, its deepest assumptions and self-articulations, have finally betrayed their untenable truth and can no longer hold. To be alive thinking must become different, it can no longer adapt to the needs of history without changing. Consequently, art, religion, philosophy, the very notion of ourselves as "rational" "subjects" of "history" must be thought in terms of their "pastness" for truth, that is to the point of their own "*Aufhebung*." If one takes Hegel to heart, then one need confess that Hegel, by thinking his as an era of the deepest encounter with limits, thinks his not only as a time that needs to give way to the future, but, as a time of limits known, more precisely, as a time calling for at least a knowledge of how to *sacrifice oneself*. It is no accident that the final two paragraphs of the *Phenomenology*, speaking of the present task of thought to which history commits us, refer us to sacrifice and crucifixion.

But one must be careful here and remember that sacrifice for Hegel is an act of reasonable knowledge. It should be clear from the outset that such sacrifice as an historical gesture is not a matter of throwing the past on some rubbish heap of history. History, for Hegel, is never a place of debris, but always of promises, and reason—under whose imperative sacrifice must be thought—is capable of refunctioning even the rubble of history. We should not forget that history—both its past and futures—takes place in the "temple of Mnemnosyne" (*VPG*, 12), and that sacrifice is one of the routes by which Spirit memorializes itself for itself. If Hegel does not have qualms about building a vision of culture on an altar of sacrifice, it is because the victims of history, those who pick up the tab for freedom, are not forgotten, but redeem their rights in memory. But that is the first point I want to make; namely, that *sacrifice, to do its work, calls forward the memory to which it is appropriated.* One might even say that sacrifice is the only possible work of memory in impossible situations, and like every work of memory, sacrifice is indexed by the possibility of recuperation and redemption. Or so, I believe, Hegel must say. At the end of the education (*Bildung*) of Spirit, at this point in time when thinking takes on new forms, "we" survivors of this history of sacrifices made—a problematic notion that for the moment I leave unproblematized—"we" know that history has always been the arena of sacrifice and might still demand sacrifice, but "we" also know that knowing our limits, "we" never need sacrifice in vain. Hegelian thought does not make history any easier to bear, it remains a hard and demanding route, but it does offer a way of redeeming that route, a way of thinking that is no longer subject to its own vanities.

When writing about Hegel, Heidegger persists in challenging Hegel's claim to have sublated the very forms of thinking that Hegel himself exposes as untenable for the future. In fact, the claim is that Hegelian thought is marked rather by its captivity to the very style of thinking that is no longer tenable, and that Hegel's attempt to record the past, to carry out the work of memory, while simultaneously thinking against it, is a delusion, the preeminent exercise of vanity. So despite Heidegger's persistent struggle with Hegel—from the earliest to the last of his texts—despite the detailed commentary on Hegelian texts, despite even the occasional concession that in Hegel "the matter of thought—namely that which of itself demands attention—is at stake" (*W*, 421), despite everything, Heidegger inevitably ultimately insists that Hegelian thought stands as metaphysical thinking par excellence. Inevitably we get the warning about Hegel: beware, ontotheology ahead. In other words, here one finds a style and strategy of addressing questions that, in its heart of hearts, is driven by the love of an image of God, and that consequently models itself after its own presumed sense of an infinite and omnipresent mind that *suffers no death.* In the end, this becomes the point Heidegger makes most forcefully against Hegel: Hegel has not, cannot have, understood the nature of the limits from which he claims to be thinking because he has not taken the full measure of death's measurelessness for us. Instead, says Heidegger, Hegelian thought persistently effaces death, and only by virtue of that effacement can the essential decisions Hegel makes be made. According to Heidegger, Hegel's sense of history, the very thought of the dialectic as articulating the movement of life, is founded on the refusal to face death, that is to confront the true meaning of loss, to face the full meaning of sacrifice without redemption, loss pure and simple. Sacrifice, an act of freedom rising up from the abyss of impossibility, like every death tolerates no calculation with respect to its own possible vanity. And so we can imagine Heidegger saying that Hegel understands nothing of either limits or sacrifice, and that while Hegel might be right to conclude the *Phenomenology* by speaking of their link and import for the task of thinking, he is wrong if he believes that he has taught us anything about either.

In "What Is Metaphysics?"—a text that goes to great lengths to separate itself from Hegel—Heidegger attempts to undercut the claims of the dialectic as the "labor of the negative" by saying that "nothing is the origin of negation, not the other way around" (WM, 116), and then he hammers the point again by saying that "more abyssal than the mere propriety of thinking that follows the route of negation is thinking that recognizes the harshness of opposition and the sharpness of loathing. More responsible is the pain of refusal and the mercilessness of an interdict" (WM, 116). And again, in his letter to Ernst Jünger, a letter itself concerned with marking the limits of history, Heidegger criticizes Hegel's conception of "work" by saying that Hegel never understood the place and meaning of pain in work (*W*, 398) and the limits to which pain, the living mime of death, takes thinking. Of course, for Heidegger, the thinker of the finitude of Being, such effacement of death is the forgetfulness of thinking's guiding appeal: Hegelian history can only take itself to be the sanctuary of Mnemnosyne because Lethe has already effaced its own life in history at every turn. Put in other words: Heidegger's claim is that the ceaseless capacity of human life to throw itself into darkness, a capacity disclosed by the "hermeneutics of facticity," persistently outstrips every Hegelian claim to have thought the possibilities of the history of such a life to its limits, to (in Hegelian language now) have confronted the "absolute master." To try to understand history and our own present according to the dialectic one finds in Hegel is to misunderstand both essentially.

What makes Heidegger's cautions about Hegel more than mere objections and a senseless set of refutations (something that Heidegger more than most knows never belongs to thinking at its best), what raises the philosophical stakes, is that Heidegger, like Hegel, claims that we can only think our times as an age of completion and exhaustion, a time in which epochal limits, a line in time etched long ago, betrays itself. Both find the danger of their respective times not something willful, nor something accidental; rather, the reversal and overturning of history to which each wants to lay claim, out of which each claims to see through his own times to its deepest truths, is itself to be understood as the *destination* of history, what Heidegger called the "*Geschick des Seins.*" Like Hegel, Heidegger writes out of the logic of history confessing its end according to its destiny, an all-powerful destiny that, citing Aeschylus's Prometheus in his own infamous "Rectoral Address" (*SA*, 11), Heidegger says overpowers all knowledge and all things. And like Hegel, Heidegger speaks of the shape of thinking to come at this fateful time by referring it to a certain relation to sacrifice: "[essential thinking] answers to the claim of being . . . which fulfills itself in the freedom of sacrifice" (*W*, 307). As is the case with Hegel, references to sacrifice in Heidegger are significant if overlooked. As an example of both the importance and neglect of such references, I might refer you to a particularly celebrated passage in Heidegger that refers to sacrifice, namely, the passage in "The Origin of the Work of Art" in which Heidegger, in the middle of proposing a relay of founding acts, acts of truth at work in history, says "another way in which truth is founded is essential sacrifice" (*H*, 50). (As an aside, I might note that this remark does not occur in the two earlier versions of "The Origin of the Work of Art," but in the second version [November 1935], written during a semester in which Heidegger is holding a seminar on Hegel's *Phenomenology*, we find Heidegger describing the notion of "world" in the work of art as a "juncture those relations [*Füge jener Bezüge*] in which all the essential decisions, victories, sacrifices and works of a people are enjoined."[2] But even if one naturally suspects that the reference to sacrifice is meant to include the Schlageter-case,[3] it is anything but natural to assume that the notion of sacrifice in Heidegger necessarily belongs to that case, and that case alone. I would simply indicate as well that during the two years immediately following his resignation from the Rektorship, Heidegger gave a seminar on Hegel's *Phenomenology* each semester, as well as a seminar entitled "Hegel 'On the State.' "[4] Given that extended engagement with Hegel, Heidegger would have been hard pressed to avoid the question of Hegel's understanding of Antigone.)

There are certainly differences between the times and that to which those times stake thinking. Differences that I might be making a grave error in neglecting (and here I would simply indicate that Heidegger never hesitates to give a name—*Gestell*—and specificity to the reign of that ending today as under the rule of technology), but such differences notwithstanding, what I want to call attention to is a certain quite peculiar matrix of questions concerning history, destiny, sacrifice, and memory. A matrix that both Hegel and Heidegger, each with different intent, takes as articulating the questionableness of history in the present juncture, a juncture in which history itself begs to be thought.

Let me try to summarize my point thus far, and also rather loosely inject a few of the other concerns that belong to this sketch of the larger horizon, namely the horizon of history, within which I am trying to situate my special question about sacrifice.

Both Hegel and Heidegger are deeply committed to the project of thinking history, both want to argue that nothing can be understood apart from its relation to history and time. Both regard that history as fated, not as something "we" (any "we") controls, but as something into which we are thrown, and yet something for which we must take responsibility. I suspect that both would concede, though with some hesitations about the language, the truth of Benjamin's remark that "there is a secret agreement between past generations and the present one. Our coming was expected on the earth. Like every generation that preceded us, we have been endowed with a *weak* Messianic power, a power to which the past has a claim that cannot be settled cheaply" (*Theses*, 2). Furthermore, each understands himself as the last consequence of that fated history, as the harbinger of history at an epochal turning point; that is, both regard history as it has been as "without a future," as between an end and new beginning. For that reason, but certainly not only nor even principally for that reason, that we are in the impossible situation of being "without a future," history stakes us to the thought of death. Consequently, both Hegel and Heidegger, and this I believe Heidegger reappropriated from Hegel, are committed to thinking the meaning of death not simply as an *"existential" event* of individuation, but as an *historical event*, and, as I hope to show, at least in the case of Hegel and intend to raise as a question about Heidegger, as a *political event*, as what Hegel calls "the supreme 'work' which the individual as such undertakes on behalf of the ethical community" (*PG*, 452).

Yet, since each is committed to understanding every time in terms of history, the past cannot be discarded—the historical slate cannot be wiped clean in the most modernist gesture possible—but remains as the first enigma of any possible future. Rethinking the past becomes the task of thinking any possible future (that is why one finds so many words in both Hegel and Heidegger that try to name the thinking that is memory: *Andenken, Gedächtnis, Erinnerung, Trauer*). The question then becomes: How is one to think the now longer tenable past? A past that was not a mere accident, but belonged to the very same history that permitted me to see its final untenability? What access do I have any longer to this inaccessible past without which I cannot, try as I might, understand myself? One sees quite clearly that the stakes of such concerns are deeply political stakes once one remembers that these are the very same questions that are being played out in the well-known and politically charged "*Historikerstreit*" in Germany today. As the possibility of the reunification becomes a visible reality, and as shifts in power relations take hold, the stakes in this quarrel over the reading of history become even more evident. The definition of history, one's pact and solidarity with the past, perhaps ultimately one's pact with the dead, is one of basic elements of the fabric of every community. The question of the *Historikerstreit,* parallel to the question facing both Hegel and Heidegger, is how one is to make a pact with a past that is impossible and that was destined to be such, not just in part, but essentially so.

That is the general problematic with which I am concerned in Hegel and Heidegger—the problematic of memory and history—one that I want to argue bears an inherent relation to the question of the community. So I want to look into the way in which both Hegel and Heidegger work through this problematic, but, since it is such an enormous field, I want to interrogate it along one rather quirky and very specific axis that follows the route of sacrifice. I have tried to defend this move by indicating that both Hegel and Heidegger make clear appeals to some notion of sacrifice that is to be understood as bearing an essential relation to history and truth at this time.

Now at this point I beg your pardon for a bit of sleight of hand. In other words, I ask you to trust the transition I now make when I say that I want to focus my concerns with this field of questions and this axis of notions more precisely still on the respective treatments of the figure of Antigone in both Hegel and Heidegger. I will forego for now the question of my own decision to make this move, though I will confess that my motives for this move are ultimately to sharpen the political dimensions of the questions I am asking. In other words, in bringing these concerns with memory, history, destiny, and sacrifice to bear upon Antigone's decision one enjoins to these concerns questions of law, violence, and justice—the very questions which it might be our need to think today. But to begin, I simply propose to ask how each thinks Antigone's act. Is her act the kind of sacrifice to which each refers us as an act of truth at work?

In raising this question in this manner I am prescinding from other, quite telling questions that come from asking about the fuller life of the text *Antigone* in another set of texts (and I prescind as well from the differences internal to the respective treatments of both the figure and the text). I am interested rather in only one restrictive point, namely, how in general each understands Antigone's act, an act that Hegel says brings about "*eine Verkehrung*," one that Heidegger says marks "*eine gegenwendige Bewegung*." Do either, or both, Hegel and Heidegger offer something by way of understanding Antigone's decision—whether it is to be thought as a criminal act, an act of resistance, of courage, blood, or love—but as act of self-sacrifice (is there any other kind?) in a situation that is destined and yet impossible?

Reversing the point: both Hegel and Heidegger speak of the possibility that sacrifice might be made requisite by history, that is, might somehow belong to the needs of thinking at least for now. Sacrifice needs to be thinkable as an act of history "truing" itself, that is unfolding its sentence. And yet neither Hegel nor Heidegger asks further about such sacrifice itself. My question is whether the fascination with Antigone—one shared of course with others, though especially relevant here is Nietzsche—gives a clue as to just what each means by sacrifice. (The choice of one's martyr here is all important—just think for a moment of the commitments which Kierkegaard makes by meditating upon sacrifice by means of his concern with Abraham sacrificing his son not himself thereby exposing sacrifice as an act of fear and trembling, of one's utter living isolation and separation from the dead, not as an act of solidarity.[5] My own choice has been to exclude sacrifice that can only be thought as an element of some ritual—sacrifice as Bataille thinks it[6]—that is, sacrifice that *symbolically* brings us to the point of revealing our own deaths. That is the sort of sacrifice that Hegel discusses in the section in the *Phenomenology* devoted to religion and the abstract work of art.)

Finally, before beginning, I need to make a confession that risks preempting and undermining all that follows; namely, that neither Hegel nor Heidegger, so far as I can tell, uses the word "sacrifice" to characterize Antigone's decision. But then, if we cannot link Antigone and the thought of sacrifice we are left again with the question of how to think the meaning of sacrifice, and we are left as well with the question of how each understands Antigone. In sacrifice don't we face the claim of Antigone: a death elected, but one that is not suicide simply because it is an *act of solidarity?*

II

Hegel's understanding of Antigone has been of course the subject of numerous commentaries, which, for the present, I want to avoid. It is typically taken as emblemizing Hegel's understanding of women, yet I would suggest that the full question of Hegel on women needs to think the figure of Antigone as the final figure in a tryptic of women: of Aphrodite, Lucinde,[7] and Antigone. (In trying to avoid the question of woman at this point, I am not suggesting that this is finally an avoidable question. In the end, I would suggest that it is no more avoidable than the question of technology is for Heidegger's concern with the question of history. Here it is not unimportant that we find the dialectic of sexual difference, of a natural difference that has been sublated into a political difference. But simply in the interests of time, I leave that aside.)

Hegel situates Antigone's act as the ultimate crisis of the realm of ethical life, that realm in which "the work of the individual for his own needs is just as much a satisfaction of the needs of others . . . [in which] the whole becomes . . . his own work, for which he sacrifices himself and precisely in so doing receives back from it his own self" (*PG*, 351). Yet, despite this preliminary sense of the ethical realm as defined by the work of the individual, this is the crisis that finally confirms the ethical superiority of the state. Her act precipitates the consummate crisis of that realm because in her act the ability of the law to satisfy and accommodate the work of the individual is called to account. The agony of the very idea of law, its doubly conflicted imperative, destines it to this crisis: articulated always only in the idiom of the universal, law necessarily enforces itself upon the irreplaceably singular and nongeneralizable life of the individual. Later this conflict in the very idea of law is explicitly linked with the relation of language to the law: language, we are reminded, is "inherently universal" (*PG*, 110) and so in the face of every true singularity it "has the divine nature of directly reversing the meaning of what is said" (*PG*, 110). But of course, that inherent distress of law appears even before it explicitly struggles with the code of language, since it is the dialectic of the universal and singular that drives the analysis of law—through the law of the heart, of virtue, and finally legislative reason—a dialectic that precedes and prepares the presentation of Antigone. But that dialectic does not reach its crisis, its real limit, until law becomes a question of death, until, that is, the singular, untransferable, natural life of the individual becomes the issue in death. In the death of the individual, that is, with the return of the individual to the point of his or her utter singularity and natural life, the transferability of the universal sway and dominion of law is called most pointedly into question.

That of course is the issue raised in *Antigone.* It is a question, one might say, of dominions and homecoming: In death has Polynices passed from the dominion of the polis and returned to the custody of the family, or do the laws of the polis extend even unto the dead? What is the lawful place of death, of what Hegel describes both as "this universality which the individual *as such* attains" (*PG*, 452) and as "the absolute master"? According to the dialectical meaning of law, the polis must bear an essential relation to death, but the question is how that relation is to be configured.

Typically, certainly by virtue of Hegel's own suggestions, Antigone's decision is explained as an act in defense of the family. (Though one shudders to think that this family is the model family for Hegel. You know the tangled lines of kinship and how those tortured lines cross into the representatives of the law so that the lines between the family and the state are thoroughly blurred from the outset—most pertinent of course is that Creon is both Antigone's uncle and her father-in-law-to-be.) But if we are to think Antigone's decision as grounded in her identity with the family, then we must begin by noting that the family, for Hegel, is an association whose rationality is governed by blood and love (*PG*, 453). Those affiliations are, according to Hegel, the most ancient, that is the most profound and yet least articulate, of all our affiliations, and consequently they remain as "the root" and natural unit (*PG*, 474) of the public life of Spirit that must be sublated, but never simply rejected in the just polis. Certainly Antigone's is, from one point of view, an act in defense of the family, and the orthodoxy has it that we can only comprehend Antigone's deed as what Ernst Bloch called a "love song" to her brother.[8] But the point that I want to make is that neither blood nor love, no rationality of the family alone, could ever give the account of Antigone's sacrifice as Hegel must think it. The limitation of love, of what Hegel calls "the most monstrous contradiction" (*PR*, 158), as the motivating ground of her sacrifice is clear: it can only happen for the living. I quote Hegel: "love proper exists only between living beings who are alike in power and thus in one another's eyes living beings from every point of view; in no respect is either dead for the other . . . in love, life is present as a duplicate of itself . . . [and] life senses life" (*FS*, 245–46). The limitation of blood is less evident until one hears the very telling way that Irigaray opens her meditation on this question by saying that "the purpose that moves blood relatives to action is the care of the *bloodless*. Their inherent duty is to ensure *burial for the dead*, thus changing a natural phenomenon into a spiritual act."[9] In other words, Antigone's cannot be understood as an act that preserves the circulation of blood—it is all important to remember that she does not die to prevent a death, nor is her elective death strictly a matter of family ties since you will recall she refuses to let her sister Ismene share in her act, saying instead "Death and the dead, they know whose act it was." *Antigone dies as an act of solidarity with the dead.* But of course one wonders about the nature of such solidarity. Here one must understand that in the figure of Antigone we witness a curious repetition of the earlier dialectic of recognition. There the proximate confrontation was between two wills, but already there we found a hidden, more profound confrontation with death. There the one who advances on the route of history is the slave, the one whose "whole being was seized with dread . . . [and] the fear of death, the absolute master . . . [the one who] trembled in every fibre of its being . . . [for whom] everything solid and stable has been shaken to its foundations" (*PG*, 194). In the case of Antigone, the one fated to defeat by virtue of her position and the grounds of her identity, *there is no anxiety*. She chooses her death because she has no anxiety, she could win no recognition—in a way one might say that she had already outlived her death.

But it is this that sheds light on the political significance of death as Hegel thinks it here. It is the imperative of ethical life to express one's solidarity with the dying, with one's fellow mortals with whom one can speak. Yet, one does not have to wait for death to come: death is present in the world and language is its memorandum. Every time I open my mouth I incur a responsibility to others and begin anew to dialogue with my own death *at the same moment, with the same gesture.* All of Hegel is an effort to teach us that without the knowledge of our mortality there is no knowledge. An act of solidarity with mortals, even if it is an act of sacrifice, has a different meaning than an act that defines itself as a union with the dead, a connectedness with those *of* whom, but not *with* whom, we may speak. If one takes both the polis and its laws as defined by the horizon of language, then the dead, those removed from conversation, the relation of all relations, can only be understood as having passed outside the polis. Yet, we bury the dead, we wrap them in shrouds and mark their place with words, we "turn a natural phenomenon into a spiritual act," precisely as an effort to protest that departure. In the end, I wonder if sacrifice is the true name for Antigone's act, since I would want to distinguish between acts of elective death dedicated to the dead and those dedicated to the dying, but I confess that I know no other name for it at least as Hegel unfolds it dialectically. But I do believe that Benjamin put his finger on a point of great insight if "we" are to think the reason in that act—perhaps against Hegel. In a context not entirely unrelated to the themes at issue here, Benjamin comments that "[one] will only have the gift of fanning the spark of hope in the past [if one] is convinced that *even the dead* will not be safe from the enemy if the enemy wins. And this enemy has not ceased to be victorious" (*Theses,* 6). We can only understand Antigone's decision dialectically by seeing it as one dedicated to history and consecrated by memory. It is a decision devoted to an inaccessible, irretrievable, past. Yet, precisely as such is stands equally under the sign of hope rather than vanity, since all acts of memory, as Hegel understands them, are anticipations of redemption, of promises deferred. *Every memory is directed to the memory of future times.* Law and the polis provide the ethical grounds and reality for the expansion of both memory and hope. For Antigone, however, history has reversed itself, while memory and hope suffer an infinite and impossible compression: memory can only serve the infinitely deferred future and hope is only directed to the irretrievable past. Ultimately, one must be able to say that this reversal of the possibilities of history happens by virtue of a requisite alteration in the relation between death and the polis at this stage of the development of ethical life.

The point I believe Hegel is making here is that there is one truth that no enemy can resist, and until or unless the state takes this truth up into itself it too can be resisted. That truth is death, about which Hegel now says that "[its] essence shows itself to be the real power of the community and the force of its self-preservation" (*PG,* 455). At the summit of the state we find death as the real sovereign, the "absolute master" from whom we can win no recognition. Not without significance does the section that immediately follows the discussion of *Antigone,* the section in which its sublated truth first begins to emerge, depict a community that Hegel characterizes as "soulless" (*PG,* 477). It is even, in a parallel section of the *Philosophy of History,* described *by the very image of death,* since there one finds this new community, which relates to its citizens as "legal persons" (*PG,* 479), described as like "living organism that decays and in which every point takes on its own life, a life which is however only the wretched life of worms" (*VPG,* 384). Having taken the work of death upon itself, the state at this new stage loses its claim to be the home of mortals and becomes instead the living embodiment of morbidity.

The dialectic of the state and its laws does not stop at this point. However, its course from this point forward has been determined essentially by Antigone's gesture: by sacrificing herself, the state is driven to assume its true, full relation to death, and by forgetting herself she memorializes our own relation to the relationlessness that is death, thereby engraving an "eternal irony in [the] community" (*PG*, 475). Antigone marks the death of illicit death. Subsequent appearances of death now only need be symbolic and attached to ritual sacrifice. The lesson of sacrifice now belongs to the memory of the state as victorious.

III

One of the most notable features of Heidegger's presentation of *Antigone* is the way in which it inevitably sits in close proximity with his concern with Hölderlin. One explanation for that is simply that Heidegger's reading of *Antigone*, which is spun almost exclusively around a commentary on, and retranslation of, Hölderlin's own translation of the chorus, centers on the question of *language* in the tragic text, especially the relation binding language, mortality, and ruin, as well as the relation between language and the polis.[10] Taking language as something like a middle term, I want to draw attention to a line in Heidegger's thought that, at least tacitly, suggests that we think the polis along with mortality and ruin.

This move should come as no surprise since I believe it is rather evident that reflections on language in Heidegger inevitably form the most secure basis for the possibility of a "Heideggerian" political thinking.[11] But then this link between language and the polis is not new with Heidegger. It is rather a thought that belongs to antiquity, one that, as Heidegger himself reminds us by referring us to Aristotle's *Politics*, simply says that "man is a *zoon politikon* because and only because he is a *zoon logon echon*" (*GA* 53, 102). This is a persistent point in Heidegger, one belonging to his project "to think 'Greeker' than the Greeks" (*GA* 39, 100), and these reflections on the special relation binding language and tragedy cannot exempt themselves from this possibility of bearing a special import for Heidegger's understanding of the polis. It is also an important point of contact with Hegel, who Heidegger called "the last of the Greeks," since Hegel had likewise suggested that the essential distress of law housed itself finally in the enigma of language, and that the task of thinking law could not remove itself from a concern with language. But if one follows Heidegger's special effort to think through this link, then one must say that, because *tragic* language bears a privileged relation to the caesura and trope, it is especially relevant for understanding how we are to think the polis in this era of historical limits, the era of a certain epochal rupture and turn. Ultimately, that privileging of tragic-poetic language in the articulation of the polis belongs essentially to the attempt to "overcome metaphysics" and the metaphysical conception of the polis that is inaugurated in Plato with the exile of the tragic poets from the polis.

In Heidegger's discussion of the language of tragedy the possibility of the polis is cast in terms of the need for a certain translation, that is, a pure passage and mediation within the polis. Thus he speaks of the "translation-neediness of [tragic-poetic] language" (*GA* 39, 79): in other words, such language calls for translation, it longs for its own complementarity and for the bonds of sameness. However, he also indicates that the language of tragedy giving definition to the polis equally marks a certain "counter-rhythmic rupture and caesura" (Höl. 5, 169), that is a certain necessary *impasse* that language itself is. The withdrawal of language prefigures both the withdrawal of the polis as well as our struggle to appear and forge relations within such a polis. The reversals and movement of language articulates the movements of political struggle. In short, like the presentation of language, one finds that from the outset, the polis is presented as the site both of essential conflict and a breech. The polis, is thus—to cite Heidegger citing Sophocles—*hypsipolis apolis.* It is established as the locus of an inherently "*gegenwendige Bewegung,*" a countervalent movement, a movement that is figured with the greatest precision in the language of the tragic chorus, namely in the strophic movement of return, the movement of *catastrophe.* The catastrophe of the polis is the collision of its imperative of passage and its destined impasse.[12] It is the nature of such a "place" as "the gathering together of the supreme and the extreme" to be like "the point of a spear" (*US,* 37). The *polemos* of the polis as an historical site needs to be thought with reference to this shattering edge, to what Heidegger calls the "overpowering" and "violence."

A more detailed look at that shattering—something I will forgo—would need to think through Heidegger's specific characterization of it as the "countervalent" relation of *dike* and *techne* (*EM,* 124). Let me simply suggest in this regard that Heidegger's rather approving citation of Heracleitus's fragment 114 in *Einführung in die Metaphysik* is relevant to that inquiry. (As an aside I would suggest that Heidegger's remarks on Heracleitus typically tend to have a strong political cast, and so not without reason does his text of self-reflections on the "Rectoral Address" go to great lengths to tell us [*SA,* 28] that in that address Heidegger was seeking a confrontation with Heracleitus's notion of *polemos* not with another celebrated presentation of *Kampf* found in Germany at that time. Still one can only wonder how far Heidegger is trying to answer Hitler's "*Kampf*" with Heracleitus's "*polemos.*") In Heracleitus's fragment 114 we find a remark that strikes a note of accord with *Antigone:* "For all human laws are nourished by a divine one. It prevails as it will and suffices for all and is more than enough." Of that Heidegger writes that these *nomoi* "of the polis, its codes . . . are the inner web of the *polis,* [which is] not a universal, not something that hangs over everyone . . . , but [is] the original unifying unity of that which is torn from within itself" (*EM*, 100). In short the struggle that defines life in the polis is to gather into a unity that which is essentially incommensurate with itself. Law, the language of that struggle, is thus only thinkable as the preservation of our deepest incommensurability. In a curious photographic reversal of its usual sense, I would propose that, for Heidegger, but maybe against Heidegger, the true measure of a law is in the measure of resistance it preserves within itself. Furthermore I would propose that we would do well to think *Antigone as the name for the impossibility of that struggle, for the requisite failure of law as that which can only endure in its own resistance.* That of course marks a real difference with Hegel, since rather than enacting the work of death as it does in Hegel, law, for Heidegger, is called to enact always its own death. According to Heidegger's reading of the tragedy, no higher reconciliation, no recompense is thinkable for us—"only a god can save us" from this persistent unworking of "the" law. If Antigone's act is to be called a sacrifice, it is not because she renders some possibility of the polis, some root of the law, sacrosanct. Nor can it be said that hers should be thought as an act of solidarity with the dead. It is rather, I would suggest, an act of confession, one that calls us to mourn the impossibility of forging any enduring solidarity with the living. As such sacrifice marks the abyssal sites of political life, the gap which no translation can bridge, no history can redeem.

But let me pull back from that point for a moment, keeping as a backdrop against the point I want to make by way of a conclusion. Instead let me draw your attention to the curiosity that in discussing *Antigone* Heidegger never directly discusses the figure of Antigone or her decision. That is simply because he does not need to focus on Antigone's decision as essentially different than any other decision one might be called upon to make in the polis as the site of history. Even if such decisions remain only "rare," they are nonetheless the decisions that define the human condition. The description of the human condition that Heidegger draws from his reading of the tragedy is not one that refers to any *unique* crisis or distress: "the Da-sein of historical man means: to be put out as the breach, to break into the overwhelming of being so that this being fractures on being" (*EM*, 124). It refers us rather to our strangeness, *the crisis of our uniqueness*, to the grace and grief alike of the human condition. "To be put out as the breach" not only means that we live as "sites of openness" (*EM*, 124), but also that as such openness we "like to hide." This doubling motion according to which Heidegger suggest that we think who we are—that even as open we encrypt ourselves—is, I would suggest, very much the same motion as the motion of love; namely, the more one draws near the other, the more one comes to recognize the final strangeness and otherness of the other. As this absorption and preservation of alterity, love reverses the distress of law which only preserves alterity in order to absorb it. From this perspective, Antigone marks the reversal of the law as the loving preservation of alterity. From this perspective, hers is not a memento of an unbridgeable abyss, but of the bonds that alterity itself, that abyss by another name, makes possible.

Let me conclude with a great leap now and say that Heidegger offers us a possibility—one he never pursues—of thinking Antigone's act as an act of resistance and love simultaneously. Furthermore, such acts provide the point from which we might come to ask about the idea of law for Heidegger. But if we are to understand these words according to their refunctioned sense as doubling within themselves, then we need to bear in mind both the necessity and the impossibility that each marks. In saying this I have of course apparently defeated my own suggestion that thinking through the figure of Antigone with Heidegger might lend some assistance in understanding just how Heidegger proposes we think the relation of history and sacrifice. I concede that defeat and worry even more about the meaning of "sacrifice" as Heidegger is thinking it.

But now I am far beyond what I believe I have earned the right to say here today, and I believe that I make claims still only in rather crude contours. It seems that I have drifted far from my original themes and promises. Maybe so. So let me conclude now, finally, with another far-flung leap, this one back to my own beginning.

I opened by invoking the widespread sentiment that for some long time now we have lived at a juncture of a certain termination of history. One gathers that sense not only from books, but from world events, all modes of cultural representation as well as from the conduct of political life. I also alluded to what I take to be Heidegger's sense of the impossibility and inevitable failure of any directed attempt on our part to either choose a future or push history toward some choice at this time. That might well be the case, and I do believe that it is, but such destined failure and impossibility of history and action does not entail a release from the demands of either. *Historical experience teaches us that there are indeed points of departure in an individual life that can exhibit elements of universality—even if only for a while.* The question I have only begun to pursue here asks how far both Hegel and Heidegger are suggesting that such acts might need to be regarded as acts of sacrifice.

I do not believe that I have an answer to that question yet, only that some preliminary remarks in that direction have been made. But I do believe that we can already make a suggestion for further reflections.

Namely, that both Hegel and Heidegger develop ultimately tragic visions of history and the polis—and as a personal note I should acknowledge that that vision is something about which I am beginning to have my doubts insofar as it draws death into the center of political life thereby bestowing upon that life a final sting. But whereas Hegel takes this tragic moment as foreshadowing a general solution to the riddles of both history and the polis, Heidegger takes this as foreshadowing the impossibility of either history or political life. To put Hegel and Heidegger on some set of scales, to try to weigh out who is "right" is as senseless an act at this point as I could imagine. It might simply be better to conclude by suggesting something that can be learned from both Hegel and Heidegger, even if only together: that somehow these tattered visions need one another, redeem one another, that somehow general solutions to questions of history and political life, while demanded of us, are only thinkable if we remember and preserve the site of resistance containing their own final countervalent impossibility.

6

The Hegelian Legacy in Heidegger's Overcoming of Aesthetics

Jacques Taminiaux
Translated and edited by Michael Gendre

In the epilogue to the essay "The Origin of the Work of Art," Heidegger calls attention to the fact that the pages of the text proper "are concerned with the riddle of art, the riddle that art itself is." Then we read: "They are far from claiming to solve the riddle. The task is to see the riddle."[1] What is the import of these sentences? Are they simply repeating one and the same thing? But why is such stress put on the "riddle"? If the entire essay itself focuses on the riddle and only prepares the reader to welcome it, why now this denial of any pretension to ever solve it? Why such an insistence on the rejection of this claim, if not because the essay itself, at least in some respects, had subscribed to it? It is difficult not to read these words of the epilogue without suspecting an ambiguity at the very core of the essay, the indication of a tendency to oscillate between the exposure to the riddle and something very different: a solution proposed to a problem. I find this conjecture confirmed by the publication of the addendum a few years after the epilogue. In it we read the following caveat: "What art may be is one of the questions to which no answers are given in this essay. What gives the impression of such an answer are directions for questioning (Cf. the first sentence of the Epilogue)" (OWA, 80).

Is the essay an approach to the riddle of art, or does it supply an answer to the philosophical question about the essence of art? Such is the ambiguity—one at the same time acknowledged and kept at bay—with which we are invited to read the essay. Yet how are we to attempt this reading? What help in our effort can this ambiguity—hardly detected so far—provide? Perhaps the following pages of the epilogue will help us to unravel the impact of such an ambiguity,[2] detected so far only in the beginning of the text.

Two other topics determine the unfolding of the epilogue: the first is aesthetics; the second is the destiny of Western art. *Aesthetics* is the name given to a specifically modern discipline that considers works of art solely as *objects* of sense apprehension, that is, objects of what this discipline conceives as a modality of subjectivity, the *Erlebnis,* or lived experience. By virtue of such an approach to works of art, *Erlebnis* is granted an ultimate normative status; it determines the essence of art, it becomes "the standard not only for art appreciation and enjoyment, but also for artistic creation" (OWA, 79). By the same token, the riddle—which the work is—is threatened. The riddle consists in this, that the work works, like speech speaks, world worlds, time temporalizes, or Being is. With reference to *Erlebnis,* the work stops working. The enigmatic consistency of its identity and differentiation dissolves and is transformed in enjoyment, emotion, and vital excitement. These are stimulations that indeed endorse the unexpected, but in which the "subject" does nothing but expand its own empire and gain self-certainty. The aesthetic imperialism of *Erlebnis* raises, therefore, the question of the destiny of art. It is impossible to come to terms with this question—the last topic in the epilogue—without addressing Hegel's words: "Die Kunst ist nach der Seite ihrer höchsten Bestimmung fur uns ein Vergangenes" ("Art is . . . for us, as regards its highest vocation, something of the past") (OWA, 80). If it is true that *Erlebnis* reigns free and that in it the riddle is dissolved, then Hegel is right: Art is for us a thing of the past, its death is under way.

Here the articulation of the ambiguity detected earlier begins to unfold. Recognizing the riddle of art means attempting to overcome aesthetics, the modern figure of metaphysics. Yet recognizing that the empire of subjectivity over art is not an invention of aesthetics, but the expression given by aesthetics to the principle that really rules over modernity, amounts to validating aesthetics under its most metaphysical figure—the one found in Hegel's *Lectures on Aesthetics,* which provides "the most comprehensive reflection on the nature of art that the West possesses, comprehensive because it stems from metaphysics" (OWA, 79).

Overcoming aesthetics and yet validating it, such is the formula that captures the ambiguity in regard to which I propose to reread "The Origin of the Work of Art." The question brought to the forefront by the recognition of this ambiguity might perhaps be formulated in the following abrupt manner: What makes the essay escape Hegel's thought?

Immediately after recalling Hegel's point on the modern death of art and stressing the impossibility of escaping its verdict, the epilogue adds:

> The question remains: Is art still an essential and necessary way in which that truth happens which is decisive for our historical existence, or is art no longer of this character? If, however, it is such no longer, then there remains the question why this is so. The truth of Hegel's judgment has not yet been decided; for behind this verdict there stands Western thought since the Greeks, which thought corresponds to a truth of beings that has already happened. Decision upon the judgment will be made, when it is made, from and about this truth of what is. Until then the judgment remains in force. But for that very reason the question is necessary whether the truth that the judgment declares is final and conclusive and what follows if it is. (OWA, 80)

Even though the essential words of this text can be interpreted in two different ways (truth in the sense of *aletheia*, and truth in the sense of absolute certainty of oneself; history in the sense of the development of the absoluteness of Spirit and in the sense of the history of Being), the overlapping of the two is obvious and deserves questioning. How can the attempt to think art nonaesthetically, that is, nonmetaphysically, intersect with and validate Hegel's philosophical position (even though such validity still remains provisional and not yet decided) when clearly Hegel's original formulation is based on an approach to art that is entirely aesthetic and metaphysical? The last sentences of the epilogue stress that the intersection with Hegel is not fortuitous, but lies at the core of the Heideggerian questioning into art:

> In the way in which, for the world determined by the West, that which is, is the real, there is concealed a specific concordance of beauty and truth. The history of the nature of Western art corresponds to the change of the nature of truth. This is no more intelligible in terms of beauty taken for itself than it is in terms of experience [*Erlebnis*], supposing that the metaphysical concept of art reaches to art's nature. (OWA, 81, modified)

In punctuating a situation of overlapping with Hegel, these words unveil, so to speak, what is presupposed in the question about the validity of Hegel's verdict on the death of art. Heidegger pointed out earlier that behind Hegel's position "stands Western thought since the Greeks, which thought corresponds to a truth of beings that has already happened" (OWA, 80). The last sentences of the epilogue invite us to recognize that this truth of beings, such as it has already been unfolding for the moderns, is actuality, *Wirklichkeit.* To be sure, this word plays a major role in Hegel, who takes it in the strong sense of achievement and result of implementation. Actuality in the Hegelian sense is that which results from an implementation, or setting-into-work, of the Spirit. Actuality is fully achieved in those works where the Spirit, seeking implementation, encounters nothing that eludes such a setting-into-work, finds nothing else but itself a situation that, to use a different language, exhibits the identity of the worker, the work, and the working. Full actuality is exhibited in modern times and is that toward which the history of the world has been developing, by presupposing it from the outset. The proposition that "for the world determined by the West, that which is, is as the real (actual)"[3] is therefore a Hegelian assertion. It is no less Hegelian to maintain that this Western unfolding of actuality includes "a specific concordance of beauty and truth" (OWA, 81, modified). This unfolding, according to Hegel, is indeed the Western maturation of actuality, and Western history is the process of its gestation.

At the dawn of Western history—without considering its Oriental antecedents—the Greek world indeed had grasped actuality, but under a form that is far from corresponding to its completion, to its truth. To the fact that the Greek world grasped beings as actuality, that is, as a setting-into-work of the Spirit, Hegel testifies by arguing that such a world is entirely artistic. It honors the Being of beings under the guise of works of art, in which Spirit (that is, its Greek form) understands its own operation. But it is the same point that also reveals the deficiency of this apprehension. Because the Greek world honors the Being of beings in works of art, it reveals that the actuality it apprehends is burdened with matter, with immediacy, with sensibility. The truth of actuality is the identity of the worker, of the work, and of the working. The Greek modality of actuality does not raise itself to such an identity, it loads this identity with a difference that it is incapable of overcoming. The specifically Greek concordance of beauty and truth is contained for Hegel in the fact that beauty reached there its full measure but that truth was affected with a deficiency. For the Greeks, he says, "beauty is the veil that hides truth." To this deficiency, with regard to the truth of actuality, Greek philosophy itself bears witness. *Wirklichkeit* is the word by which Hegel translates the Aristotelian *energeia.* By his thinking of *energeia* as *entelecheia,* Aristotle, according to Hegel, proves that he understood it as "in itself goal and realization of the goal." *Energeia* provides Aristotle with a way of grasping the speculative identity of actuality, "the pure actuality that originates within itself" and "negativity focussing on itself."[4]

But because in Aristotle this notion is subordinated to an entirely positive philosophy of nature, it fails to acknowledge negativity and mediation, and is credited by Hegel only with reaching the first level of the self-movement of the Spirit.

The overcoming of this first level entails the overcoming of nature, of immediacy, of sensibility, in a process at the end of which actuality in its modern form accomplishes its truth: namely, the Spirit being certain of itself within its own actuality. From truth as harmony with a given nature, the Spirit has progressed to truth as absolute self-certainty. At the end of this process, we find the specifically modern concordance between beauty and truth. It is the inverted form of the Greek concordance, because truth, which has now reached its full measure, manifests the deficiency of beauty. From now on, beauty is nothing but an elementary modality of self-certainty, a situation exhibited by modern art according to Hegel, in that it makes a game of every form and content.

It is therefore possible to lend a strictly Hegelian interpretation to Heidegger's claim that "to the transformation of the essence of truth corresponds a history of the essence of Western art" (OWA, 81, modified). Since the point at issue in this history of the essence of Western art is the manifestation of Being as actuality, in a development that after the summit of Greek art is for Hegel one of decline, the last sentence of Heidegger's epilogue also lends itself to a Hegelian reading: the full measure of the essence of art is revealed neither by beauty as an abstract concept, nor by the psychological effects that works of art spark in the lived experience of individuals.

This close kinship between Heidegger and Hegel and the importance it has in the very text of the essay "The Origin of the Work of Art" is what we now proceed to interrogate. As it turns out, its importance has manifested itself in our previous analysis of the epilogue. Before actually returning to the text itself, let us bring together the manifold ways in which this importance emerges by articulating these questions: What unites or separates the meditation on the riddle and the theory of the essence of art? What unites or separates the overcoming of aesthetics and its metaphysical completion in speculative dialectics? What unites or separates the history of Being and the history of the Spirit? It can be argued that these three questions point to a fourth one that is more fundamental: Concerning art, what unites or separates the setting-into-work (or *energeia*) of *alētheia* in the Heideggerian sense and the setting-into-work (or *energeia*) of the Spirit in the Hegelian sense?

To address these questions, the end of the epilogue gives a guideline. By stressing that neither beauty considered in itself nor the lived experience (*Erlebnis*) gives the measure of the essence of (Western) art, this text calls to mind the methodological outline found at the beginning of the essay. These considerations of methodology now require our attention.

It has sometimes been noticed that, because of the similarity of their central themes, these considerations of methodology bear a relation, at least formally, to Hegel's introductory remarks at the beginning of his *Lectures on Aesthetics.* In both, the central theme is circularity.

Heidegger's very provisional stance among the "common ideas" allows him to undermine their evidence by gradually highlighting something to which they are blind: the circular movement of the questioning into the origin of the work of art. If one asserts that the origin of the work of art is the artist, one must add—immediately and conversely—that the work is the origin of the artist, since without the work his title would be undeserved. Here we have the first, still elementary, figure of circularity, which immediately rebounds by virtue of a third term. "Artist and work are each of them by virtue of a third thing which is prior to both, namely that which also gives artist and work their names art" (OWA, 17). But if we investigate the essence of art understood as the origin of both artist and work, we cannot fail to notice another, more deeply rooted, figure of circularity: "What art is should be inferable from the work. What the work of art is we can come to know only from the nature of art" (OWA, 18). Thus we have a circle that "common sense" compels us to avoid, but into which wakeful thinking is bound to enquire: "This is neither a makeshift nor a defect. To enter upon this path is the strength of thought, to continue on it is the feast of thought, assuming that thinking is a craft. Not only is the main step from work to art a circle like the step from art to work, but every separate step that we attempt circles in this circle" (OWA, 18).

Undermining the evidence of common ideas, the emergence of circularity to broad daylight now allows us to discard two antithetical forms of philosophy of art: the first derives the essence of the work of art from cumulative empirical symptoms, the second derives it from higher concepts. Both are equally blind to the figure of circularity without which, however, no inquiry could be pursued. This double rejection, which furthermore is akin to the phenomenological reduction of the natural attitude, is Hegelian in style because of what it discards, because of its insistence on circularity, and because of the manner in which circularity is approached.

It is indeed easy to isolate in Hegel the two figures of circularity that we have just identified in Heidegger. The first one is the reciprocity of the artist and of the work, itself founded on a third term extending over both is the theme of the individual figure of consciousness that the *Phenomenology* names "the spiritual animal kingdom and deceit, or the 'matter in hand' itself."[5] This figure describes the creator who erects his own individuality into an absolute. In the consciousness of this individual, the determined character of his nature is perceived not as a limitation, but as a universal element inside which his nature unfolds without obstacle and is "pure reciprocal relationship with itself in its actualization" (see *PS*, § 396). In this actualization, a differentiation emerges that affects the simplicity of his original nature: this consciousness sets a *goal* for itself, represents to itself the means of realizing it, and achieves it in a *work*. But these differences do not shatter the simplicity of that consciousness; they are inessential and rather confirm it in its circularity, in its pure act of relating itself to itself. No matter what the nature of the consciousness, the circumstances that it finds at its disposal, its goals, its means, its works, all elements produce a pattern of circularity with that consciousness at the center: "There is nothing for individuality which has not been made by it, or there is no reality (actuality) which is not individuality's own nature and doing, and no action, nor in-itself of individuality that is not real (actual)" (*PS*, § 403, p. 242). Yet this circularity of the individual and of its work is only the animal anticipation of a deeper and properly spiritual type of circularity of the individual and of its work is only the animal anticipation of a deeper and properly spiritual type of circularity that exceeds the confines of this individual. The experience pursued and undergone by the individual shows the deceptive character of the circularity to which that consciousness is linked. Deeper than this elementary circularity, the "matter in hand" that inevitably confronts such an experience is a third element: this element shatters the simple reciprocity of elementary circularity and foreshadows within the individual, and beyond him or her, the true circle of the Spirit.

For in the work the individual does not claim to accomplish anything but its singularity. But as soon as the work exists, the individual creator from whom it came and who thought that nothing except this person's individuality had been brought into it, undergoes the realization that, inasmuch as it is being offered to others, the work lends itself to operations other than its creator's. The work is thus exposed to a transindividual operation that causes a shift and opens a new process of becoming. Facing this process, the individual creator experiences the contingency of what he or she originally felt compelled them and contained a necessity—his or her talent, the goal pursued, the circumstances, the means available, even the work. Since the work turns out to be ephemeral, consciousness dissociates itself from it and erects its concept as the perdurable. The true work, therefore, is not this product, which from now on turns out to be contingent, but the "matter itself" (*Sache selbst*) as the identity of Being and setting-into-work.

The true thing, the matter at issue, the *Sache*, is not the work, but art. But as soon as the individual creator raises the issue of art, he or she either tends to reduce it to a kind of universal predicate unifying the various aspects of the creator's operations, or turns the issue of art into a pure abstraction without any possible determination as he or she dismisses the accusation of merely pursuing self-interest in such works. As a consequence, the artist oscillates between two fallacies, one being the false reduction of the universal to the singular, and the second being the false dissociation of the universal and the singular. Since the cause that this consciousness invokes is in fact nothing without the operation of everybody, including its own operation, this individual consciousness experiences that the matter is neither an abstract universal, the predicate of individual species, nor a pure ideal. "It is rather substance permeated by individuality, subject in which there is individuality just as much qua individual, or qua this particular individual, as qua all individuals; and it is the universal which has being only as this action of all and each" (*PS*, § 418, p. 252).

Concerning the second figure of circularity—in which art is grasped exclusively from the work, yet every reception of a work presupposes the understanding of the essence of art—we only need to recall that it plays a fundamental role in the introduction to the *Lectures on Aesthetics*. To be sure, the first pages of this lecture course take great care to stress that the train of thought about to unfold does not provide us with the full measure of the essence of art, because the circularity characterizing the essence of art at the most essential level cannot be sufficiently clarified in the narrow framework of a lecture course. In order for a theory of art to be fully philosophical, or scientific, in the Hegelian sense, it must satisfy the "highest scientific need which requires that, even though an object exists, its necessity be nevertheless demonstrated."[6] Hegel remarks that regarding the object of any science, two points must be taken into consideration, "first, that such an object is, and second, what it is" (*LA*, 11). In the ordinary sciences, which in this regard are aligned with the common notions, the existence of such an object is tantamount to an absolute beginning, to a point of departure from which the sciences proceed toward the appropriate essence. Thus, the point of departure of ordinary aesthetics consists in the fact that some works of art can be "shown." From this one assumes that an appropriate method can be found to determine the essence of these works. But in a science worthy of the name (only the whole of philosophy—the encyclopedia of philosophical sciences—is granted such a status in Hegel), nothing must be accepted as pure and simple fact subjected to the so-called contingencies of existence. That there are works of art is not a factual occurrence that philosophy should take for granted from the outset. For philosophy, the occurrence of works of art is more than a fact, it exhibits a necessity that can and must be demonstrated. This necessity is derived from the concept, or essence, of art and this concept itself results and derives with utmost necessity from the Spirit itself. Therefore aesthetics has the status of a science only when it is understood as a sphere inserted as a broader circle of the system that explicitly demonstrates the necessary unfolding of the Spirit in its totality. In science, thus understood as system,

> there is so to speak no absolute beginning. By absolute beginning, what is often meant is an abstract beginning, a beginning that would be nothing else but a beginning. But since philosophy is a totality, as such its beginning is everywhere. Now, essentially this beginning is everywhere a result. It is necessary to conceive philosophy as a circle coming back upon itself. (*LA*, 20)

But the *Lectures on Aesthetics* cannot exhibit the connection between the various spheres of the system and clarify its circularity by demonstrating how the phenomenal production of works follows a necessity of essence arising from the Spirit and how, conversely, their production was necessary in order for the Spirit to complete its essence. As a result, the *Lectures on Aesthetics* take their departure in ordinary notions and the common theories associated with them: "First of all, we have to consider only one thing, i.e., that there are works of art. Such a consideration is appropriate to give a sound starting point" (*LA*, 14). From this ordinary notion, we must gain access to the circle and show how the latter is at the same time presupposed and ignored by the common representation.

It is at this juncture that the introduction to these *Lectures* and the very beginning of Heidegger's essay intersect and overlap. Both cases involve the rejection of empiricism and of intellectualism. In addition, these rejections are for the same reason: both approaches fail to recognize circularity. According to Hegel, empiricism is flawed because it leads either to negative results—there is no essence of art—or to very abstract and general definitions: for instance, that art aims at eliciting pleasurable sensations. Moreover, not only can these definitions be simply contradicted by antithetical ones, but their realm is so vast that it can extend to many other domains. In no way can empiricism remedy this void or expansion without surreptitiously and contradictorily permeating its approach with a nebulous view of the essence.

Against all this, Hegel draws on Plato: "One must consider not particular objects, that are called beautiful, but the Beautiful." The idea is what provides us with the right beginning. Yet this new beginning would be as misleading as that of empiricism if it only consisted in holding the idea as a unique ethereal principle antithetically opposed to the self-proclaimed concreteness of the sensible, or as the pure intelligible entity heterogeneous to phenomenal production. This notion, in effect, too, would fail to recognize circularity. Hence the idea in the Hegelian sense cannot be set apart from its setting-into-work. It is essential for the idea "to differentiate itself, to particularize from within itself, by developing into the variety, the multiplicity, into the differences, into the many and different forms and figures of art" (*LA*, 19).

From the previous assessment, we see that it is a Hegelian, as much as a Heideggerian, proposition to assert that neither lived experience (*Erlebnis*) nor beauty taken in itself proves equal to the essence of art. Yet one can object that it is not the same kind of circularity that is at stake in both cases: Hegel's is the speculative circle; Heidegger's, the hermeneutic circle. Thus it is toward a comparison of these two figures of circularity that we must strive. It is such a comparison that will guide our questioning.

The circularity of the question of art in "The Origin of the Work of Art" is reminiscent of another circularity previously treated by Heidegger, namely, the circularity of understanding. Insofar as the question of art entails the "understanding" of the essence of art, the circularity of this question presents itself as a particular instance of the hermeneutic circle mentioned in § 32 of *Sein und Zeit.* This circle was announced as early as the "exposition of the question of the meaning of Being." In order to be taken up expressly as a problem, this question requires, indeed, a preliminary elucidation of the entity that is taking the problem up and of this entity's mode of being. Heidegger stresses that this circular procedure does not beg the question, but rather acknowledges that an understanding of Being is what the entity that we are has always already been involved in.

This analysis acknowledges the "remarkable 'relatedness backward or forward' which what we are asking about (Being) bears to the inquiry itself as a mode of Being of an entity."[7] This ambiguous connectedness between the inquiry and what is under inquiry is essential in the hermeneutic circle.

The existential structure of this ambiguous relatedness is what the analytic of *Dasein* exhibits. The analytic stresses that every interpretation moves within a circle. Yet this point is not tantamount to saying merely that there must be an antecedent, in the form of pretheoretical understanding, to every interpretation that adopts a theoretical comportment in the attempt to explain a given being in the light of its properties. The elucidation of any being as such certainly depends on an everyday mode of being of the entity that we are. This mode of being has always already been grounded on the basis of a prior understanding of the manifestation of the world and has always already produced perspectives and meanings, if not anticipated new ones. However, this circle of interpretation and antecedent understanding is only the expression of a deeper circle whose source originates in the circular ontological structure of Dasein itself.

To refer the hermeneutic circle to Dasein's structure amounts to associating the latter to the existential triad of thrownness-in (situation), understanding, and fallenness. Such a triad shows a circular structure, because there is an overlapping of all the terms: every thrown situation is understood as such, every understanding is engaged in a situation, yet neither is free from obliteration, and thus both allow for the emergence of fallenness which consists in forsaking their inalienable character. This structure is ontologically circular, because the mutual overlapping of these terms discloses Dasein as a *project* of Being always already *thrown* into the openness of Being, yet a project such that it is always in danger of letting this openness be obliterated, hidden from itself, and masked by the public and everyday evidence of beings present-at-hand (*Vorhandenes*).

The hermeneutic circle announced in the exposition of the question of the meaning of Being unfolds its existential structure in the analytic of Dasein. But the analytic only exhibits the foundation of this circle when the existential components[8] of interpretation, provided that they are held together in the unitary structure of care, lend themselves to an originary interpretation that, while integrating the results of the analytic, reveals temporality as the ontological meaning of Dasein, and time as the transcendental horizon of the question of the meaning of Being. Accordingly, the foundation of the hermeneutic circle turns out to be the knot tying together the three ecstasies of finite temporality. The phenomenon of care, in which Dasein maintains itself open to its ownmost possibility of Being, reveals that Dasein is always self-preceded, inasmuch as it presupposes its inscription in the openness of Being. In other words, Dasein's coming to itself (future) matters to it only inasmuch as it has already been (past). And we can say that there is reciprocity between these two dimensions, because every recasting entails an anticipation and vice versa. "Eigentlich Zukunftig *ist* das Dasein eigentlich *gewesen*. . . . Dasein kann nur eigentlich *sein*, sofern es zukünftig ist" ("As authentically futural, Dasein *is* authentically as *having been*. . . . Only so far as it is futural can Dasein *be* authentically [as having been]") (*BT*,

373/326). At the intersection of anticipation and repetition, a relation to the present takes place. It is also this chasm that the relation to the present always threatens to obliterate, when that present antecedently dissociated from its ec-static foundation is granted a primordial status.

If such is indeed the teaching of *Sein und Zeit* regarding the circle of understanding, one can justifiably conclude that its circularity excludes any privileging of the present and precludes its hypostasis as eternal *nunc stans.* The privileging of the present can only bear witness to the obliteration of circularity. The second conclusion is that understanding, which is grounded upon the finite temporality of Dasein, is not amenable to a totalization that is not finite. It is not amenable to a totalization that would trespass the limits of the intrinsically mortal project constitutive of Dasein, as well as the limits assignable to the interaction of finite projects whose radical historicality is a dimension precisely not totalizable in any global history.

If one now pays attention to the fact that we have an understanding of Being inasmuch as it is no being, one could conclude finally that the circle at issue is intrinsically differentiated. It is not enough to say that the project is always a cast-forth project, that anticipation is always retrospective; one must also add that the movement of transcendence constituting Dasein emanates not so much from Dasein itself as from what transgresses all entities, namely, from Being, of which the entity existing ec-statically is itself nothing but the "there." In other words, in the circularity of understanding, we detect the insurmountable, originary, and ever-present difference between Being and beings, a difference that supports the ec-static nature of Dasein, but that the latter does not constitute.

These three points show that the hermeneutic circle is heterogeneous to the speculative circle. Recall the famous proposition by which the speculative circle is presented in the *Phenomenology of Spirit:* "[The true] is the process of its own becoming, the circle that presupposes its end as its goal, having its end also as its beginning; and only by being worked out to its end, is it actual" (*PS,* § 18, p. 10). This circle grants a privilege to the present, to totalization, and to saturation. It entails the privilege of the present, because in the *Phenomenology* this self-becoming is nothing but the phenomenal or temporal succession of the moments of the Spirit. But the present is privileged also in the sense that the phenomenal or temporal moments, defined by their contribution to the increasing actualization of the Spirit, exhaust their effectiveness in their own contribution and are thus linked to a determined epoch, representing a determined degree in the maturation of the Spirit: after or beyond such a degree, the past no longer offers the possibility of retrieval or repetition (*Wiederholung*), but only of commemoration (*Erinnerung*). Finally, the present is granted a privilege, in the sense that the goal both presupposed and sought by the self-becoming of the Spirit certain of itself, or by the concept knowing itself as such eliminates the form of time, that is, the succession of presents, in order to be actualized in the *nunc stans* of the full presence, "the eternal Idea that is in and for itself eternally actualizing itself and reaching its goal in absolute spirit" (*Encyclopedia*, § 577). This form of circularity entails totalization: it is the same thing to say that "the true is its own self-becoming" and to say that "the true is the whole." Here understanding what is true amounts to totalization. In particular, understanding calls for the totalization of the meaning of history and of the institutions that came into existence in its process. It is equally obvious that this form of circularity also entails saturation: in Hegel differentiation never has a primordial status; it is only a preface to identity, identity's provisional alienation, the element through which the equality of self-sameness makes itself absolute.

If such are indeed the respective consequences of the hermeneutic circle and the speculative one, then the methodological similarities that we identified earlier—the rejection of empiricism and of an intellectualistic a priorism, the preliminary detection of a double circularity (the first regarding the work and of the artist with reference to art as a middle term, the second concerning the work and of the essence of art), the progression toward circularity on the basis of common notions—these similarities contain absolutely no evidence of a core kinship between these two approaches. In every respect there is heterogeneity between the fundamental features of each form of circularity toward which each path progresses independently.

However, the question remains open as to what treatment is given by the essay "The Origin of the Work of Art" to the three consequences of the hermeneutic circle. In other words, we still have to ask what its own circular progression can assert regarding the privilege of the present, totalization, and the excess of Being over beings. It is only by investigating the treatment of these topics that we shall be able to clarify the ambiguity that set this inquiry in motion: How does the Heideggerian overcoming of aesthetics, as a figure of metaphysics, come to intersect and overlap Hegel's aesthetics, which is the most metaphysical aesthetics of all?

So far, only in the epilogue did we find a more or less implicit acknowledgment of this overlapping. However, another text, roughly of the same period as the essay, expressly recognizes and underscores this recognition to such an extent that this very overlapping now seems to result in the abolition pure and simple of the heterogeneity between the hermeneutic and the speculative circles. I have in mind an important text of the 1936 course on Nietzsche, "The Will to Power as Art." The text in question bears the title "Six Basic Developments in the History of Aesthetics."[9] These developments—brought together by Heidegger at the time of his debate with the Nietzschean interpretation of the essence of art—are said to "characterize the essence of aesthetics, its role in Western thought and its relation to the history of Western art" (*N*, 79–80). Of the six alleged facts or developments, the first four are of central interest to us, because their very formulation acknowledges the overlapping we are investigating. Let me reintroduce them:

1. "The magnificent art of Greece remains without a corresponding cognitive-conceptual meditation on it, such meditation not having to be identical with aesthetics" (*N*, 80).

2. "Aesthetics begins with the Greeks only at that moment when their great art and also the great philosophy that flourished along with it comes to an end. At that time, during the age of Plato and Aristotle, in connection with the organization of philosophy as a whole, those basic concepts are formed which mark off the boundaries for all future inquiry into art. One of those basic notions is the conceptual pair, *hyle-morphe, materia-forma,* matter-form" (*N*, 80). To this first pair is associated the next one: *techne-physis.* The first pair owes its origin to Plato's determination of beings in view of their appearing: *eidos,* or idea. As in other texts of the same period, here as well Heidegger insists on the fact that *eidos* (originally only an effect of *physis*), as soon as it became predominant as a determination, by virtue of the fact that it had acquired a founding and normative status with respect to *physis,* not only detached itself from its origin but obliterated the pre-Platonic sense of *physis* as the unconcealment of the totality of beings (*aletheia*). Since the distinction *hyle-morphe* is regulated by the new priority of *idea,* it starts to function in the context of an obliteration of *physis* (or *aletheia*). It was to *aletheia* that the initial use of the word *techne* was connected, designating the knowledge by means of which man, immersed in *physis,* orients himself, goes about his activities, and copes with beings according to what they let be revealed out of themselves. But by associating itself with the *hyle-morphe* distinction, now regulated by the new priority of *idea, techne* "loses this primitive force of meaning" (*N*, 82, modified) and undergoes an interpretation which gives it the sense of the aptitude to confer a form upon a material. As soon as we notice, says Heidegger, that this aptitude does not belong to the realm of the fine arts but to the realm of the fabrication of tools, we are bound to be overcome by serious doubts concerning the relevance of the fundamental concepts of the philosophical questioning of art.

3. "The third basic development is the beginning of the modern age. Man and his unconstrained knowledge of himself, as of his positions among beings, become the arena where the decision falls as to how beings are to be experienced, defined, and shaped" (*N*, 83).

The *cogito me cogitare* acquires the highest-court status for judging all beings. "I myself, and my states, are the primary and genuine beings. Everything else that may be said to be is measured against the standard of this quite certain being" (*N*, 83). At this juncture, in close connection with the modern metaphysics of subjectivity, aesthetics is born: it is the discipline specifically devoted to the study of the beautiful in art, inasmuch as the beautiful is related to the emotional states of man as to an exclusive normative principle. "A mode of observation (is recognized) for which the way had long been paved" (*N*, 83), Heidegger stresses. It presupposes indeed the Platonic heritage evoked earlier and consists essentially in a transposition: "'Aesthetics' is to be in the field of sensuousness and feeling precisely what logic is in the area of thinking" (*N*, 83)—logic that had been born out of metaphysics, and that since its birth has bound truth to enunciation and to judgment and its rules.

Therefore, the third fact is the birth of "aesthetics" as the modern discipline conceived as a logic of sensibility. In this discipline, "the artwork is posited as the 'object' for a 'subject'; definitive for aesthetic consideration is the subject-object relation, indeed as a relation of feeling" (*N*, 78).

It is concerning this third fundamental fact that the question of the intersecting and overlapping that we are pursuing is presented with the utmost clarity. Heidegger writes:

> Parallel to the formation of aesthetics and to the effort to clarify and ground the aesthetic state, another decisive process unfolds within the history of art. Great art and its works are great in their historical emergence and Being because in man's historical existence they accomplish a decisive task: they make manifest, in the way appropriate to works, what beings as a whole are, preserving such manifestation in the work. Art and its work are necessary only as an itinerary and sojourn for man in which the truth of beings as a whole, i.e., the unconditioned, absolute, opens itself up to him. What makes art great is not only and not in the first place the high quality of what is created. Rather, art is great because it is an "absolute need." Because it is that, and to the extent it is that, it also can and must be great in rank. For only on the basis of the magnitude of its essential character does it also create a dimension of magnitude for the rank and stature of what is brought forth.
>
> Concurrent with the formation of a dominant aesthetics and of the aesthetic relation to art in modern times is the decline of great art, great

> in the designated sense. Such decline does not result from the fact that "quality" is poorer and the style less imposing; it is rather that art forfeits its essence, loses its immediate relation to the basic task of representing the absolute, i.e., of establishing the absolute definitively as such in the realm of historical man. (*N*, 83–84)

I hope to be forgiven for this long quote. Even though no mention is directly made of Hegel, no great familiarity with speculative aesthetics is required to recognize the obvious echo of the Hegelian concept of great art. It is more than an echo, because the expression *absolute need* put in quotation marks by Heidegger is clearly borrowed from Hegel. He thought that art is great, is art fully, only when it comes as the response to the "absolute need" to manifest the "unconditioned" or the "absolute"; for him, this need was historically connected to the Greek world, because only in it was art truly "necessary." Hegel also claimed that the period of blossoming of great art preceded the birth of philosophy with Socrates and Plato a birth that would soon spell the demise of Greek art. Because of the fact that the sequence of the first three fundamental facts advanced by Heidegger is pivotally centered on the idea that the only "great art" was Greek, and more precisely pre-Socratic, and also because of the fact that it expressly subscribes to the Hegelian definition of great art as the necessary response to the absolute need to exhibit the absolute with its speculative connotation, for these reasons this sequence is a very close duplication of the Hegelian succession of the ages of the history of art:

1. The great Greek art, without corresponding conceptual reflection;
2. The Greek end of great art at the time of the birth of metaphysics with Socrates and Plato, within which is foreshadowed and announced at a distance the advent of aesthetics;
3. The properly modern decline of great art at the time when metaphysics moves into the era of subjectivity, thus making possible the birth of aesthetics proper.

Therefore, it is not surprising that the fourth fundamental fact advanced by Heidegger should be formulated by him in the very same terms that Hegel used:

> The achievement of aesthetics derives its greatness from the fact that it recognizes and gives utterance to the end of great art as such. The final and greatest aesthetics in the Western tradition is that of Hegel. . . . There the following statements appear: ". . . In all these relations art is and

remains for us with regard to its highest determination, something of the past." (*SW* 10:1, 16)

The magnificent days of Greek art, like the golden era of the later Middle Ages, are gone. (*SW* 10:1, 15–16) (*N*, 84)

It is extremely surprising, however, that this sequence of fundamental facts should endorse a properly metaphysical concept of art without questioning it, at the same time as, in the wake of a meditation on the most primordial semantic units of Greek thinking, it points toward a nonmetaphysical essence of art. What an amazing tangle! For what could be more metaphysical than to assign to the fine arts the essential task of exhibiting "the truth of beings as a whole, that is to say the unconditioned, the Absolute" (*N*, 84)? What could be more surprising than to hear that only Greek, pre-Socratic art took upon itself this properly metaphysical task for which it alone deserves "greatness," at the very same time as it is stressed that the most significant words found in the pre-Socratic thinkers and poets—*aletheia* and *physis*—point not toward an unconditional and supreme being as the ground of beings as a whole, but toward the twofold unity of revealing and reserve at the very core of Being? What could be more amazing than the fact that Heidegger points out, at the same time, that the Greek word *techne* initially referred not to making, to fabricating, to the imposition of a form upon a material, but to a knowledge, to an opening to the twofold unconcealment of *physis*, to a know-how involved in dealing with it, in co-responding to its very twofold nature?

What are we to make of this intertwining? One may wonder whether it does not constitute the unthought of the Heideggerian overcoming of aesthetics and whether it does not create within his texts devoted to art a tension that they never overcame.

Before detecting the evidence of such a tension, let us first remark that, inasmuch as the Heideggerian conception of the history of Western art expressly endorses the Hegelian definition of great art, it is led to discard the three consequences of the hermeneutic circle upon which we insisted earlier. Indeed, the recasting of that Hegelian definition entails the privilege given to the present, the totalization of history, and the reduction of Being on the level of beings or of their beingness. A privilege is given to the present with the notion that once, during the Greek dawn, there had been a time, a present, when art was art fully. There is also a totalization of history in the sense of the sequence of the four fundamental facts mentioned previously, a sequence that furthermore is complemented with a fifth development: the Wagnerian aspiration to the integral work of art in the unfixed, evanescent, and measureless element of blind and superficial *Erlebnis;* and finally a sixth:

the Nietzschean reaction against that nihilistic vertigo with the notion of art as an intoxication of the will willing its own overcoming, that is, its ever-renewed intensification. These last two facts cannot indeed be found in Hegel, but they confirm and continue a series whose style we may identify as Hegelian because they imply that in this present day and age of planetary technology, whose metaphysical essence Nietzsche anticipated in the twin doctrines of the will to power and of the eternal return, art does nothing but perpetuate its nonessence. This sequence of facts entails the abolition of the difference between Being and beings, which can easily be understood by noticing that the Hegelian concept of "great art" that regulates it derives its meaning not from the twofold unity of revealing and reserve at the core of *aletheia*, but rather from the manifestation of an unconditioned and absolute foundation of the totality, in short from a supreme being.

Yet, as we saw, the book *Nietzsche* combines this purely metaphysical concept of art with a nonmetaphysical one, and this fusion generates in it an internal tension whose signs we can now attempt to detect in "The Origin of the Work of Art."

It is remarkable that in it we should also find the expression *great art*. At the beginning of the second section of the essay, Heidegger stresses the fact that "only great art is under consideration here" (OWA, 40). The immediate context of that sentence leaves no doubt on the Hegelian origin of this expression. Not only does the expression aim, as it does in Hegel, at the Greek world and the Christian Middle Ages (Heidegger evokes the Aegina sculptures, Sophocles's *Antigone*, the temple in Paestum, but the Bamberg cathedral, too), but also in a very Hegelian style it evokes both worlds as irrevocably gone, their works being no longer what they were as a result of the collapse of their worlds and, more importantly, of the fact that we, moderns, approach them as we do objects, by means of representation (*Vorstellung*).

Heidegger writes:

> World-withdrawal and world-decay can never be undone. The works are no longer the same as they once were. It is they themselves, to be sure, that we encounter there, but they themselves are gone by. As bygone works, they stand over against us in the realm of tradition and conservation. Henceforth, they remain merely such objects. Their standing before us is still indeed a consequence of, but no longer the same as, their former self-subsistence. Their self-subsistence has fled from them. The whole art industry, even carried to the extreme and exercised in every way for the sake of works themselves, extends only to the object-being of the works. But this does not constitute their work-being. (OWA, 41)

It is difficult not to hear in these words the echo of Hegel's words in the *Phenomenology of Spirit* that evoked the collapse of Greece and "the disappearance of the works of the Muses":

> So Fate does not restore their world to us along with the works of antique Art, it gives not the spring and summer of the ethical life in which they blossomed and ripened, but only the veiled recollection of that actual world. Our active enjoyment of them is therefore not an act of divine worship through which our consciousness might come to its perfect truth and fulfillment; it is an external activity—the wiping-off of some drops of rain or specks of dust from these fruits, so to speak—one which erects an intricate scaffolding of the dead elements of their outward existence—the language, the historical circumstances, etc. in place of the inner elements of the ethical life which environed, created, and inspired them. All this we do, not in order to enter into their very life but only to possess an idea of them in our imagination. (*PS*, § 753, 455–56)

Once more it is in close agreement with Hegel that after stressing that the works of the great art are no longer for us moderns "what they were [*die Gewesenen*]," Heidegger claims that "as work, [the work] belongs uniquely within the realm that is opened up by itself. For the work-being of the work is present in, and only in, such opening up" (OWA, 41). The privilege of the present lies in this: the works of the great art were truly works only within the realm that they opened up in a bygone age; only then were they truly present. For us now, they no longer actualize that opening, for they have changed to objects.

Another affinity with Hegel lies in the particular choice for the work of art selected to apprise the reader of the advent of this opening: the Greek temple. Such a choice brings in a special load of meaning, for it unmistakably presupposes that the works that truly work—that is, the works of great art—can be nothing but sacred, that the world that they erect is the one in which a "people" embraces the seal and figure of its destiny, and also it supposes that they remain works only "as long as the god has not fled from them" (OWA, 43). Hegel, likewise, maintained that art was fully art only in the artistic religion of the Greek people and as long as this religion remained alive.

Yet, striking though it is, this parallelism cannot be extended too far. Even though the Heideggerian description of the features characterizing the work as opening up a realm is reminiscent of Hegel, it nevertheless escapes the Hegelian ascendancy. At the same time as the work erects and consecrates a world, it manifests from the very depths of that world that there is something that the world cannot absorb: the earth, another name for *physis*. What the work manifests, arranges, administers, and organizes, is consequently referred and entrusted to something ungraspable, to an enigma, to a secret. Such is the polemical essence of the work, which Hegel indeed recognized in the great art of Greece, but in which he sought to acknowledge nothing but a provisional conflict, the tension between substance and subject before the absorption of the former by the latter. Nothing of the like is to be found in Heidegger. The earth, or *physis*, is not the substance that the Spirit is called upon to dissolve in the process of acquiring total self-certainty. More importantly, the earth is the unfathomable reserve at the core of what is disclosed, for which it is the ever-presupposed and ever-renewed resource.

At this juncture comes to the fore the tension between the Hegelian theme obscurely espoused by Heidegger and another theme that escapes it. It is one thing to maintain, in line with Hegel, as we read in *Nietzsche*, that great art corresponds to the absolute need to exhibit "the truth of beings as a whole, that is to say (of) the unconditioned." It is quite another thing to say that it brings into the open the struggle between earth and world.

In this struggle, by virtue of which only the work is truly work, the polemical nature of *aletheia* is at stake. *Aletheia* is what sets itself to work in the work. But the meditation on the nature of *aletheia* is precisely what shatters the first superficial evidence of the notion of "great art," along with the entire network of Hegelian echoes brought in the wake of this notion.

Let me call attention to the indications of such a shattering. The simple fact that a painting by Van Gogh should be entrusted with the mission of conveying an example of the setting-into-work of *aletheia* is not compatible with the Hegelian connotations present in the Heideggerian concept of the great art. Which "historical people" could possibly be summoned to embrace its historic destiny by this modern painter whose works were frowned upon by his contemporaries? Yet the peasant's shoes painted by Van Gogh are granted the virtue of making reliability (*Verläßlichkeit*) manifest, that is, of manifesting the link between the world and the earth, more profoundly rooted than the readiness-at-hand of equipment. Moreover, the very meditation on *aletheia* to which the description of the Greek temple leads, entails a relativization of the aletheic privilege of Greek Dasein, and thus shatters the artistic privilege of Greece. Indeed, Heidegger writes: "The nature of truth as *aletheia* was not thought out in the thinking of the Greeks, nor since then and least of all in the philosophy that followed after. Unconcealedness is, for thought, the most concealed thing in Greek existence, although from early times it determines the present of everything present" (OWA, 51). The sequence

([1] artistic but nonphilosophical Greece; [2] philosophical but no-longer-artistic Greece), Hegelian in origin, is therefore not the last word, since *aletheia* remained concealed to those very thinkers of the artistic not yet philosophical or metaphysical age of Greece, even though it did "flash out" through their most pregnant linguistic coinages. Their saying, therefore, is less the vestige of a treasure to which they had privileged access than a constellation of signs that have been awaiting, up to this very day, a meditation that always is to come.

There is more. This meditation on *aletheia*, on unconcealedness, proceeds along a way that avoids all normative application. At the core of this meditation it turns out that "the clearing in which beings stand is in itself at the same time a concealing [*Verbergung*]" (OWA, 53), and that the latter rules over beings as a whole in a double mode, in the mode of the refusal or concealing, which we best reach when "we can say no more of beings than that they are" (OWA, 53), and in the mode of displacement, that is, of dissembling (*Verstellen*), which occurs when, inside the clearing (*Lichtung*), something in a being masks something else of that being or passes itself off as something that it is not. Of this double mode Heidegger writes: "Concealment can be a refusal [*Versagen*] or merely a dissembling [*Verstellen*]. We are never fully certain whether it is the one or the other. Concealment conceals and dissembles itself" (OWA, 54). And further on: "Truth occurs as itself in that the concealing denial, as refusal, provides its constant source to all clearing, and yet, as dissembling it metes out to all clearing the indefeasible severity of deception" (OWA, 55, modified). Here indeed the most severe shattering of the Hegelian theme is expressed: How can one convincingly talk about great art, and consequently suggest a clear distinction between great and inferior, if one cannot decide whether concealment, inseparable as it is from unconcealment, is encountered by us in the mode of refusal or in that of dissembling? How then could it be possible to distinguish, in Hegel's manner, between the age of art's greatness and the age of its decline?

Isn't Heidegger's position worlds apart from the Hegelian "greatness," worlds apart from the exhibition of the unconditioned, worlds apart from the monumentality, the resolute and given unanimity of a historical people, when he writes later on in the essay the following assessment?

> The simple *factum est* wants to be held forth into the Open by the work: namely this, that unconcealedness of what is has happened here, and that as this happening it happens here for the first time; or, that such a work is at all rather than is not. . . . Precisely where the artist, the process and the

> circumstances of the genesis of the work remain unknown, this thrust, this "*that* it is" of createdness, emerges into view most purely from the work. (OWA, 65)

And further:

> The more solitarily the work, fixed in the figure stands on its own and the more cleanly it seems to cut all ties to human beings, the more simply does the thrust come into the Open that such a work is, and the more essentially is the extraordinary thrust to the surface and the long-familiar thrust down. (OWA, 66)

It is at this point, a point almost characterized, one might say, by insignificance, since it resists all knowledge and all power when the work simply offers itself and reveals the enigma that it is, rather than is not, that the Heideggerian meditation is radically irreducible to the speculative circle.

Therefore, there is present in the text of "The Origin of the Work of Art" a tension between the terms we singled out at the beginning: on the one hand, attention is given to the enigma; on the other hand, we have the suggestion of a solution to the philosophical problem of the essence of art. It is true that the language of the essay remains questioning throughout, in contradistinction to that of *Nietzsche,* which is massively assertive. Consequently, the weight of speculative circularity is less predominant in it than in *Nietzsche.* However, the speculative circle is still present, and it reemerges implicitly when the essay expressly reiterates what the hermeneutic circle teaches in relation to art. I have in mind here the pages of the third section, dealing with poetry (*Dichtung*) conceived as the essence of art:

> The nature of poetry [*Dichtung*], in turn, is the founding of truth. We understand founding here in a triple sense: founding as bestowing [*Schenken*], founding as grounding [*Gründen*] and founding as beginning [*Anfangen*]. Founding, however, is actual only in preserving. Thus to each mode of founding there corresponds a mode of preserving. (OWA, 75)

This is, the text adds, "the structure of the nature of art." The fact that we are dealing here with a variant of the hermeneutic circle, of the circle of the cast-forth project that understanding is, such a fact is unmistakably indicated in the text by the qualification of *Dichtung* as "poetic projection," which opens up "that into which human being as historical is already cast" (OWA, 75). The inclusion within the structure of the *Dichtung* of the previously analyzed characters of the hermeneutic circle is undeniable, because the *bestowing* here evoked designates the excess of Being over beings, because the *founding* here evoked consists in entrusting that which is instituted by the work of art to the already-there of the earth, or *physis*, and because the beginning also evoked consists in opening a space of safekeeping and retrieval. In a way, such a circle is untotalizable, because in it we face the ever renewed intersection of the three ec-stases of time, that is to say, an ad-vent (*Geschehen*) that preserves itself at the very core of what happens. One can suspect, however, that the shadow of speculative circularity looms within the meditation on this ad-vent, which is the very history of Being. Isn't it this shadow, which at a distance in the text rules over Heidegger's outline for art history, articulated along three major epochs: Greek, medieval, and modern? Isn't it the same shadow, most importantly, that makes it necessary to construe each of these eruptions of history as the "awakening of a *people* to what it has been entrusted to accomplish"? Isn't it also the same shadow that compels Heidegger to ask at the closing of the essay whether art can still be today an "origin" or "whether it is to remain a mere appendix and then can only be carried along as a routine cultural phenomenon"?

Beyond the text that we have just scrutinized, two other signs give additional testimony to the fact that the shadow of the speculative history of Spirit is brought to bear on Heidegger's meditation on art. The first sign is the precipitation with which Heidegger confined the adventure of contemporary art within the limits of technology, that is, of what he called *Gestell*, taken to be the completed figure of metaphysics, as we can see both in the 1967 Athens conference and in the posthumous interview by *Der Spiegel* magazine. Why such precipitation, when the lecture *The Question concerning Technology* seemed to suggest quite a different approach? This lecture indeed first undermined the naive certainties about the instrumental conception of technology and then proceeded to show how contemporary technology, which is the achievement and the completion of the modern metaphysics of subjectivity, still remains in the midst of the generalized challenge that constitutes it a mode of unconcealing, that is, of *aletheia*. Its essence, therefore, is ambiguous: at the same time as the *Gestell* entails the ruling of the darkest forgetfulness of Being, because beings are reduced to their availability for manipulations and calculations, it contains the way Being has of calling us to attention while preserving its secret. The kinship between danger and saving power, says Heidegger, is comparable to the two sides of a coin. Precisely because of this ambiguity, the essence of technology is not at all technological. Heidegger then draws the consequence that an "essential reflection upon technology and decisive confrontation with it must happen in a realm that is, on the one hand, akin to the essence of technology, and, on the other, fundamentally different from it. Such a realm is art."[10] Is he here contemplating art in the morning of Greece? Perhaps. But if so, why would a privilege be given to Greece if it were not by dint of some unquestioned Hegelian reemergence? Why couldn't contemporary art itself testify to this "ambiguous essence"? Even acknowledging that contemporary art invents and exhibits itself under the mode of challenge and defiant provocation, an acknowledgment that in my opinion should be made without hesitation or condition, doesn't the very fact that such works are offered to the public eye amount to letting others glean the enigma that they are, and therefore detect the ambiguous essence that appeared to the thinker on the lonely path of the meditation on Being?

The second sign is the insistence with which Heidegger stresses that aesthetics, the offspring of the modern metaphysics of subjectivity, turns the work of art into an "object" of private experience, of *Erlebnis*. Precisely because art has now moved into the horizon of aesthetics thus circumscribed, it is destined to a decline of its essence, an essence that consists in setting *aletheia* into work. Yet Heidegger himself taught us to recognize that one aesthetics, at least, one properly modern philosophy of subjectivity, escapes such a characterization: the *Critique of Judgment* (*N*, 109). He called attention to the fact that, when Kant characterizes the attitude by which we receive the beautiful thing as favor (*Gunst*), in a sense Kant causes the collapse of the modern correlation of subject and object, because such a favor stands beyond any possible conceptualization, any purposefulness, and any subjective complacency, and is rather the pure openness to the unconcealed as such. The surprising thing is that this profound reading of Kant is in no way integrated by Heidegger in his meditation on the history of art, insofar as the history of art is linked to the history of aesthetics. Everything happens as if, in his acceptance of the various epochs of that history, determined though they might be by the increasing forgetfulness of Being and not by the *parousia* of the Spirit, Heidegger is taking Hegel as the only guide. In Kant, however, we find in strict conformity with the doctrine of favor an invitation to cast another look on the history of art, one that would amount to considering it not in terms of progress or decline, but as "a domain of originality," that is, of an enigmatic irruption of nature that does not cease to be renewed in the interplay with the tradition that inspired it. This view is akin to a Kantian approximation of the hermeneutic circle: the past of art is not something dead, merely handing down the remnants of bygone ages; it is a myriad of signs pregnant with future possibilities. This approximation of the heremeneutical circle in Kant is not brought to the fore by Heidegger. Had he pointed in its direction, he might have been led to concede that the modern ushering of art inside the horizon of aesthetics is less the sign of a decline or of a terminal captivity inside the closing of subjectivity than of a new opening to the enigma of unconcealment.

7

Hegel's Art of Memory

Martin Donougho

My topic, for no very dialectical reason, has three different if overlapping emphases. An initial emphasis will be on Hegel's conception of art (or the work of art) as a form of memory and historical recollection. A second will be on his speculative recuperation of art's past, which may be observed not just in the notorious thesis on the "end" or "death" of art tout court, but equally in Hegel's preference for an historical treatment of the various arts (all that is save music).[1] A third emphasis will be on what *we* can make of Hegel, or at least of "art" as dialectically reworked at his hands: what does the theory amount to "for us," at a distance of over one hundred fifty years, with all manner of interim developments within as well as outside art (and bearing in mind that the invocation "for us" may no longer carry a dialectical charge)? In short: How does Hegel think art collects and recollects the past? In what ways does he reenact the past in and as his philosophical system? And to what extent might his own angle on art be preserved—or forgotten—today? That is, if "we" were to mount a Hegelian retrospective, so to speak, what would it look like? More briefly still—and with all the slippage and oblivion as well as self-reflexivity that such a process would involve—how might we recall Hegel's memory of art-as-memory?

A subtext of course is Heidegger's own *Andenken/Verwindung* both of *art* so-called and of Hegel's *philosophy* of art, all part of his own effort at overcoming aesthetics.[2] "The Origin of the Work of Art" (dating from 1936) includes a brief afterword written somewhat later in which Hegel's *Lectures on Aesthetics* (and specifically the lecture series of 1828–29) is cited as "the most comprehensive, because thought from within metaphysics, consideration [*Besinnung*—it can also mean remembrance] of the essence of art that the West possesses."[3] Heidegger raises here the question of the *truth* of Hegel's claim as to the death or end of art. His reason for doing that is not so much to reach a final decision—the jury remains out, he says, and behind its eventual verdict will lie the entire history of Western metaphysics—but more to draw attention to what is at stake. Art would be "for us" at an end, he says, only if subjective experience or representation (*Vorstellung*) remained its element. On the other hand, the possibility remains open for art's coming to be (*Werden*) (*H*, 67/66), or for what Heidegger calls the "setting to work" or "unconcealedness" of truth. He sees a parallel between the *Seinsvergessenheit* of the metaphysical tradition and a historical narrowing of art's horizons in the West. Art itself has become forgetful of truth, a tendency Hegel's claim amply documents. At the same time, it remains an open possibility that "great art" might yet emerge out of the ruins of representation, just as it remains possible that metaphysics might yet be overcome.

Thus Heidegger. Derrida in turn raises a question about the "end-ism" or "closure" in Heidegger's *own* thinking—for example, in his plangent gestures toward the end and what is to come. The question can equally well be put to Derrida, and of course, to the present writer too—though modesty forbids further appeal to the reader (assuming you are with me, that is)—the question as to what possible position from which to invoke the sense of an ending. For everything is provisional. There seems no end to what John McCumber usefully terms "demarcation" (the pointing to nonclosure, work left to do, . . .).[4]

Before stepping into that particular river, however, a few preliminaries—reminders of matters familiar enough to be forgotten. We face at least two sorts of difficulties: at one pole, establishing our initial "text," whether Hegel's or Heidegger's; and at the other, deciding how it is to be taken or interpreted. "Hegel's philosophy of art" is hard to track down in its native habitat. We might easily finish up like the worthy constable in Thomas Hardy, with the suspect we were looking for but not the one we wanted. Despite recent successes in identifying sources and contexts, the archival record remains thin and ambiguous. As for the *Aesthetics* itself, that is largely a compilation of student notes to lectures given over several years at the University of Berlin. Even if we were able in a critical manner to sort out some of the interference patterns in their transmission, we should still have to take account of the circumstances of delivery and reception, not to mention Hotho's sometimes quirky editing. Hegel shared with Fichte and Schelling a distaste for publication; the few works he did publish may indeed be heavy yet are no less difficult to weigh. All of which is complicated by the fact that a good deal, especially in the *Aesthetics*, consists of the low-level observations of an intelligent "amateur" (though in this respect it often seems difficult to say *anything* theoretically valuable about art, which tends to resist the aesthetician's solemn offer of categories and explanations).[5]

The resulting impression of bland orthodoxy is an immediate obstacle to understanding Hegel's philosophy of art, as Paul de Man (that fastidious reader of Hegel) pointed out in a late essay.[6] What to do about it?

> One either has to reduce the *Aesthetics*, as Heidegger does, to the gnomic wisdom of its most enigmatic pronouncements—the end of art, the sensory appearance of the idea—and treat it as the mute sphinx that ends all conversation, or like Adorno and some of his followers, one has to consider it as the Achilles heel of an entire system, in the very specific sense that the *Aesthetics* would be the place where the inadequacy of Hegel's theory of language would be revealed.

Enough has already been said to throw doubt on this almost casual placement of Heidegger as transmitter of the Hegelian wisdom. Only recall the way in which Heidegger's citation of Hegel's *Aesthetics* is carefully "framed" (if that is the word) within a *Nachwort* to realize that Heidegger keeps his distance from Hegel's metaphysical "*Ge-stell*," a distance that allows for questioning—on both sides—as much as acceptance or resignation. He lets Hegelian theses resonate, but as part of his own attempt to question "aesthetics" and its metaphysical "take" on art and beauty, an attempt also to move beyond the terms of representation and subjectivity. Echoing Heidegger, but from a different angle, my argument in what follows will be that Hegelian dialectic displays the limits not so much *to* art as *within* art (qua practice and category); it opens up a logic of delimitation and deferral continuing to our own day.

In any event, de Man clearly takes the *second* path indicated above, one he associates with Peter Szondi and his criticism of the shabby treatment the *Aesthetics* accords to figures and tropes (in the chapter on "Conscious Symbolics").[7] Yet here too de Man shortchanges Adorno and Szondi, both of whom employed what might be called a "nontotalizing" dialectics—but dialectics all the same—and whose approaches to "theory" were accordingly quite unlike de Man's strategy of rhetorical "displacement" or "deconstruction." I should add that I too see no reason to equate "dialectic" with "totalizing" thought or the speculative accumulation of conceptual capital, even in Hegel: it includes, e.g., a dissolving of all fixed oppositions, the overturning of masterful hierarchies, as well as the rendering explicit of what was merely implicit. In McCumber's terminology, while Hegel himself may well have tended to conflate demarcation and narrative and thereby impose a happy ending, "for us" the story is always one "to be continued": there remain lots of loose ends, in other words.

Accordingly there are several alternatives open to us in seeking a way into (and out of!) Hegelian systemics. Just as we are unsure what the Hegelian teaching *is*, "originally" or "*an sich*," so various attitudes impose themselves or may be taken, short of bare acceptance or rejection. Not to labor the point, we still do not know what to make of Hegel's philosophy of art.

In what follows I look first at art qua memory (as theorized in the *Encyclopedia*), then turn to the two-fold death of art, first as Greek *Kunstreligion*, and again as a romantic (and ultimately Romantic)[8] sundering into subjectivism and prosaic externality, before finally taking up the legacy "for us" of the Hegelian account of art.

Minders and Reminders

Lecturing in 1951–52—the first year he had been allowed back to teach after the war—Heidegger expressly links thinking (*Denken*) with devotion (*Andacht*), thanks (*Dank*), remembrance (*Andenken*), and memory (*Gedächtnis*). He recalls, from beyond the metaphysical tradition, the mythic figure of Mnemosyne, mother of the muses: "Dame Memory [*die Gedächtnis*] . . . the gathering of recollection, thinking back . . . the founding source of poetry [*Dichtens*]."[9] And he is moved to cite Hölderlin's poem "Mnemosyne," particularly its uncanny lines:

> Ein Zeichen sind wir, deutungslos. Schmerzlos sind wir und haben fast
>
> Die Sprache in der Fremde verloren.

Toward the end of the summer term Heidegger declares:

> Thought is remembrance [*Andenken*]. But remembrance is something other than a fleeting actualization of the past.
>
> Remembrance considers what affects us [*uns angeht*]. We are not yet in the proper space to reflect ([*nachzudenken*] upon freedom, or even to speak of it, so long as we *also* close our eyes to this annihilation [*Vernichtung*] of freedom.[10]

Let me briefly note some features of Heidegger's way of thinking here: (1) Language, thought, memory, and poetry are brought into close kinship; (2) "We" are asked to listen to a call to recollect, gather and keep what is important in our (local or regional) past or our epochal destiny (*Geschick*); and (3) The poet or thinking interpreter recalls both what is incumbent on us and of how difficult it is to think it—the most thought-provoking thing (*das Bedenklichste*) in our thoughtful time is the lack of a space for thought. Heidegger had come to think that art—especially poetic language—offered a privileged access to such remembrance beyond modern objectivism and subjectivism, though in principle many "things" could call on us to open up relations or contexts of meaning.

Far removed from Hegel, you might think—yet really not so distant. Hegel too spoke of the need for philosophy and art in a time of reflection and crisis. Art for him comprised both popular expression and a means by which a people becomes conscious of what it is—or rather *was*, and not (as for Heidegger) what it is "called" to be: the artist draws on and articulates a communal past.[11] The essential (*das Wesen*) resides in what has *been* (*gewesen*), Hegel was fond of saying—though (as he also recognized) not just any past would do, only a past such as the "Heroic Age" of Homeric Greece where universal ethos shines through individual *Gestalt* (which of course raises problems for an aesthetic rendering of modern technologically "prosaic" society). The crucial difference here is that Hegel's picture is presented as being *pre*subjective, portraying a solidary, embedded self such as we imagine it to have been in ancient Greece, whereas Heidegger thinks of art as a *displacement* of selfhood, that is, of the modern "distanced" subject.[12] After his renunciation of the Hellenic ideal and thinking modeled on art, Hegel tried to account for how such a subject might find a place (if at all), in the state as well as in his system. In the process, I would argue, Hegel renders both art and subjectivity problematic, certainly nothing to take for granted.

At Jena Hegel had early developed a theory of language as memory (*Gedächtnis*)—"*the Mnemosyne of the ancients*"[13]—through which a people gives itself a *name*, hence a conscious and considered (*gedacht*) place, so stepping out of the sheer undifferentiated flow of space and time. Along with labor (or its tools) and recognition (*Anerkennung*), language in its anamnetic capacity serves to *constitute* a people, who in turn constitute themselves in and as a memorable *work*. Language is accordingly a supra-individual medium, the form of its memory communal. A fragment dating from 1803 speaks of "Mnemosyne or the absolute Muse, Art" and continues, "the work of art is the work of all; there is just one who brings it completed into the daylight, in that he is the last to work on it, and he is the darling of Mnemosyne."[14] The artist functions, in short, as the mere channel for communal memory.

Hegel soon came to give a more inflected account of memory, as if this epic fusion of the self with Mnemosyne and the artist with his muse could not stay unmediated for long. From the time of the Nuremberg *Propaedeutic* through the successive editions of the *Encyclopedia* (1817, 1827, 1831), while the linkage between *Gedächtnis* and Mnemosyne is retained, it enters only at the end of a tortuous process of self recollection (*Erinnerung*) and forgetfulness.[15] (Oddly enough, considering the importance of *Gedächtnis* both before and after the *Phenomenology*, that work mentions the term just once, in an important aside on the abstract superficiality of "observing reason": particular items are recalled in mechanical fashion, preliminary to the hard work of penetrating their universal essence.[16] The movement characteristic of the *Phenomenology* is less the memory work of empirical science than it is the "internalizing" of *Erinnerung*, with which at one point [*PG*, 531; *PS*, 441] Mnemosyne is expressly identified.)

The relevant sections of the *Encyclopedia*, especially those dealing with the peculiar relation (or lack of relation) between *Erinnerung* and *Gedächtnis*, have received so much attention recently that there seems little to be said.[17] Accordingly, my comments can at least be brief.

The first point to note is that art plays a crucial anamnestic role, in the guise of "phantasia"—a medium accorded great importance in the medieval "art of memory,"[18] on which Hegel heaps scorn later in § 462. Of *Phantasie*—a mode of *Vorstellung* (representation), according to Hegelian "Psychology"—the *Encyclopedia* remarks: "This constitutes the formal aspect of *art;* for art presents the truly universal, or the Idea, in the form of *sensuous existence*—of the *image* [*des* sinnlichen Daseins—*des* Bildes]."[19] All the more annoying then is the text's reticence at this point. Hegel apparently spent more time lecturing on art than Boumann's "*Zusatz*" to § 456 leads us to suppose. Karl Rosenkranz—himself the author of a "Psychology"—complains that Hegel does nothing to explain the role of the different species of artistic phantasy, or indeed what art is doing here in the first place.[20]

Phantasy comes under "*Einbildungskraft*" ("imagination"), the second division of "*Vorstellung*" (literally "setting before"), which in turn follows upon "*Anschauung*" (or "looking on") and precedes "*Denken*" ("thinking"). "*Einbildungskraft*" is flanked by two modes of remembering: recollection (*Erinnerung*, "internalizing memory"), and memory (*Gedächtnis*—that's for thought, *Gedanken*). Art is accordingly "central" to the entire section, as well as to Hegel's theoretical account of memory and selfhood. Yet that central place turns out to be difficult to locate.

Erinnerung begins with a concrete image (*Bild*), the legacy of "intuition." But the image as such is fleeting and nonexistent; as subject, intelligence finds it already "internalized" (*erinnert*), "unconsciously preserved" (*bewußtlos aufbewahrt*), kept at intelligence's disposal.[21] Images are contained in "this nocturnal (mine)shaft" (*diesen nächtlichen Schacht*) of the self: an extraordinary metaphor that has attracted Derrida's and others' attention. The metaphor had already cropped up in § 403, under "Anthropology," where Hegel remarks that the self in its independence preserves determinations by negating them—whence the inner darkness:

> It is indeed this determination that we have before us with regard to representations or remembrances. Every individual constitutes an infinite wealth of sensory determinations, representations, information, thoughts, etc.; yet *I* am something wholly *indivisible* [*ein ganz Einfaches*],—a featureless shaft, in which all this is preserved without existence. It is only when *I* recollect *a* representation (*mich* an eine *Vorstellung erinnere*) that I bring it out of that interior into existence, for consciousness.[22]

These are dark goings on between me and my self, in which the "*Er*" (or "he") of recollection is strangely impersonal in this most personal matters. *Who's minding the store?* That is the crucial question, for memory is always a matter of representing, staging, "putting before" (us? itself?) the self or subjectivity and not simply any old idea or meaning. Memory, and hence art, turn out to comprise an attempt at self-construction.

The transition from *Erinnerung* to *Einbildungskraft* is secured by an active synthesis between the reservoir of images and some existent image, resulting in a "proper" content (*Inhalt*). With this we have *Phantasie*—Coleridge's "esemplastic" imagination, original rather than merely associative, the mere "fancy" of a "bundle"-sort of self—which Hegel subdivides without further comment into "symbolizing, allegorizing, or poetic [*dichtend*]" phantasy.[23] Yet the *real* content is subjectivity itself, the "subject of enunciation" one might say; a feature that emerges only if there remains no resistance in the imaginary material—grain in the wood, so to speak—to phantasy's self-transparent nature. That is, (1) iconic resemblance is abandoned for the anonymity of the sign, and (2) significance is derived not from an already existing (and iconic) relation but from the subject's *giving* the intuition (or signifier) a meaning. This is "sign-making phantasy," also termed "productive memory (the initially abstract Mnemosyne)" in the remark to § 458.[24] Only now does the intuition as such *mean*, and mean something *else*: a "soul" quite independent of the imaginary material.

Hegel proceeds to contrast sign with symbol: "The *sign* is any immediate intuition which represents a content wholly other than what it has per se;—the *pyramid*, in which a strange soul is placed and preserved."[25]

This memorable image I would interpret as saying that while in the symbol intuition shares some determinate feature with what it is meant to express, the sign exhibits no such relation. In its featureless exterior the pyramid symbolizes the *non*symbolic, *non*iconic nature of meaning, as well as a semantic "afterlife" in the realm of thought.

That is to get ahead of myself, of course; but in fact I shall not spend much time with the second sort of remembering, *Gedächtnis*, only point up changes in the view. Where recollection constituted the self as an interior vault, full of vague shadows, memory is like an emptying out of the self into a lexicon of "names," into a language (or symbolic order) which "I" manipulate but cannot be said to produce (as "I" could with sign-making phantasy). How the self does this excites Hegel's wonder; and indeed, his description is quasi-Lacanian, almost as if the self is "interpellated" by this linguistic order, the inner life coming to itself only through what Lacan would call an "*extimité.*" Extreme internalization (*Erinnerung*) coincides with extreme utterance (*Entäußerung*), in Hegel's version (§ 463A). As abstract subjectivity, "I" become(s) the power "of" (not over) various names or words, as if "I" survive(s) in their recital. "I" am/is "the empty *bond* [*Band*] that fixes [*befestigt*] within itself strings of names and retains them in a fixed order,"[26] a "mechanism" of subjective externality (Hegel refers to the philosophy of nature on mechanics). Intelligence can become thought only through this wholesale expulsion of subjectivity; it is what McCumber calls "death by habit."[27] The inner life gets strung out in external series or algorithms—chains of signifiers, so to speak. Yet that is wholly to renounce the specular or Cartesian self, an "*Ich*" founded on the model of reflexion, even if thought or the concept supposedly will attain an absolute self-presence.

Now where does art enter in this strange flitting on the part of intelligence between night and day, remembering and forgetting, self and nature? It enters somewhere *between* internal and external memory, *between* our drawing upon subjectivity as a reserve (*Vorrat*) or pit of images, and the emptying out of the self into mechanical (but willed) recitation. More exactly, the artist enters *between* a merely associative and a sign-making imagination: a "symbol-making" phantasy, we might dub it (where "symbol" encompasses allegorical, symbolic, as well as poetic processes). Art—which the *Aesthetics* presents as a union of "*Gestalt*" and "*Bedeutung*"—will always deal in imagery, its meaning concrete and figural, even when language is its medium (for the *meanings* remain metaphorical and figural). Yet there is now undeniably a certain fuzziness to the activity of artistic representation, in Hegel's account of it. Thus:

1. The manner in which imagery achieves or receives its meaning is underdetermined. Compare the way Hegel theorizes the symbol in the

Aesthetics.[28] There it is pointed out that although the symbol is more than a conventional sign—because its "*Gestalt*" shares some quality with its "*Bedeutung*"—it remains constitutionally *ambiguous,* since the observer is uncertain *which* quality is the right one. Nonambiguous meaning requires specification, whether by the individual or by convention (custom). (The argument here parallels Eco's or Goodman's critique of iconic "resemblance.") Paradoxically, then, the symbol devolves upon the relation of indifference (*Gleichgültigkeit*) that characterizes the sign. That the symbol is, dialectically if not *an sich,* nothing but a fancy sign is precisely the point evident (for us) in (or on) the pyramid, and (somewhat differently) as we read the chapter on "Conscious Symbolics." Can we go further, and claim that art, as (a) at bottom symbolic (i.e., implying a "relation, affinity, and concrete interpenetration [*Ineinander*] of meaning and shape"),[29] is in the last analysis (b) no more than semiosis, a sign, a prosaic separation of the two sides? That is the move de Man makes (along with several further "displacements," slipped in very fast, where luckily we need not follow him).[30] And his point is not gainsaid by pointing at the classical artwork, which (as Hegel puts it) does not so much *have* as *embody* a meaning—literally so, for beautiful body and soul (character, Ideal, etc.) are somehow fused. The issue de Man rightly brings up is precisely *how* sense and intellect are one; and that remains a mystery.

2. Given the way Hegel has set things up, it follows that the artist never quite succeeds in expressing, presenting, or constructing his or her "self," since that happens only with the production of *signs,* and more radically, with the total "uttering" of the self into language and the (supposed) reconstruction of subjectivity as thought. (We might compare Hölderlin's lines cited above: individual selves are mere signs. But in addition we are dealing with the paradoxical aesthetics of Romantic "expressivity," which can give no proper account of the creative process that results in the expressive product, or of its terms, on pain of undoing them; the product is a sign merely that "art has been there.")[31] If representational memory comprises an act of self-creation, then the *artist* turns out to be somewhat "beside" her/himself. It is as if s/he forgets her/himself somewhere on the road from the "shaft" via the "pyramid" to the serial existence of language and thought. As Adorno for one clearly saw, the Hegelian subject (at least the finite ego rather than the infinite "whole") is never a fixed term of reflexion.

3. Hence the artist's *activity* becomes occluded, even dissimulative (though we should bear in mind that "Psychology" speaks only in "theoretical" not "practical" idiom). For example, in the *Aesthetics* the step from mere association to artistic production occurs in the transition from Zoroastrianism to "phantastic symbolics," i.e., primarily Hindu

iconography, which immediately precedes "symbolism proper," that in ancient Egypt. "Phantastic symbolics" is marked by a "difference" or "struggle" (*Kampf*) between meaning and "its" shape (*LA*, 430; *HA*, 332–33). Here we have not so much a "beautiful union" of the two, more what is "passed off" (*hingestellt*) as such, and as art. This ruse is discovered only in the phantastic search for the right image for an as yet undetermined meaning. Egypt—land of riddles—then appears as a kind of demystification of such a deceptive quest. Two sorts of solutions to the oriental enigma are possible at this point. Either the pyramid is to be read as alluding to the *separation* of appearance and idea—and so we move to the sublime (topic of the chapter following) and to figures and tropes (the last chapter of "Symbolics"). Or else the sphinx—itself half human, half nature—may be said to pose a riddle whose answer ("man") will stand for classical Greece tout court, i.e., for the properly beautiful union of meaning and shape (topic of the section on the classical worldview). Similarly, the inscription over the statue to Isis—"I am what is, was, and what will be. No mortal has yet lifted my veil"—which Kant and the Romantics had considered the epitome of the sublime, may be resolved into human and self-possessed terms; a man lifts the veil and recognizes himself, at least in the human shape of the Olympian deities.[32]

The Hegelian narrator could at this point declare that with the Greek ideal a union of meaning and shape *is*, has been, perfectly achieved. As the audience, though, we might have our doubts about such a projected happy ending. Mindful of our passage to Egypt, we might wonder instead whether the Ideal too isn't just (someone's) "*Hinstellung*"—a bluff which the sublime has in effect already called.

Happily this is not the place to enter into the complexities of Hegel's perspective on the sublime.[33] Let me do no more than suggest that the contrast of Hegel as representative philosopher of beauty with Heidegger as thinker of the sublime yields only a half-truth.[34] On the face of it, of course, Hegel seems to absorb the sublime into the beautiful, expressly choosing Schiller's "Ideal" as a name for this merging of ethical striving with classical harmony.[35] Yet, as we shall see in the following section, their union is one of convenience only, and convention too. Moreover, Hegel's sublime cannot be redeemed in the coin of speculative subjectivity. Like Heidegger, he resists the plangencies of what has become known as the "Romantic" or "hermeneutic" sublime.[36] Nor does he pledge the sublime to some "higher" economy of thought. I would argue that the Hegelian sublime is remarkably like the mechanical memory or *Gedächtnis* just analyzed; in both formations the self finds itself emptied out, reified, finite, profane, at its wit's end, and in both this stems from a failure to give the sacred an aesthetic shape. In that sense the sublime appears as the *defining*—rather than de Man's "defective"[37]—cornerstone of Hegel's philosophy of art, an edifice which is definitely *not* bathed in a classical sweetness and light. The art that comes after the sublime is condemned to the same fate, the same finitude. Whether as the Greek Ideal, or in romantic (and ultimately Romantic) supernaturalism, art will reduce to "the prose of the world."

Odds and Ends—or, Inside the Hegelian Museum

During the years Hegel was lecturing on philosophy of art at the University of Berlin, Schinkel's great museum was being built on the island opposite Hegel's house. Here for the first time paintings were to be arranged "scientifically," by historical school. We find parallel shifts in the new historical philology, or with the founding of concert-halls to play "masterpieces" from the past, and so on. Of course, Hegel appears happier (or at least resigned) to art's new-found museal status than is Heidegger in the "Origin" essay. For Hegel the museum is a mausoleum, art what it (in one sense always) "has been," a shape of life grown old. More important, the Hegelian account describes art as having grown old at least twice over—the first time *qua* art, the second time with the end of religion.[38] The irony runs deeper still: as we have just seen, the sublime prompts the question whether art was not already dead before it even had a chance to mature—an extension of Hegel's quip (made in connexion with Caesarism) about historical events occurring twice over, the second time to ratify what was already decided fact.

What, then, are these two endings prefigured in the sublime?

1. A classical death: Hegel tells his undergraduate listeners that with Greece "we" (Germans?) feel at home (*heimatlich*). Yet what follows is often uncanny enough to have given them nightmares. We *would* feel nostalgic for such a place and such a time, he adds—with the implication that in fact we *cannot,* since there is no room for nostalgia, even in philosophy. We ought I think to pay special attention to the way Hegel frames, presents, "mounts," puts on his classical centerpiece. The beautiful picture painted, the figure shaped, the drama reenacted, are hardly to be taken at face value; a certain ambiguity and *Verfremdungseffekt* seem built in, deliberately or not.

The *Philosophy of History* portrays ancient Greece as having achieved a precarious balance between a total lack of subjectivity in the oriental cultures and its overemphasis in modern subjectivism. Breaking with the fantastic or sublime culture of the East, the Greeks sought the *meaning* of nature everywhere, finding that in their own image, in their organic existence and corporeal beauty. It is, he says, as if the Greek spirit sculpted *itself* into beautiful shapes (*Gestalten*):[39] all the artist had to do was imitate what lay before him. Yet where the *Aesthetics* places such "beautiful individuality" in a (perhaps imaginary) Age of Heroes, in these lectures individuality is institutionalized, as a threefold aestheticization of *life* ("the subjective work of art"), *religious culture* ("the objective work of art"), and most important, the *polis* ("the political work of art"), which effectively unites both the other aspects. The political fusion of individual consciousness and ethical substance reaches its acme in Periclean Athens: "In democracy the main thing is that the character of the citizens be sculptural [*plastisch*], shaped from one piece," we read (*PH*, 312). By either account, what is lacking is the principle of subjective inwardness (*für sich frei werdende Innerlichkeit*). In Hegel's narrative of birth, efflorescence, and decay, the emergence of this principle leads to the downfall of the polis. Ironically the meaning of the beautiful Ideal turns out to be equivocal; the polis is at once too natural and too subjective; pressing on one moment brings down the weight of the other. The dramatist rather than the sculptor does justice to this particular dynamic—it is as if (says Hegel) the Greeks represented the fall of their aesthetic Ideal aesthetically, in tragedy.

Several features come together in this familiar picture:[40] At first glance Greece was *organic* through and through, nature spiritualized and spirit naturalized, etc., and even its death is a natural process. It was also *mimetic*, in the sense that the polis repeats and mimes natural processes, which the artist in turn simply repeats (or completes) in the form of art—likewise a natural activity. As such the Ideal centers on the *work*, with the polis its ultimate embodiment (in a noninstrumental sense, i.e., not as "labor"). Early on Hegel writes as if individual works (the "beautiful fruit") are of a piece with the whole organism, its integral expression. That is, the work belongs to the *community* (*das Gemeinwesen*) or people as a whole, of which the individual—including the artist, the "darling of Mnemosyne"—is just a member (*Glied*).

Doubtless such an aesthetico-political Ideal has had an enormous influence, not just in Germany; and it conditions a good deal of Hegel's thinking too, not least on education. Whether it matches the full Hegelian presentation is another matter. If Hegel did at one time hold to this organic model, even one projected into a mythic Golden Age, after 1804 we find the inflections that mark out his mature view: (1) art is the "veil" (*Schleier*, a Goethean image) that hides rather than presents the truth, a semblance or "*Schein*";[41] and (2) it is the artist's subjectivity that prompts him to portray (and *be*tray) his world—the work as death mask and mourning.

Our initial picture turns out, upon reflection therefore, to be riven with conflict. And on still further reflection, "picture-thinking" itself is thrown into question. Already in the 1802 *Natural Law* essay we find the right of subjectivity clashing with that of substantive mimetics, though the context remains dramaturgical in form (an unmediated "*Anschauung*" on the scenes of a world history displayed as tragic repetition). By the time of the *Phenomenology* (1807)—whose "shapes of consciousness" are more or less deliberately mounted in a "gallery of images"—we find an extensive discussion of the "subject of enunciation" that is generically enacted in tragedy. In the section devoted to Greek "*Kunstreligion*" Hegel speaks of the self (*das Selbst*) giving itself shape through the production (*Hervorbringung*) of a consciousness such that it observes its own self in action. It is the tragedian not the sculptor who epitomizes self-consciousness, *qua* "spirit, inwardly certain, which mourns over the loss of its world, and now from the purity of its self creates its own essence, raised above actuality . . ." i.e., as a representation. The dramatist's ethical substance has turned into its opposite, pure self-consciousness or form; and this in turn is "the night in which substance was betrayed and itself made into subject. It is out of this night of pure self-certainty that ethical spirit is resurrected as a shape freed from nature and its own immediate existence" (*PG*, 514; *PS*, 426)—a parody on the Passion story, of course (even if it is unclear exactly who plays the part of Judas). The tragedian selects an individual to bear the burden of this sorrow, and puts him on stage.[42]

> Spirit is present in this individual as his universal—as his pathos, by giving himself over to which his self-consciousness loses its freedom. But that positive power of universality is subdued by the pure self of the individual, the negative power. This pure activity, conscious of its inalienable strength, wrestles with the shapeless essence. Becoming master over that, it has made the pathos into its very being [*Stoffe*] and supplied its own content, and their unity emerges as a work, universal spirit individualized and set before [*vorgestellt*] us. (*PG*, 515; *PS*, 427)

That is, the antagonists on stage embody the universal *pathe* of ethical substance and the self. Selfhood wins out, precisely through fashioning the work that *represents* the conflict. But what a strange act of authorial witness this amounts to, combining as it does mourning, betrayal, and hypocrisy (for presumably this display is only "for us," and the artist too is self-deceived about the deception).

In this doubly ironic view, the organic "work"—political or artistic—is subverted from within. As Hegel tells the story in chapter 7, the subversion works its way generically from hymn, via epic, to tragedy, in a metadrama of hypocrisy (see *PG*, 541; *PS*, 450), in which both players and the characters they portray rely on oblivion (*Lethe*) for continuing to act as they do. The drama thereupon dissolves into comedy, when the mask (or persona) is dropped, the person (the abstract, legal self) comes to the fore, and we all become equal in the sight of God or (if unavailable) the emperor. All the same, the *real* "*eiron*" of the piece is less the mimetic playwright/person than—as we at the other end of history can see—the self-formative Romantic ego, pretending to adopt a mimetic model of art when in fact it is staging the whole scene in its fertile and creative imagination.

2. A romantic death: from a religious perspective, art and the aesthetic are, in the aftermath of the classical death of art, either devalued by Judaeo-Christian iconoclasm, or given a subaltern role in presenting the human aspect, e.g., of divine love, religious community, bodily pain, etc. In its own terms, art is internally split, spirit hovering over the formless waters (as Hegel puts it, borrowing from Genesis), at once absolute inwardness and utter externality. Romantic art thus exhibits opposite tendencies: toward realism (e.g., Dutch painting),[43] and toward subjective form-ing (music, the lyric, "humor," etc.). Conversely, looking back, what we see is a gradual fall from embodying or at least imitating the divine presence—a declension from the "high mimetic" mode of classical art—to naturalism and irony. Parody and formal displacement are the watchwords of post-Hellenic fabrication, in this "entropology" of art. Of course, one might still interpret this decline as redemptive, at an imaginative remove, as with Northrop Frye's renewal of the romance tradition, or with Bakhtinian "carnival." But more likely the formalist displacements serve only to foreground the imperialism of literary artifice. Prospero's magic has its audience spellbound even in the gesture of casting aside his staff; better to get rid of this piece of histrionics altogether! Hegel's view is thoroughly secular, not specular, without illusions of transcendence, even those of fiction.

Two figures mark this second dissolution of art: "the beautiful soul" (in the *Phenomenology*), and "*Humanus*" (in the *Aesthetics*). The first enters, as a hypertrophic form of the transcendental ego, at the end of chapter 6 of the *Phenomenology*, a chapter that, among other things, tells a story of "subjectivation," construction-cum-representation of selfhood. The first such "self" had emerged from the trial of Greek tragedy/comedy, which forged the persona into the abstract "person" of Roman law and Christian doctrine.[44] The second was the "*citoyen*" of the modern state, resultant of centuries of cultural discipline and "alienation." The third is the Kantian subject, taken in its moral aspect as "conscience" (*Gewissen*—a term of art in Fichte and Schleiermacher).[45] All three "selves" comprise an attempted fusing of inwardness and externality (we are reminded of the "*extimité*" of mechanical remembrance). All are wrecked on the shoals of finitude. All involve linguistic "utterance," e.g., as the language of flattery by which the nobles try to legitimize themselves and their king, or as the beautiful soul's assurances that it speaks the truth.[46] It is the gap between what it says and what it not merely means but also means by saying it that finally pulls this third "self" apart, lays it open to the *sparagmos* of mere finitude (consumption, madness, Roman Catholic idolatry—it's all the same). Lastly, all three are theatrical in mode, not just the first. Think only of the notion of "representation" in the state, or of Kant's viewing of the French Revolution as a moral spectacle. The fall of "the beautiful soul" too is theatrical: its role-playing, *Verstellung* (displacement, sliding, shiftiness), and hypocrisy are finally unmasked and "recognized," not least by itself, in a "reversal" that is staged in an expressly confessional mise-en-scène.

More to the point, this final scene presents a spectacle of the downfall of theatricality as such, the fall of ironic impersonation and of a reflexively grounded subjectivity. But what then remains of Hegelian subjectivity, after the threefold ruination of the (finite, individual) self? For Hegel the recuperation via atonement and forgiveness is a "die to live" that results in a kind of dialogic notion of subjectivity (and I note in passing how much Habermas's notion of communicative interest derives from Hegel's early notion of "love" as "surrender" or *Hingebung* to the other).

Our second figure, *Humanus,* is likewise shrouded in mystery. It enters in the last part of the section devoted to "the end" of romantic art, as an allusion to Goethe's early poem, "Die Geheimnisse."[47] At this stage it is clear that the modern artist no longer has a natural or mythological "*Heimat*" mimetically to put forth, a content to interpret or give form to. His activity, says Hegel, is much like the dramatist's peopling of his stage with alien personae. But it turns out—in the usual dialectical move that makes this very act of forming the new content—that the alien forms and their staging are both aspects of the creative artist's humanity, and that what the new "saint" Humanus stands for is his mining of himself for his material: mimesis as self-expression! Difficult though it may be to gauge Hegel's tone from what is after all an obscure fragment, we can say that Hegel neither condemns this as idolatry nor praises it as creative. Rather, the ironic or parodic shimmer is at once minimalist and utopian: it makes of such art a paltry thing, while pointing, perhaps, to something posthumanist. It has been argued, e.g., by Dieter Henrich, that for Hegel art survives only as "postaesthetic," renouncing the unity of form and content found in the classical Ideal. Henrich argues further that Hegel was already responding to the shrinking of art to "Biedermeier" proportions.[48] And it is true that the intimate sphere of art came to challenge the public sphere of a prosaic and increasingly repressive political regime. We saw that if the "beautiful soul" ultimately finds its apotheosis as the philosopher's "absolute knowing," it does so only via acknowledgment of a common and finite humanity, a loss of self. It may be—if Hegel had a crystal ball—that art after "Humanus" will be similarly finite, disenchanted, at once ecumenical and eclectic: a museum without walls, but erected in a domestic interior.

In sum, Hegel was not calling for the return of the Greek Ideal to the lifeworld: any residual neoclassicism or utopianism was abandoned in his youth, and the Berlin Lectures complete this normative distancing.[49] Nor did he endorse a romantic or Romantic quest for transcendence, remaining highly critical of its subjectivist aesthetic. The contrast with Heidegger is nevertheless striking: for we have with him a true Romantic, at least in his openness to the possible happening of "great" art, the punctual and inspired "jutting forth" of earth into world. For Hegel, great art—in the sense of a novel and hermeneutic imaging of religious content—was a thing of the past, indeed, something in a museum: that is precisely the challenge enfolded into the layers of Heidegger's "Origin" essay. How art can be "essentially" past is the subject of my last section.

"Lazarus, Arise"—or, Beginnings and Endings

> Two things stand out: the first is the absorbed intenseness of a resurrecting and evocative memory, a memory that says to every object: "Lazarus, arise"; the second is a fire, an intoxication of pencil or brush, almost amounting to frenzy.
>
> —*Baudelaire, "The Painter of Modern Life" (1863)*[50]

> Today has no margins, the event arrives
> Flush with its edges
>
> —*John Ashbery, "Self-Portrait in a Convex Mirror"*

If "*Aller Anfang ist schwer*" (according to that well-known aesthetician, Karl Marx), no less difficult are endings. In particular, there seems no end to discussions of Hegel's claim or prognosis as to the "end" of art.[51] I don't propose to add to them, but offer instead a paradox or riddle. How is it that Hegel could pronounce art dead at the very moment when art (as both practice and category) was coming into being? What does that say about a putative "philosophy of art"? The puzzle is hardly solved by lexical sorting, as if there were different "objects" at issue. They are intimately linked, and indeed there would not *be* a philosophy of art at all without the shift from "the fine arts" or "art" as distributive quality, variously defined, to a new Romantic notion of "Art" as embodied in a "work" of art, product of original and creative self-expression, etc.

We do not of course have to sift the archive of "*Begriffsgeschichte*" or "keywords" to come to the conclusion that "Art" (as "*Dichtung*") is wholly different from the tradition descending from Greek "*techne.*" Doubtless one could give a historical narrative of how the ancient term and the practices it designated were transformed into or displaced by a modern understanding. I shall instead sketch a few ways in which art, the arts, and the work of art came to be marked and demarcated as such, in theory and practice, suspending for now judgment as to whether similar mechanisms can without anachronism be discerned in the distant past.

1. We could give a differential or—perhaps better—"reactive" account, almost a Nietzschean "just so" genealogy, of art qua "distinction" (to apply Pierre Bourdieu's term), where the aesthetic is a mark of social prestige and status, one that compensates for the loss of transcendental or feudal warranty. Although canons have existed at least since medieval times (Curtius noted how "classic" derives from a taxation category), such distinction really begins in the sixteenth century, with the Italian (and thence French and English) notion of a "gentleman," whose accomplishments centrally include knowledge of the arts. This "courtesy" meaning to "art" (in R. G. Collingwood's terminology) also presupposes a "court society" (as described by Norbert Elias) and its regime of biomechanics. The French idea of the "*honnête homme*" performs a similar function in the following century, courtiers seeking to delimit a sphere of value separate from the king's court yet superior to "popular" culture. Later still, the Scottish and French Enlightenments develop an ideology of aesthetic *taste,* a capacity analogous to the "moral" faculty, cultivated in the public sphere of polite conversation (which some imagine still exists). The cachet of a hard-to-acquire aesthetic competence has hardly lost its value in today's society of course: it constitutes much of the *value* in aesthetic value, after all. Nowadays art occupies its own autonomous sphere, though Peter Bürger remarks that this institutionalization took place only in the late nineteenth century; Niklas Luhmann has argued that that forms part of the wider movement toward specialization typical

of modernity.[52] One could even give a formal description of the institution of art (e.g., the "institutional" theory of art of Dickie, for whom "aesthetic value" is as given as it is empty for Bourdieu). More convincing (because more historical) is Arthur Danto's theory of "the artworld," with its mix of semantics and pragmatics of artworks versus "real things." That is, the constitution of art does not for him *reduce* to the sociology of what Goffman called the "frame effect," a mere enfranchising gesture: it produces qualitative meanings for the "artworld" as a whole.

2. This last flurry of remarks should bring home the impossibility of separating the reactive mechanism above from another, more semantically inclined one: the Romantic assertion of the autonomy of artistic imagination. Romanticism provided an intrinsic rationale for the value in and of art; it promised redemption from a fallen and reified modern world. The fine arts, as they came to be defined and practiced in the seventeenth and eighteenth centuries,[53] were never conceptualized *as* art, even though the several branches could be thought of as sharing certain properties or as being similarly motivated or functional. The conceptualization of "Art" came only with a properly Romantic aesthetic toward the end of the century. In brief, autonomous art or its artwork becomes the ultimate status symbol, a mark and expression of humanity itself, of the human self considered as creative and self-expressive in and through work, whose paradigm is language. Such an aesthetic is endorsed by a fundamental shift from a metaphysics of "form" to one of "form*ing*," Fichte being its first explicit proponent; or to rephrase, a shift from a *mimetic* to an *expressivist* model of production, based on the principle of "creativity," as Hans Blumenberg has shown.[54]

In this respect we continue to live in the shadow of Romanticism, not least under the aegis of modernism/modernity in its various forms, which can be seen as maintaining the promise of poetic originality and hence escape from a reified society.[55] But the dialectic of modernism quickly becomes complex and occluded. For a start, the marked term ("originality") becomes a badge of distinction in the previous socially reactive sense (as for the avant garde or Abstract Expressionism, and as guyed by Duchamp or Warhol or Jeff Koons); it may have little meaning *apart* from that. And although it is still possible to find unadulterated modernists—e.g., Clement Greenberg, whose formalism is founded upon the "purity" of Kantian self-critique—the very gesture becomes contaminated by the very world of commodities it would shun. Michael Fried accordingly reworks the formalist dialectic in terms of "absorption" versus "theatricality," while acknowledging that the first will always involve a theatrical gesture.[56] Similarly, Adorno criticizes the Romantics' over-attachment to sheer "apparition"—expression, originality—arguing that the sheen of commodification—its "*Schein*"—is part and parcel of the modernist dynamic. Artworks and "real things" (i.e., reification) are always in cahoots. Hence "every theory of art must also be a critique of art"[57]—there is always work to be done. Such a logic of demarcation might then lead us straight to a third line.

3. This last "discrimination" of art is harder to pin down—a self-reflexiveness that is surely part of its point. Best viewed as the wholesale ironizing—displacement or "remove," rather, because no stable self or viewpoint is presupposed, even in ironic mode—of the previous line, it amounts to a redescription of Romanticism as a rhetorically masterful set of gestures. It questions the claim to autonomy implicit in artistic presentation (*Darstellung*). Formulations may be found in Derrida, Lacoue-Labarthe and Nancy, or (in another vein) de Man.[58] Their model is Heidegger's questioning of a metaphysical tradition dominated by the "*Ge-stell*" of technological thinking, his preference for creative *Dichtung* over mere (because aesthetic) "literature." Heidegger of course distances himself from Romantic subjectivism, inclining rather to the other pole of creativity embodied in language: it speaks us. Still, the ambiguity haunts the Heideggerian account of art from the mid-thirties on, and in his late essays on poetic thinking he remains Romantic in his search for originary redemption. Here Blanchot is the chief intermediary, especially his study entitled *L'Espace littéraire* (or "the literary remove"), in part an obscure parody of the notion of the "work" of art in Heidegger's "Origin" essay. Another likely source of transmission is the essay "Literature and the Right to Death," from his *La Part du feu*,[59] another odd parody, this time of Hegel's "Animal Kingdom of Spirit" from the *Phenomenology*. In suggesting that Literature begins only when it is in question, that Literature is built upon its own ruins, Blanchot draws our attention to its self-invention, as it nominates the work—the thing, *die Sache Selbst*—as the writer's peculiar achievement when in fact it is a snare, a deceit. The writer is an artifact of the French Revolution, like Hegel's concept, in enduring death and maintaining itself therein.

Next in line comes Derrida, who sees in Art/Literature the obverse to philosophy, as if each were called into being simply to call the other into being, rather than—as with Romanticism, on the above account—to guard against a prosaic, second-hand, inhuman, and reifying society. Let us rename the entire constellation the "system-subject" to bring out how—in response to the inadequacy of the Kantian, merely formal self—a philosophy of the subject comes to occupy center-stage.[60] The "subject" (cited in quotes to indicate its problematic status) comes into being through an artistic self-presentation (*Darstellung*); that is, through human autoproduction in work, especially the artwork. Or again, the "subject" is an effect elicited by philosophical discourse, an "eidaesthetics." The authors of *The Literary Absolute* mimic yet stay at one remove from this mythology of "forming form" or "autopoiesis" espoused by the *Frühromantiker*, seeing even the ironist's play of subjectivities as so much rhetorical paperwork rather than a true response to the Kantian crisis. They reject out of hand what they see as the masterful grasp of Hegelian dialectics, as it tries to put art in its proper speculative frame. (I note in passing a parallel with Paul de Man's wrestling with the angel of aesthetic ideology.)

Now, we don't have to suppose that Hegel saw things in such distanced terms to hold that they condition his own interest in art, if only for us, in retrospect. He reads (may be read as reading) them back, anachronistically, into the "art" of the past—how could he (we) not? Two conclusions may be drawn.

In the first place, Hegel's philosophy of art can easily be situated within my *petits récits*. Thus, while Hegel does not focus on matters of prestige or social pragmatics, he does attend to how such gestures of "artistic identification" (Danto) are encoded in theory or concepts, and hence in the differentiation of artworks from real things (or as he would say, of absolute from finite spirit). Nor is it surprising that Danto sees himself as retelling a Hegelian narrative of gradually heightened self-reflexiveness. Hegel would add that our world turns out to lack all transcendental sanction—worldliness without end, we might say. Hegel takes it as culturally given that *Kunstreligion* and religion proper are already dead, that there is no longer any content that form could hermeneutically (re)present and whose "value" it could reflect. As to my second tale, ours is a world in which the Romantics' attempt to escape prosaic heteronomy has come to grief: autonomous creativity or human authenticity are no longer credible as prevailing norms. Hence (in the last place) self-contained critical reason will forever be differential, never pure. Hegel himself thematizes the logic of limitation, reserve, or supplementarity put to work here (even if he also thinks philosophical thought has, at least in principle, overcome its finite terms). He certainly does not himself place credence in the normative force of a specialized artworld (à la Habermas), a region marked out by "autopoiesis."

Second, Hegel's dialectic renders art and artwork "exotopical" (as Bakhtin would say), that is, discernible only from the outside and in retrospect. Derrida writes of "the equivocality of the *end*, in the play of *telos* and death."[61] The past can be viewed either *teleologically*, as a story of art's triumphant coming to itself, in absolute self-knowing; or else *dialectically*, as a tale of decline and formal declension. In the second view, the name "art" becomes almost an epitaph, naming what *has been* but never actually *was.* Hegel's well-known lines in the *Phenomenology* concerning the fate of Greek spirit—"beautiful fruit already picked from the tree," etc.[62]—would support both readings. It is an ambivalence that permeates Hegel's "memory" of art, and hence our own reflections on that.

Of course, much has happened since Hegel proffered his narrative of decline—a fact some have hailed as speculative philosophy's comeuppance. In particular, Hegel could scarcely have anticipated the burgeoning of a "culture industry" in the midnineteenth century, or the subsequent spread of commodification throughout society, in a wholesale "aestheticization" of the lifeworld.[63] Adorno is a witness to that process, as in another way is Heidegger (whose well-known essay could well be retitled "The Origin of the Work of Art in the Age of its Technical Reproducibility"). Paradoxically, both thinkers have shown how Hegelian dialectic outruns his own system, how demarcation escapes narrative closure by disclosing its own "unthought." In other words, the story—or at least the *petit récit*—goes on.

Was it was unfair of me to have cited Baudelaire on the painter of modern life, especially when we consider that Baudelairian "memory" becomes Benjamin's "*Gedächtnis*"—hardly what one expects of the speculative philosopher's "internalizing" glance? I hope I have said enough to suggest that Hegel's philosopher (like Baudelaire's painter) is fully a "man of the world," and further that his aesthetic philosophy is neither classicist (it does not subsume everything to sculpture) nor modernist (it does not dissolve all into subjectivity). Habermas calls Hegel the first thinker for whom modernity—that is, subjectivity, the claim to self-certification (*Selbstgewisserung*)—becomes a problem.[64] Oddly enough, Habermas thinks that Hegel himself subscribes to the program of self-critique and absolute autonomy. But that I see as more Kantian: the Hegelian move is precisely to put in question the margin that defines any such "autopoiesis." Responding to Habermas's "project of autonomy," Vincent Descombes cites Baudelaire's defense of Flaubert: it is absurd to expect a genre to "frame" or "indict" itself—"c'est au lecteur qu'il revient de tirer les *conclusions de la conclusion.*"[65] I would approach Hegel's theory of art-as-memory from the same angle. The "appeal-structure" of his lectures on aesthetics is akin to the one he sees in art itself—a conclusion that resists definitive closure. . . .

8

Heidegger on Hegel's Antigone: The Memory of Gender and the Forgetfulness of the Ethical Difference

Kathleen Wright

Memory selects, and thus also forgets. In this essay, I shall explore the way Heidegger's memory of the ontological difference in his reading of Sophocles's *Antigone* in 1935 and 1942 forgets Hegel's reading of it along with what I shall call the ethical difference.[1] For Hegel, this play presents the most basic ethical conflict that is possible, which is the conflict between obligations to the family and obligations to the state.[2] Lines 369–75 of the choral ode known as the "Ode to Man" sum up the wisdom to be acquired from this tragic conflict. They read in Elizabeth Wyckoff's translation as follows:

> When he honors the laws of the land and gods' sworn right [*dike*] high indeed is his city [*upsipolis*]; but state-less [*apolis*] the man who dares to dwell with dishonor [*tolma*]. Not by my fire [*parhestios*], never to share my thought, who [*hos*, masculine, singular] does these things.[3]

According to Hegel, both laws—the law decreed by Creon as the ruler of the state and the law or justice (*dike*) decreed by the gods which dictates the burial of Polyneices—are binding upon each and every individual with equal force. Antigone and Creon enter upon their collision course when each of them honors only one of these laws. In so doing, each dishonors the other law. According to Hegel's reading, Antigone and Creon are both guilty, and each of them are punished by becoming "stateless," Antigone in her death, and Creon at the end of the play. Hegel's reading depends on the closing lines of this ode—"Not by my fire, never to share my thoughts, the man who does these things."—referring equally to Creon and to Antigone. R. C. Jebb lends support to Hegel's reading when he perceptively observes that "The choral ode has closed with an allusion to the unknown man [*hos* . . .]. At this moment Antigone is led in by the Guard."[4]

Heidegger and Hegel seem to be equally fascinated by Sophocles's *Antigone.* Hegel, for example, announces near the end of his *Lectures on Aesthetics* that "of all the masterpieces of the classical and the modern world—and I know nearly all of them and you should and can—the *Antigone* seems to me to be the most magnificent and satisfying work of art of this kind."[5] As if to rival this, Heidegger makes an even stronger claim. Sophocles's *Antigone* is not simply the most magnificent work of art within the history of the West. It is unique because it originates the history of the Greeks and therefore the history of the West. "[T]he poetry called *Antigone,*" Heidegger informs us, "is as poetry a founding of the whole Greek world (Dasein)."[6] Heidegger's provocative counterclaim should not conceal from us how much he nevertheless agrees with Hegel about the singular importance of Sophocles's *Antigone.*

In his *Aesthetics,* Hegel bases his claim that Sophocles's *Antigone* is "one of the most sublime and in every respect most excellent works of art of all time" on the fact that it is an outstanding represention of the tragic "clash" (*Gegensatz*) between divine and human law, between the obligations to the family and the obligations to the state.[7] In his *Philosophy of Right,* Hegel tells us even more explicitly that Sophocles's *Antigone* is "one of the most sublime presentations" of "family piety," which is "principally the law of woman." This law, he continues, "is opposed to public law, to the law of the land. This is the supreme opposition [*Gegensatz*] in ethics and therefore in tragedy; and it is individualized in [Sophocles' play, *Antigone*] in the opposing natures [*Gegensatz*] of man and woman."[8] For Hegel, then, the supremacy of *Antigone* as a work of art rests on its presentation of the "supreme opposition in ethics."

We note that Hegel appeals here to "the opposing natures of man and woman," that is, to sexual difference, and not to generational difference (uncle and niece) or to power difference (ruler and ruled) to describe the opposition between Creon and Antigone, the representatives of public law and family piety, respectively. The opposite sexes "individualize" opposite laws; Antigone the law of woman, and Creon the law of the land or "of man."

How does Heidegger's reading of the *Antigone* differ from Hegel's? The most obvious difference is that by focusing exclusively on the "Ode to Man" in 1935, Heidegger's reading neglects the plot and the rest of the play. Even when Heidegger includes Antigone's conversations with Ismene and Creon in his 1942 interpretation of the "Ode to Man," he focuses his attention upon them only insofar as they relate to the first and last lines of this one choral ode. Heidegger's focus, we find, renders peripheral the complex familial and political differences between Creon and Antigone in this tragedy, that they are uncle and niece as well as ruler and ruled. We find that by decentering the family and the state in his readings of the *Antigone*, Heidegger attempts to forget Hegel's rival reading which makes the ethical difference or conflict between the law of the family (e.g., family piety) and the law of the state central to this tragedy. Without ever explicitly naming Hegel, Heidegger nonetheless implies through his use of quotation marks that Hegel is his rival when he states that the conflict in this play is not between the "state" and "religion" (*GA* 53, 147; *HHI*, 118).

The competition between these two readers of Sophocles's *Antigone* emerges even more clearly when we consider the role and function of sexual difference in Heidegger's account. We have been told by Jacques Derrida in "Choreographies" that Heidegger "almost never" speaks about sexuality or sexual difference.[9] Derrida has pointed out one such occasion, Heidegger's reference in 1928 to sexuality when he insists on the neutrality of Dasein as discussed in *Being and Time* (1927).[10] Heidegger's two readings of Sophocles's *Antigone* are another occasion as I will show in part one of this paper. In parts 2 and 3, I will examine Heidegger's understanding of those Greeks, including Creon, who are male, and of the Greek woman, Antigone.

After establishing what Heidegger thinks about sexual difference, I will turn in part 4 to how Heidegger's reading of Sophocles's *Antigone* differs from Hegel's. Instead of using the ontological difference, Heidegger's own framework for his thinking, I will explore the picture Heidegger offers of sexual difference within the ethical framework provided by Hegel for the *Antigone*. When examined within this framework, we find that sexual difference in Heidegger is not used to support the "supreme opposition in ethics." We discover instead that Heidegger employs sexual difference in his reading of the *Antigone* to undermine the very possibility of an ethics.

Heidegger nowhere encourages us to relate his thinking to that of Hegel. On the contrary, he insists repeatedly on his proximity to Hegel's contemporary, Friedrich Hölderlin, and his distance from Hegel.[11] Nonetheless by relating Heidegger's interpretation of Sophocles's *Antigone* to that of Hegel, we find one reason why an ethics remains the unthought in Heidegger's own thinking.

Heidegger on Sexual Difference

We cannot discover Heidegger's thoughts about sexuality or sexual difference if we concentrate only on the presence or absence of words like sexuality or themes like the body which are related to sexuality. Instead we must look at how gender operates in translations, in interpretations, and between the 1935 and the 1942 translations and interpretations of the same word, line, ode, or text. Let us start with Heidegger's translation of the Greek *ta deina* (neuter, plural) which occurs in line 333 of Sophocles's *Antigone.* Heidegger chooses to translate *to deinon* (neuter, singular) as *das Unheimliche* (neuter, singular) in 1935 and 1942. English translators of Sophocles such as Jebb and Wyckoff choose to translate *to deinon* as "a wonder." Freud's translator employs "the uncanny" for *das Unheimliche.* I prefer a more modest translation, "the unsettling," because it preserves what are for this essay important features of the classical Greek *to deinon* and the modern German *das Unheimliche.*[12]

In 1935 and again in 1942, Heidegger insists that the word *deinon*, condenses the meaning of the whole of the *Antigone.* Unpacked, the meaning of *deinon* radiates out and determines the meaning of the first two lines of the choral ode, which read, in my translation, "There is much that is unsettling, but nothing more unsettling than human being." Lines 333–34, when in turn unpacked, disclose the meaning of the choral ode as a whole (lines 333–375). The ode, which is the second of five choral odes in the play, is said to determine the meaning of the play as a whole, a play which, Heidegger believes, "founds" the whole of the Greek world (*Dasein*). Where in this word, line, ode, play, and finally in this world is sexual difference to be found?

In Heidegger's 1935 reading of the "Ode of Man," he unpacks what is concentrated within the word *deinon* by identifying two characteristics of the unsettling (*das Unheimliche*). It is "overwhelming" (*das Überwältigende*) and it is "violating" (*das Gewalttätige*). In 1942, Heidegger identifies a third characteristic: it is "unfamiliar" (*das Ungewöhnliche*). We notice that this new characterization, the unfamiliar, contains a reference to the familiar (*das Gewöhnliche*) and to dwelling (*Wohnen*), thus to the family home as the traditional domain of women. The characterization of the unsettling in 1942 which introduces the feminine allows us to recognize that in 1935 the unsettling was thought of in wholly masculine terms. We find therefore that there is a sexual difference between Heidegger's earlier and later characterizations of the unsettling (*to deinon* and *das Unheimliche*).

Heidegger's interpretation of lines 333–34 of the ode also changes from 1935 to 1942, and again we find that the difference is sexual.

Heidegger initially interprets the ode to sing the praise of those human beings who venture forth to say and do what has never before been said or done. The groundbreaking speech acts and deeds of these human beings who are "the most unsettling of all" are said to include "poetic utterances," "thought projects," "conquering and developing new territories," and "creating new states." In 1942, however, Heidegger interprets the Chorus to single out Antigone, and to bestow upon her their highest praise. Antigone, he argues, is unique among all those who have said or done what has never before been said or done, and as such she is the most unsettling of all. Heidegger's insistence in 1942 that the Chorus refers to Antigone in lines 333–34 leads us to realize that in 1935 Heidegger made no mention at all of Antigone. And with this realization comes the recognition that the groundbreaking speech acts and activities he referred to in 1935 were possible only for those Greeks who were male.[13]

Let us pause for a moment to note that Heidegger nowhere explicitly acknowledges that he has introduced sexual difference into his account in 1942. What he does admit is that Antigone is different from Creon and the others who are unsettling (*deina*). She is said to be "authentically unsettling" (*eigentliche Unheimischsein*) and they to be "inauthentically unsettling" (*GA* 53, 128, 146; *HHI*, 103, 117). We note, however, that Heidegger does not revise or reject his 1935 reading in 1942. Instead he frames what he had said earlier about what it means to be unsettling by referring first to Ismene and Antigone and then at the end to Antigone and the hearth. Women and, most tellingly, Antigone are completely absent from Heidegger's 1935 reading. The addition of women and of the hearth, a place associated with women, in 1942 "sexualize" what the ode as read by Heidegger in 1935 is said to praise. Instead of referring neutrally to all human beings regardless of their gender, what Heidegger praises in 1935 in fact applies only to those human beings who are male. What Heidegger says about the world of the Greeks in 1935 applies to it, therefore, only insofar as it is, in Nietzsche's words, "a culture of men."[14]

We find that in his two readings of Sophocles's *Antigone* Heidegger does just the opposite of what Derrida maintains in "Geschlecht: Sexual Difference, Ontological Difference." Instead of neutralizing the sexuality of Dasein, Heidegger sexualizes Dasein. He implicitly masculinizes Dasein in 1935 and explicitly feminizes Dasein in 1942. How does Heidegger think the two terms of this sexual difference? Does Heidegger take over the traditional construal of sexual difference?

According to this (now disputed) view, sexual difference is binary (either male or female) and it is hierarchic (the male over the female). Heidegger, it would seem, rejects this construal of sexual difference at least in the case of Antigone. For in spite of her status as a woman, she emerges as superior ("the most unsettling") to all men. At the same time, however, Heidegger elevates Antigone above all other women as well as above all men. Where, then, does Heidegger stand in relation to the binary opposition and hierarchic relation of the sexes, a relation which we find expressed in Hegel in terms of the "opposing natures of man and woman"?[15] To answer this question, we must turn to the larger picture and examine what Heidegger says about sexual difference when we combine his 1935 and his 1942 interpretations of the ode as a whole.

Man, the Controversial

Hegel, we recall, stated in his *Philosophy of Right* that Sophocles "individualized" the opposing laws of state and family in his characters, Creon and Antigone. And he made the additional claim that it was solely by virtue of their sexual difference that each character represented in their lives and actions the laws that they did. Although Heidegger first identifies Creon and Antigone by name in 1942, the "nature of man" as Heidegger developes it in 1935 is best exemplified by Oedipus.[16]

Heidegger focuses on the choral ode in Sophocles's *Antigone* because he believes it "comprehends in the form of poetry the being of human being [*Menschsein*] for the Greeks."[17] The word *deinon,* we are told, is the key to how the Greeks comprehended their being-in-the-world, their being-there (Dasein). This word, he claims, means two conflicting things (*zweideutig*) (*EM,* 114; *IM,* 126). It means both what is fearful (*das Furchtbare*) and what is powerful (*das Gewaltige*). Heidegger elaborates on each of these two characteristics of what I shall call from now on the Greek experience of existence.[18] Existence is experienced fearfully "in the sense of something that overwhelms as it governs [them] [*das überwältigende Walten*], compelling [in humans] an equal degree of both sheer panic, that is true anxiety [*Angst*], and waves of concentrated and wordless awe" (*EM,* 114–15; *IM,* 126). A Greek also experiences his existence powerfully "in the sense of a man who [*dessen, der*] uses force [*Gewalt*]. He does not just have force at his disposal. Rather he is actively powerful [*gewalt-tätig,* violent] insofar as using force [*Gewaltbrauchen*] is for him [*ihm*] the fundamental trait not just of his action [*seines Tun*] but of his existence [*seines Dasein*]" (*EM,* 115; *IM,* 126; emphasis added). Heidegger, we note, does not gender the first characteristic of the Greek experience of existence. However, the second characteristic implicitly introduces gender. Those whose experience of their existence is powerful are exclusively gendered male.

These two characteristic experiences of existence (Dasein) are in conflict with one another. Man's experience of vulnerability is at odds with his experience of power. This conflict is, however, the source of what is most unsettling about man, which is that his deeds (*Tun*) increase rather than diminish the conflict characteristic of his being. Man acts violently (*gewalt-tätig*) by turning against that which overwhelms his existence (*EM*, 115: "*gewalt-tätig inmitten des Überwältigenden*"; *IM*, 126). What Heidegger describes as Greek is a type of man that is contro-versial (*gegen-wendig*).

In this account, the *Heimliche*, the homelike, is said to be what first threatens to overwhelm man's existence. The *Heimliche* includes "the familiar, the ordinary, the usual, and the secure" (*EM*, 115: "*das Heimische, Gewohnte, Geläufige, Ungefährdete*"; *IM*, 127). Man is the *Un-heimliche*; he unsettles, that is, he projects himself beyond (*hinauswirft*) the average and the everyday world of the familiar and the secure (*EM*, 116; *IM*, 127). This drive to escape the ordinary brings man to act: "*chorei*, he abandons his place [*Ort*], he moves out—and puts himself at risk into the superior force of the placeless [*ortlos*], the ocean's tidal waves" (*EM*, 118; *IM*, 129).

Heidegger warns against reading the deeds of man described in lines 335–62 in terms of "the development of humans from hunters in the wild and primitive [one-mast] sailors to founders of city-states and men of culture" (*EM*, 119; *IM*, 130). For this reading tames the controversial character of the men of Greece that drove them to leave behind the familiar and to expand and to colonize the ancient world. In his own reading of these lines, Heidegger emphasizes *Gewalttätigkeit*, the violence of these deeds.

Among those powers that threaten to overwhelm the man who abandons the familiar and journeys by sea are the sea itself and the earth, along with what inhabits them, the birds, the fish, and the wild horses and bulls. Heidegger reads man's setting out to sea as a violent "break out" (*Ausbruch*) and his cultivation of the earth as a violent "break through" (*Umbruch*). Man's relation to the other things that live in the sea and on the earth is just as violent. With his snares and his nets, man wrests these creatures out of their own natural cycles to destroy or to imprison them (*EM*, 118; *IM*, 130).

The powers within his own self, his abilities to speak, to reason, to be in a mood, to feel passionately, and to found new settlements, also threaten to overwhelm man (*EM*, 119; *IM*, 131). Once again what man does is violent: "The violence [*Gewalttätigkeit*] of the poetic utterance, of thought projects, of conquering and developing new territories, and of creating new states is not just an activating of capacities which man has. Rather the violence [of these speech acts and deeds] tames and brings to submission these powers by virtue of which being discloses itself as such insofar as man invades it" (*EM*, 120; *IM*, 132). Heidegger's 1935 account of the being of human being (*Menschsein*) among the Greeks describes the existence and deeds of those Greeks who are male. The controversy (*Gegenwendigkeit*) between power and vulnerability is at the core of their existence (Dasein), and violence (*Gewalttätigkeit*) marks the speech acts and deeds (*Tun*) of all those who excel.

Heidegger concludes this account by redefining two Greek terms, *techne* and *dike*. *Techne*, he says, is the Greek word for this doing of what is violent (*Gewalt-tätigkeit*), and *dike* is the word for the experience of being overwhelmed, the first characteristic of what is *deinon* (*EM*, 122; *IM*, 134). We have found that *techne*, as Heidegger defines this word, is attributable only to Greeks who are male. We will find that Heidegger also proposes a concept of man's *dike*, one that is directly opposed to "law," which is the way Hegel understands the Greek word *dike*. We shall come back to man's *dike* and how it differs from the way *dike* functions in relation to the woman Antigone after we look at what Heidegger has to say about the existence (Dasein) and action (*Handeln*) of Antigone.

Antigone, an Eccentric Woman

We find that his 1942 interpretation focuses in the play on the same choral ode. Heidegger makes two changes to his reading of the ode itself which make it possible for him to include Antigone among those who are referred to as unsettling.[19] He adds that those who are *deina* also experience their existence (Dasein) as something unfamiliar (*das Ungewöhnliche*) (*GA* 53, 77; *HHI*, 63). With this new characterization of what is unsettling about the existence of these Greeks, Heidegger brings out their own experience of being superior, of being extra-ordinary (*außergewöhnlich*): "The powerful [*das Gewaltige*] always exceeds the ordinary [*gewohnten*] and the familiar [*gewöhnlichen*] powers and capacities. For this reason, the *deinon* is at the same time the unfamiliar [*das Ungewöhnliche*]" (*GA* 53, 77; *HHI*, 63).[20] Those Greek males who excel in the ways described before experience their existence as superior to that of other Greeks as well as of non-Greeks. Antigone, too, Heidegger now argues, experiences her existence as out of the ordinary and the familiar.

In Heidegger's 1935 account, the Greek male who felt himself overwhelmed by the familiar and ordinary (*das Heimliche*) mastered this by abandoning his home as he set out (*chorei*) to sea and to settle new territories (*EM*, 118; *IM*, 129). Clearly the same deeds (*Tun*) cannot be attributed to Antigone even though she also leaves the home. Heidegger therefore alters his reading of the ode again in 1942 by choosing not *chorei* (line 336) but *pelei* (line 333) as the word for this distancing of oneself from the home and the familiar. Heidegger translates *pelein* as to "rise up" in the sense of to "stand out," to be "outstanding" (*sich regen* and *das Hervor-ragende*) (*GA* 53, 87–89; *HHI,* 71f.). This shift to *pelein* allows Heidegger to include Antigone's action (*Handeln*) among the acts of those who are unsettling (*das Unheimliche*) referred to in lines 333–34. For even without leaving Thebes, Antigone "rises up" out of the home and "stands out" among those like Ismene whose place is the home.

Controversy (*Gegenwendigkeit*), Heidegger argues, is at the core of Antigone's existence (Dasein) just as it is in the case of those Greek males who are unsettling. However there is a difference, which becomes the basis for what makes her distinctive above all those otherwise outstanding Greek men. Antigone's conflict, Heidegger tells us, is directed "inward" (*inwendige Gegenwendigkeit*); theirs is directed "outward" (*außer sich*) (*GA* 53, 103; *HHI,* 84). They turn against the overwhelming to ward it off by acts of violence (*techne*). She turns toward what is overwhelming her and calmly takes it upon herself (*Aufsichnehmen*) (*GA* 53, 127–28; *HHI,* 103). Earlier I used the word "controversial" to designate the deeds (*Tun*) of the men of Greece. The word "eccentric," I believe, best captures what is said by Heidegger to be controversial about Antigone's action (*Handeln*). She is ec-centric because even as she removes herself and stands out from the home and the familiar, her action relates back to the home and to the hearth which is its center.

We do not understand Antigone's action, Heidegger tells us, if we think that it is the act of burying Polyneices according to the cult of the dead and of what is due to blood relations. For in Heidegger's reading of the play, *Antigone* is not about the tragic conflict between Creon, representing the state, and Antigone, representing the divine and eternal law of the family upheld by women (*GA* 53, 147; *HHI,* 118). Rather, Antigone's action turns out to be not Polyneices's burial but her acquiescence to the death which will befall her. To put this in Hegelian terms, Antigone's action is not her crime but her punishment.

What matters for Heidegger in this play is the distancing of oneself from the ordinary and everyday that occurs along with one's being-toward-death. What the play presents is the aversion (*Gegenspiel*) between two ways of being "unsettling" (*unheimlich*), of being "not at home" (*unheimisch*) in the world in one's being-toward-death (*GA* 53, 147; *HHI,* 118). These two opposed ways of being not at home in the world do not, in Heidegger's reading, come together to clash as if drawn together by a centripetal force. Rather he reads them as opposing each other by repelling each other, each turning away from the other. The first way of being not at home in the world is that which we have identified in those Greeks who are male. The second way is that of Antigone. To differentiate Antigone's way of being not at home in the world from that identified with *techne,* Heidegger calls hers a "poetic" dwelling on the earth (*GA* 53, 150: "*Das unheimisch Heimischsein des Menschen auf der Erde ist 'dichterisch'* "; *HHI,* 120).

Heidegger reads the confrontation between Antigone and Ismene which occurs in lines 88–99 to confirm that Antigone's action amounts to dwelling poetically in being toward her death. These lines, he says, express the hostility of the sisters toward one another and not their solidarity against Creon. As word clashes against word "like sword against sword," Antigone distances herself from Ismene, from the home, and from all that is familiar (*GA* 53, 122; *HHI,* 98). What Ismene disputes is how Antigone is comporting herself toward the *deinon,* that which is unsettling her. *Deinon,* mentioned on line 96 by Antigone, can be read to refer to a particular threat, the death sentence decreed by Creon upon anyone who would dare to bury Polyneices. In Heidegger's reading, *deinon* remains indefinite and introduces the ontological difference. As a result of Heidegger's reading, Antigone does not comport herself toward anything in particular (*ein Seiendes*) or something that comes from outside of herself. The *deinon* comes instead from within her by virtue of the death that befalls her simply by her being (*Sein*). Antigone acquiesces. Without resistance, she turns toward the unsettling, letting it take place within her (*pathein to deinon*) (*GA* 53, 127–28; *HHI,* 103). She "strives" (*erjagen*) above all to "take it upon herself—to endure [the unsettling] through to the end." Hers is, Heidegger maintains, "the authentic experiencing [of being unsettled, *unheimlich,* in being-toward-death]" (*GA* 53, 127: "*Aufsichnehmen— . . . das Durchmachen bis zum Ende: das eigentliche Erfahren*"; *HHI,* 103).

When we examine Heidegger's reading of these lines, we do not find an Antigone who turns against and resists Creon's decree. We find instead that in distancing herself from Ismene she resists and turns away from what is familiar. We also discover that she turns away and avoids that way of being unfamiliar, of being not at home in the world, which we have come to identify with those outstanding Greeks who are male. For Heidegger, the Greek word *katastrophe* designates most appropriately the lives of those who attempt to master what threatens to overwhelm them, including death, through *techne.* The word "catastrophe," he tells us, means a "turning around that turns a human being away from what is his own [or proper] way of being" (*GA* 53, 94: "*eine Umkehrung, die ihn vom eigenen Wesen abkehrt*"; *HHI,* 77). Antigone is distinctive among those who are not at home in the world in their being-toward-death because she avoids catastrophe. Only Antigone comes to "dwell," that is, becomes settled in (*Heimischwerden*) being not at home in the world (*Unheimischsein*) (*GA* 53, 128–29; *HHI*, 104).

In Heidegger's account, Antigone's "supreme action" (*das höchste Handeln*) is this acquiescence to dying, and not her "premature death" as a result of Creon's decree (*GA* 53, 136, 129; *HHI*, 109, 104). Heidegger sums this action up using the last line of Hölderlin's late and fragmentary poem, "In lovely blueness . . .": "Life is death, and death is a kind of life."[21] For Heidegger, the word *Heimischwerden* or "dwelling" designates most appropriately the "drama" (*to drama*) of Antigone's life as an acquiescence to death because it suggests an uninterrupted memory of the home and of the hearth which is its center (*GA* 53, 128, 144; *HHI*, 104, 115). The chorus, Heidegger argues, recognizes Antigone as one who belongs to the hearth. In its last line, "Not by my hearth. . . . ," it explicitly banishes all of those who are outstanding except Antigone (*GA* 53, 146–49; *HHI*, 117–19). What the chorus intimates in this line is that Antigone's "dwelling" is distinctive because she is not forgetful of Being and of her "belonging to Being." (*GA* 53, 147: "*Heimischwerden aus der Zugehörigkeit zum Sein*"; *HHI*, 118). For the "hearth" (*Herd*), Heidegger informs us, is secretly "the word for Being [*Sein*]" (*GA* 53, 150; *HHI*, 120; also *GA* 53, 136; *HHI*, 109).[22]

According to Heidegger, the woman, Antigone, "is herself a poem." Her existence is the "poem of dwelling in being not at home [in the world]. Antigone is the poem of the most sublime and authentic being not at home [in the world]" (*GA* 53, 151: "*Antigone selbst ist das Gedicht des Heimischwerdens im Unheimischsein. Antigone ist das Gedicht des höchsten und eigentlichen Unheimischseins*"; *HHI*, 121). What enables Antigone to exist as a poem, to dwell poetically in her being-toward-death, is her remembrance of the ontological difference, that both in her life and in her death she belongs not to something or someone (*ein Seiendes*), but only to Being itself (*GA* 53, 150: "*das Unheimischsein im Heimischwerden. Dies ist die Zugehörigkeit zum Sein selbst*"; *HHI*, 118).

Heidegger and the Forgetfulness of the Ethical Difference

Hegel had based the opposition, *Gegensatz*, between state and family law on the opposing natures, *Gegensatz*, of man and woman. As characters, Antigone and Creon concretize in their gendered existences these obligations—she woman's law, the law of the family, and he man's law, the law of the state. Heidegger, we find, continues to maintain that conflict or controversy, *Gegenwendigkeit*, is basic to human existence, but this controversy is not for Heidegger that between the opposite sexes. Instead each person, be they man or woman, experiences controversy within their own existence. There is, however, a sexual difference inasmuch as Antigone responds differently to the conflict she experiences in her existence (Dasein). Whereas the Greek man acts violently (*Tun*), extending his mastery of the world through *techne*, Antigone actively endures (*Handeln*), dwelling poetically on the earth.

Heidegger's account of sexual difference in the *Antigone* undermines Hegel's reading of this play by attacking Hegel's idea that law, in one case divinely sanctioned state law and in the other case divinely sanctioned family law, determines the gendered existences of man and woman. Heidegger insists that the word *deinon*, "the fundamental word of the choral ode," is "the fundamental word of this tragedy, and yes of the Greek culture [*Griechentum*] itself" (*GA* 53, 76; *HHI*, 63). This challenges Hegel's claim that *dike* understood as law (*Gesetz*) is central to this tragedy because it governs the deeds and actions of those who are *deina*. Heidegger claims instead that *deinon* governs *dike* with the result that *dike* no longer serves as a foundation for ethics. Let us examine Heidegger's rival account of *dike* in relation to the gendered existences of man and woman.

The Greek men who are unsettling (*deina*) experience in their existences a conflict between being overwhelmed and acting powerfully. Heidegger tells us that *dike* is the name for that which overwhelms (*das Überwältigende*): "If one translates *dike* as 'justice' and understands this legally and morally, then the word loses its fundamental metaphysical meaning. The same holds for the interpretation of *dike* as norm. In all of its domains and powers, that which overwhelms is in regard to its mightiness that which puts [man] to the test [*der Fug*]" (*EM*, 123; *IM*, 135). In response to such testing, these men embark upon the mastery of the world around them by means of *techne*. We can say that *dike*, that which overwhelms man, determines him to act ever more violently (*techne*). Thus in Heidegger's reading, the *dike* that governs man has the opposite effect of law. For *dike* compels man to "hubris and presumptuousness [*Übermut und Vermessenheit*]" (*EM*, 125; *IM*, 138).

Antigone, we are told, distinguishes herself from those Greek men who are hubristic through *techne*. We find, however, that Heidegger does not grant her this distinction because something like law, for example, the law of the family, governs her action. Antigone's confrontation with Ismene, according to Heidegger's reading, dissociates her action from all ties to the family and the familiar. Her death befalls her simply by virtue of being a human being. Lines 450–57, Antigone's response to Creon, provide Heidegger with additional support for his claim that no law, not even *dike*, governs Antigone's action. This is what Antigone says in Wyckoff's translation:

> For me it was not Zeus who made that order [*tade*].
> Nor did that Justice [*dike*] who lives with the
>   gods below
> mark out such laws [*nomous*] to hold among mankind.
> Nor did I think your orders were so strong
> that you, a mortal man, could over-run
> the gods' unwritten and unfailing laws [*nomima*].
> Not now, nor yesterday's, they always live,
> and no one knows their origin in time.[23]

Most interpreters, Hegel included, understand Antigone to say that her action of burying Polyneices obeys the gods' unwritten laws. Heidegger challenges this interpretation by reading the demonstrative pronoun *tade* in the first line not in reference to Creon's order to leave Polyneices unburied but to Antigone's "action" understood as her authentic experiencing of being unsettled, *unheimlich*, in being-toward-death. For Heidegger, no thing, *kein Seiendes*, demands this of her, and especially not something like a law, be it manmade or god-given. What determines Antigone instead is Being itself (*Sein*), which "holds sway [also] over the sky gods (Zeus) and the cthonic gods (Dike)" (*GA* 53, 147; *HHI*, 117). Antigone's action, so Heidegger argues, cannot be dictated by state or family law for she belongs not to the state or to the family, but solely to Being. (*GA* 53, 143–44: "Zugehörigkeit zum Sein"; *HHI*, 118).

Heidegger challenges Hegel's reading of the figure of Antigone by denying that her action is dictated by the "law of women," those unwritten laws having to do with the underworld which Zeus, the reigning god of the world above, also enforces. We find instead an Antigone whose way of being is unrelated to such ontic matters such as her brother's burial since she understands herself to be related only to Being (*Sein*). Heidegger is, I would argue, vying with Hegel for Antigone. To claim as Heidegger does that Antigone, the woman, is the "purest poem" (*Gedicht*) is to counter Hegel's claim that the play *Antigone* is "one of the most sublime presentations" of "family piety" (*GA* 53, 149; *HHI*, 121). According to Heidegger's reading, Antigone is not the purest poetic expression of family piety. She is instead purely poetry, and altogether unrelated to family piety, woman's law, and ethics.

In presenting the rivalry between Heidegger and Hegel, I have tried to show in what way Heidegger's reading of the play *Antigone* can be understood to challenge Hegel's reading. What we have found is that

Heidegger's reading undermines Hegel's by doubly denying the role of law in the deeds (*Tun)* of controversial men like Creon, and in the action (*Handeln*) of the eccentric woman Antigone. The violent decree, the "law" unlike any before, enacted by the Greek man, Creon, is hubristic: his deed (*Tun*) exceeds all established law. The response or "action" of the Greek woman, Antigone, is quiescent: what she undergoes (*Handeln*) is unrelated to Creon's "new law" and to the older established laws of the state and of the family.

Is Heidegger successful in this competition against Hegel for Antigone? Heidegger does succeed in transforming the play *Antigone* from one that is about the ethical difference between family law and state law into one that is about the ontological difference between poetic dwelling on the earth and the technical mastery of the world. Insofar as Antigone stands at the end of Heidegger's reading as the purest and most concentrated form of poetic dwelling, Heidegger succeeds in obliterating the memory of Hegel's rival reading of Antigone as standing for family piety. But does Heidegger really gain the woman Antigone? I find that what remains forgotten in the Antigone Heidegger remembers is the possibility of criticism or resistance to technical hubris. Thus I conclude that Heidegger fails to gain the woman Antigone, since he succeeds against Hegel only by silencing Antigone as a voice of resistance against the inhumanity of hubris. This Greek woman's voice of resistance is silenced by Heidegger in his reading of *Antigone* in 1942 in Germany just when it was so much needed. It remains missing and forgotten along with an ethics in Heidegger's thinking.[24]

9

Stuff • Thread • Point • Fire: Hölderlin on Historical Memory and Tragic Dissolution

David Farrell Krell

> What are we? personified almighty points.
>
> —*Novalis,* Vorarbeiten *1798 (2, 329)*

> To climb down a mountain, to embrace the region with one's eyes, and all the while to feel an unsated craving. Passionate lovers who do not know how to achieve unification (in Lucretius) [.] The knower demands unification with the things and sees himself apart from them—that is his passio. Either everything should dissolve in knowledge or he himself will dissolve in the things—that is his tragedy. (The latter is his death and its pathos. The former is his striving to make everything into spirit: enjoyment in conquering, vaporizing, and violating matter. Enjoyment of the atomism of mathematical points. Cupidity! [)]
>
> —*Nietzsche, Notebook M III 1 (Spring–Fall, 1881), 11 [69]*

The point, the point of all dialectical, internalizing remembrance (Hegelian *Erinnerung*), as of all commemorative thinking (Heideggerian *Andenken*), is to hold in memory and to preserve from obliteration the contents (Hegelian and Heideggerian *Inhalt*) of thought and experience. For both Hegel and Heidegger, to remember is to heed, hold, and keep.[1] Sometimes the same seems to be true of Hölderlin. Yet at virtually every moment in his theoretical writings, from the Jena through the Homburg periods, and perhaps especially in the final years *he only mourns* all dialectical punctuation catches fire. In that fire all historical memory as traditionally conceived, and every form of traditionally conceived interior life, are consumed. The ostensible inwardness (*Innigkeit* as it is usually rendered) and internalizing remembrance (*Erinnerung*) that Hölderlin appears to endorse, as well as the punctuated line of time as such, remain only as ash. Thus the ambiguous fate of Empedocles, who is Hölderlin's obsession during the years in which most of the theoretical sketches were composed: Empedocles feels himself to be fettered by time as succession, and yet is unable to find liberation in a death that would be freely chosen at a certain *point* in successive time; he remains on the verge of the crater, so to speak, consumed in the the very delay that wards off his "one full deed at the end." However, if *Der Tod des Empedokles* remains but a fragment, or three fragments, forever disrupted and disruptive, returning always only as tragedy, then the ardor or intensity (*Innigkeit* as I shall render it throughout these remarks) of its very fragmentation incinerates the time of succession, consumes the time of identity, purges the time of *mimēsis.* In Hölderlin's punctilious yet hardly punctual time of tragic dissolution, a time bereft of punctuation, all points, as we shall see, become fireballs.

All points. For example, points of view, points of commencement and culmination, starting, middle, and end-points, points of rest, unification, dissolution, and scission (*Gesicht[s]-*, *Anfangs-*, *Mittel-*, *End-*, *Ruhe-*, *Vereinigungs-*, *Auflösungs-*, *Scheidepunkte*). Even what Hölderlin calls the elongated or distended point, *der verlängerte Punkt,* is productive, not of a line, or of a usable, weavable thread, but of a burning fuse. *All* points in Hölderlin's theoretical writings are consumed by the fire of heaven, which is not so much an ethereal, crystalline, mnemonic preservative of a bygone life as an ecstatic, intense reliving of the same life—in ineluctable downgoing. As Nietzsche too will have known.

I shall restrict myself in what follows to comments on several passages from "Wenn der Dichter einmal des Geistes mächtig" (which earlier editors of Hölderlin's works called "On the Poetic Spirit's Manner of Proceeding"), "Das untergehende Vaterland" ("Becoming in Passing Away"), and the "Grund zum Empedokles."[2]

The Reproductive Act

"If the poet should ever attain power over the spirit," begins Hölderlin, such spiritual power would enable her or him to reproduce himself or herself in the same or in an other. Such power would guide all inclination and appropriation (*Zueignung*), would allow the poet to capture and secure (*festhalten, versichern*) both self and poetic work through "the reproductive act." Such spiritual power would reproduce itself (*sich reproduzieren*) in the very stuff of poetry as it does in an individual's memory—through the harmonious alternation and interplay of spiritual import and form. Yet alternation and interplay of content and form in and of themselves are insufficient. The reproductive stuff of life and of dramatic action remains to be *found*. And even when it is found, appropriation of it commands a certain temporal order of differentiation and deferral, distribution and delay:

> Thus the stuff must be distributed, the total impression must be delayed, and the identity must become a striving forward from one point to another, whereupon the total impression naturally finds itself, so that the point of commencement and the mid-point and the point of culmination are most intensely drawn to one another, in such a way that closure occurs, with the point of culmination turning back to the point of inception, and the point of inception to the mid-point. (*S* 14, 143)

The point of poetic creation articulates a thread of circular unity, a unity of linear unification and linear opposition or juxtaposition—as in the central junction or intersection in the sign for infinity: ∞. For the poetic process is alive, seasonal, and cyclical, drawn at one and the same time or in rhythmic alternation toward its mid-point and its extremes. Life alternates endlessly, precisely because it is the only alternative. Life itself is the elongated or distended point, *der verlängerte Punkt,* which strives simultaneously for intensity (*Innigkeit*) and distinction or difference (*Unterscheidung*). The identity of the extenuated point *That I am still in the cloister is a result of my mother's request. For her sake I can certainly afford to let a couple of years go sour* cannot come to rest absolutely, for that would be its death. Nor can that identity depend on a sequence of infinitely isolated moments ("as it were, a row of atoms"). It must be constituted by "*a thoroughgoing and characteristic drawing into relation*" (*Beziehung*). Such identity, which is always something more than mere serial unity, confronts as its "ultimate task"

> having a thread, a remembrance, in harmonic alter(n)ation [*Wechsel*]; so that the spirit never is in a single moment and then again in another single moment, but is perdurance in one as in another, remaining present to itself in its various attunements precisely as it is altogether present to

> itself *in infinite* unity, which on the one hand is the point of disjunction of the singular as singular, while on the other is the unifying point of the singular as juxtaposed, and finally both at the same time, so that in it the harmoniously juxtaposed is neither juxtaposed as singular nor unified as juxtaposed, but is felt *for the past few days my work has stumbled to a halt, at which point I always employ reason concerning it* as both in *one*, as singularly and inseparably juxtaposed, and is invented as so felt. (*S* 14, 150)

Thus the artist who seeks an inspired voice and vision in foreign climes and distant times struggles to achieve self-identity and a measure of autonomy, but also to distinguish himself or herself in the world, all the while yearning to preserve a harmonious relationship between self and world. The poet usually either collapses back into childlike innocence or prods the self with merciless commands and bootless contradictions—all the traps and trappings of ambition. *Yet this wretched alternative is all but unavoidable. . . . The boy has to deal with men.* Only one maxim, applied to the poet's life, can rescue her or him from what at one point Hölderlin calls "this sad alternative," namely, the alternate regression into a childhood of intense personal feeling and sallying forth into a hostile world of distinctions and differences. The only maxim that will help the poet survive such alter(n)ation is the following: "Posit yourself *with free choice* in harmonious juxtaposition to an external sphere, precisely in the way you are in *harmonious* juxtaposition within yourself, by nature, and yet unrecognizably so, as long as you remain within yourself" (*S* 14, 153–54). Presumably, the only obstacle to a successful application of the maxim *You have become clearer about who you are than I have* is how one can *avoid* remaining within oneself, how one can sally forth at least long enough to recognize (on the outside) the harmony of oneself (within). Hölderlin's fascination with Empedocles may be due to the circumstance that the ancient Greek magus develops a unique approach to this struggle between inner self and outer world, although in the three drafts of Hölderlin's play the poet is unable to bring Empedocles to the point of radical (dis)solution, to the idealized deed of suicide.

Hölderlin's essay, "The Fatherland in Decline," indicates that the poet is never alone, whether in harmonious or cacophonous juxtaposition. Born to be a singer, he may find that his age requires him to be a sacrifice. To be sure, the essay generally takes the larger, more distant view, according to which the new world and new life *I am in a new world* come to be from the passing away of the prior ones. For a point of time, or in between two points of time, the new age seems to hover tremulously between being and nonbeing; nevertheless, Hölderlin attributes to the new age all three modalities—possibility, actuality, and necessity. Looking fore as well as aft, in anticipation of what Nietzsche will describe as the Apollonian dream-state, Hölderlin calls the process of becoming and passing away (insofar as it is captured in the unconstrained and therefore scarcely mimetic art of tragic-dramatic poetry) "a terrifying yet divine dream" (*S* 14, 97). Terrifying inasmuch as the divine dream is invariably haunted by disruption and dissolution; divine inasmuch as the thread of remembrance can ostensibly nonetheless be woven into the "stuff" of the drama.

> Thus the dissolution, as necessary, from the viewpoint of ideal remembrance becomes as such the ideal object of newly developed life, a backward glance to the path that had to be traversed from the beginning of the dissolution to the point at which the new life [produced] a remembrance of the dissolved; and from that, as an explanation and unification of the gap and of the contrast that takes place between the new and the bygone, remembrance of the dissolution can proceed. Ideal dissolution does not terrify. The point[s] of commencement and culmination are already established, found, secured; hence this dissolution is always more secure, more relentless, bolder; and it presents itself as it properly is, as a reproductive act, whereby life runs through all its points and, in order to attain the entire sum, tarries on none of them, dissolving itself in each in order to produce itself in the next; except that the dissolution is more ideal to the degree to which it distances itself from its point of commencement, whereas the restoration is more real to the same degree, until finally from the sum of these sensations of passing away and originating, infinitely run through in a moment, a whole feeling of life comes to the fore; and also from this, the sole excluded element, what was primally dissolved in remembrance (by the necessity of an object in its most accomplished state). And after the remembrance of the dissolved, the individual, unites with the infinite feeling of life through remembrance of dissolution, and after the gap between them is filled, there proceeds from this unification and comparison of the past singularity and the infinitely present the new situation proper, the next step that is to succeed upon the past. (*S* 14, 97)

Early on in the long and tortuous passage I have reproduced here, Hölderlin interrupts the phrase "a backward glance to the path that had to be traversed." He introduces into his manuscript three quick sketches, drawings, graphics, or doodles. The ink drawings, evidently in a hasty hand, look something like this:

The first of the three sketches (counting from the left) is partly gathered up by a scooping, sweeping line that appears to have been meant to encompass the figure as a whole, but inadvertently sunders it:

The drawings are as difficult to "read" as the text is. Do they depict the problem of the contiguity of points, or of the communication between points, in Hölderlin's historical continuum, or "thread," two points juxtaposed and conjoined by some unknown "X" of "ideal" or "tragic" dissolution? Does the middle sketch depict a single point of the dissolved past, trebled and infinitized within itself? (Does it not look like an open eye, the eye of Franz Baader's and F. W. J. Schelling's sun, heart, and theocosmic eye?)[3] Does the final drawing represent the periodic wave of a halved infinity, replacing the usual straight line of succession? Are the straight lines in the final figure introduced in order to graph or measure the waves of the period, to calculate the rhythmic intensities of peak and valley? The problems of such a retrospective "window" (the window itself seems an Egyptian eye, the eye of Manes, accustomed to the longer historical view) on the past point of dissolution, a window that would itself be an opening of ongoing life, *futural* life, are, as Hölderlin well knows, immense.

Hölderlin's "explanation and unification of the gap and of the contrast that takes place between the new and the bygone" remain mysterious indeed. Ideal dissolution may not terrify, but it certainly baffles. Yet the one thing it surely does *not* do is preserve some historical past as a past present, or present past, in the perfection of the present perfect tense. It does not grasp at the Hegelian and Heideggerian *Gewesen*. Further, even if the points of inception and termination in the process, according to Hölderlin, are "already established, found, secured," the reproductive act that runs through them and provides the thread seems hardly as straightforward, relentless, and bold as, say, Descartes's *enumeratio* does.[4] In the following paragraph of Hölderlin's text, which consists of a single sentence, the optimism of the reproductive act (odd equivocation, as though *reproduction* alternated somewhere between memory and life, or between memory, life, love, and the poetic work) reaches its apogee: "Thus, in remembrance of dissolution, the latter, because both its ends stand firm, becomes altogether the secure, relentless, and bold act that it properly is." Whether it is engaged in affairs of love or history, the ubiquitous, vigorous, and yet altogether ambiguous reproductive act *It's peculiar—I'll probably never fall in love except in dreams* appears to disseminate its power and surrender its act to tragic dissolution as such. Dissolution envisaged and remembered therefore seems to involve much more than merely filling a gap. Could it be the daring leap of Empedocles into Etna? And yet is not that vaunted leap *I know that everything godlike / Must go down* postponed endlessly? As though given infinite pause *I shall not go yet, old man!* by Hölderlin's sudden recollection of Empedocles stranded on the brink of his reproductive act of tragic dissolution, the next paragraph of the text begins with an *Aber,* "However." An *Aber* that takes us from foreign *stuff* to the temporal, historical, significative *thread* and from thence to a *point* that is ablaze with *fire*—it is an *Aber* that would have served as the midpoint of these remarks of mine, had they been so bold, secure, and relentless:

> However, this ideal dissolution is distinguished from the actual also by the fact that it goes from the infinitely present to the finitely past, such that (1) at every point of the same dissolution and restoration, (2) at one point in its dissolution and restoration with every other, (3) at every point in its dissolution and restoration, it is infinitely more interlaced with the total feeling of dissolution and restoration, and everything is more infinitely permeated, touched, and confronted by pain and joy, strife and peace, movement and rest, form and formlessness, so that a heavenly fire rather than an earthly one works its effects. (*S* 14, 98)

One should never underestimate the very real devastation wrought by idealized heavenly fire in the ideal dissolution of ideal points. Does it not seem as though every point of dissolution in Hölderlin's historical vision, taken in itself and also in its relation with every other, whether of the beginning, middle, or end, whether of unification or disjunction, is incinerated? Would not cinder and ash alone be left as the barest signs or traces—always something less than punctual points—of the bold reproductive act? Where stuff, thread, and point are met by fire, all inwardness melts in ardor and intensity, all economies of evidentiary punctuality and containment shrivel in what Bataille will have called the general economy of solar expenditure without reserves. *O you well-known to me, you magic, / Frightful flame! how quietly you dwell / Here, then there, how you shy from yourself / And flee yourself, you soul of the living!*

The next paragraph of "Das untergehende Vaterland," the last I shall cite, begins with the word *Endlich,* "finally," but also "finitely."

Endlike. To be sure, the passage commences with the optimism of an infinitely present present, the pure presence of perfect (re)production, (re)presentation, and restoration (*Herstellung*), and an ideal envisagement of a dissolution that is ostensibly always safely past:

> Endlike, once again, because on the other hand the ideal dissolution goes from the infinitely present to the finitely past; ideal dissolution differs from the actual in that it can be more thoroughly determined, it does not have to conflate in anxious disquiet several essential points of dissolution and restoration into one, does not have to wander anxiously in the direction of things inessential, toward the feared dissolution, nor toward things that would hinder the restoration, things quite properly dead; it also does not have to limit itself, one-sidedly, anxiously, and to the bitter end, to one point of dissolution and restoration, so that it is made to go toward its proper demise. Rather, it goes its precise, straight, open way, at each point of dissolution and restoration being entirely what it can be at that point, and only at it, hence truly individual; naturally, nothing foreign or distracting, nothing itself insignificant forces itself onto this point; but it traverses the individual point freely and completely in all its relations with the remaining points of dissolution and restoration that lie between the first two points that are *capable of* dissolution and restoration, namely, the juxtaposed infinitely new and finitely old, the real whole and the ideal particulars. (*S* 14, 98)

Hölderlin himself *I am on the way to becoming a really good boy* concedes and even emphasizes the advantage of proceeding from the infinitely present to the finitely (or finally) past, from the ideally "real" totality to the really "ideal" yet truncated particulars of a history in which much is "quite properly dead." To proceed the other way would require that one go to encounter disquiet, anxiety, contingency, and death proper. Unfortunately, this "other way" is the only way available to those who act or think *in* time and history, without the idealized and idealizing window on the "real," which is to say "finite," past. *You know me and you and death and life not.* If heavenly fire consumes the points of dissolution and restoration in the ideal, the infinitely present, then the gaps between these incinerated points themselves become infinite—in the sense of the unbounded and indeterminate. If the theoretical fragment in question begins with the phrase "The fatherland in decline," and if it peters out in a Fichtean lucubration (*Ich/Nichtich*) and a fragmentary recollection of tragic unification, nothing in Hölderlin's meditation can halt or even slow the irremediable decline, the downgoing, diminution, and decease, behind all the brave reproductive racing back and forth between points of ideal dissolution and restoration.

The Bypassed Terminus

There is in Hölderlin's text what one might call "the missed terminal" or "bypassed terminus," *der verpaßte Endpunkt.* (The locution is not Hölderlin's.) Not the elongated point that produces a narrative thread and the dramatic stuff of historical life, but a repeated point of repetitious culmination, which the text itself repeatedly reaches but then bypasses into endless rumination and redundancy. Such a missed opportunity for closure occurs in "Wenn der Dichter einmal des Geistes mächtig," and I will therefore return to it for an instant, to the very point at which I stopped citing earlier. After naming the thread of remembrance that binds beginning and end and mid-point, thus transforming a series of atomic and discrete units into one continuous invention or narrative cycle *Thus it had to be. / Thus the spirit wills it / And the ripening time. / For sometimes we / The blind need a miracle* Hölderlin indicates the "properly poetic character" of that thread. Remembrance in the poet lies beyond the powers of both art and genius, and its thread is spun and twisted in the direction or sense (*Sinn*) that the poet will fatefully come to have. Such direction or sense or meaning, *der Sinn,* constitutes poetic individuality. "To such individuality alone is given the identity of inspiration, the accomplishment of genius and art, the presentification of the infinite, the divine moment [*die Vergegenwärtigung des Unendlichen, der göttliche Moment gegeben*]" (*S* 14, 150). Full stop.

Phenomenology itself, whether Hegelian, Husserlian, or Heideggerian, would doubtless be more than satisfied with such givenness and presentification, such perfection of evidence. Philosophical speculation of every kind would certainly accept a full stop or a period or (as the French say) a *point* to terminate the sentence and the paragraph. For what more could be given or written after this divine moment of infinite presentification? Fortunately, Hölderlin never knows when to stop fully. Never fully knows when to stop. Never knows fully when to let the period fall. It is as though he were drawn, spun, and twisted in the direction of disquiet, death, and dissolution—as though he were born to play with heavenly fire. *Daily I must call upon the vanished godhead. When I think of great men in great times, and how they spread holy fire on all sides and transformed everything that was defunct, everything wooden, all the straw of the world into flames, so that it soared heavenward with them; and when I think of me, of how often I drift about like a flickering little lamp begging for a drop of oil so that I can shine a bit longer through the night—behold! a wondrous shudder passes through all my limbs, and softly I say to myself a terrifying word: the living dead!*

The living dead are the not quite properly dead, those who linger, those who clutter the stage between the historical past and the infinite present with all the contingencies of their mortal narratives. Those who, like Empedocles, never go to meet their end in one idealized act, one complete deed, at the end. Those who pass their apotheosis by without recognizing it. Those who are poets for the duration.

The bypassed terminus. Never knowing when to stop. Always either hyperbolic or elliptical. The (in)famous first sentence of "Wenn der Dichter einmal des Geistes mächtig" contains 109 lines and over a thousand words; a semicolon appears in line 50 in order to slow the sentence down for a brief interval, for it is all about control and points of rest (*Ruhepunkte*), although it is also about strife, alter(n)ation, and the receptivity of poetic stuff, which is almost always recalcitrant. The poetic process can therefore never be purely *Do you know what the cause of it is? Human beings are afraid of one another, afraid that the genius of the one will consume that of the other; that's why they gladly provide one another with food and drink, but nothing that nourishes the soul, and they can't bear it when something they say or do starts up like a flame of spirit in the other. The fools! As though anything human beings might say to one another were more than kindling, which burns only when it is ignited by spiritual fire, inasmuch as it came to be out of life and fire. And if only they were to grant one another nourishment, both parties would live and illumine, and neither would consume the other* about purity. Pure presentification of the infinite in the infinitely present, the divine moment, does not avail. It is not the end point. More is needed, more of something else must be found, if such a thing dare be said. "In its operations, the poetic spirit's manner of proceeding can never end with this. If it is true, something else must be found in it [*aufzufinden sein*], and it must show itself to be the case that the procedure that gives the poem its significance is merely the transition from what is pure to this to-be-found [*der Übergang vom Reinen zu diesem Aufzufindenden*], as also backwards from this to what is pure. (Mediation between spirit and sign)" (*S* 14, 148). As long as the to-be-found remains to-be-found, ensconced in the gerundive of necessity and encrypted in the sign, the regression to purity *Do you recall our unruffled hours, when we and we alone were rapt to one another? How triumphant! The two of us, so free and proud and alert, blossoming, gleaming in heart and soul and eye and face, and each alongside the other in such heavenly bliss! Even then I sensed it and said it: one could travel the world over and still not find anything like that again. Daily*

I can feel it, and ever more gravely remains problematic. The Ariadnic thread that might have guided us back point-by-point smolders. It burns as a fuse. It untwists and ravels to ash. Mediation between spirit and sign loses itself among signs of sheer intensity (*Innigkeit*). No stop can be a full stop, no point a point to which the poet might return and from which he or she might set out boldly, relentlessly, securely, straightforwardly, on the way (back) to spirit. The very possibility of mediation loses itself in the interminable hiatus of the caesura—as Hölderlin long ago observed, and as Walter Benjamin, Maurice Blanchot, and Philippe Lacoue-Labarthe have recently reminded us.[5]

The only possible punctuality or punctuation for a discourse that perdures in the white heat of caesura and hiatus *Many people excel in this or that. But a nature like yours, where all is gathered in an intense indestructible living union, is the pearl of our times. Whoever has known her, and whoever knows that her own happiness, born of heaven, is also her profound unhappiness, he too is eternally blessed and eternally wretched* consists of the rare comma, the sparse semicolon, and . . . *der verpaßte Endpunkt.*[6] After Hölderlin invokes the presentification of the infinitely present, the divine moment of perfect givenness, his paragraph ends . . . but his text goes on, beyond the pure word, in search of what remains *aufzufinden,* locating only a dead and deadening unity (*eine tote und tötende Einheit*). Defunct unity appears in the form of "a positive nothing" (*eines positiven Nichts*), "an infinite cessation" (*eines unendlichen Stillstands*), and matchless "hyperbole" (*es ist die Hyperbel aller Hyperbeln der kühnste und letzte Versuch des poetischen Geistes*) (*S* 14, 150–51). This boldest and most reckless leap beyond perfect givenness would take us to the question of freedom, and to what was earlier invoked as "this sad alternative": the poet happy in his or her childhood, like Empedocles in his garden, but wretched in the world of distinguished men—distinguished, but always vying, always envious. *Ah! I'd rather you knew nothing / Of me and all my mourning. No!* A hyperbolic or elliptical leap would never grant the poet a sign that might guarantee the safe return to purity; it would be a leap into endless complications, where there would always remain something to be found, something beyond the repeatedly bypassed termination. . . .

At the Burning Point

Can we learn a little more about the point of combustion? When, where, and how in Hölderlin's text does the *point* of every *thread* of all narrative *stuff* catch *fire* and burn itself out?

From the outset, Hölderlin was fascinated by the necessity of separation (*Trennung*). Every point, including the mid-point, was for him *I live a very lonely life, and I believe it does me good* the point that opens upon a sheathe of separation (*Scheidepunkt*). Even in the early essay, "Judgment and Being," composed early in 1795, "original separation" was the primal division and allotment that others were calling *Urteil,* "judgment." For Hölderlin it was more like an ordeal, an *Ur-Teilung,* more like crisis and divorce than confident critique. From the outset the ordeal was as much of life as of thought. *I am happy and unhappy as a result of your kindness. . . . Dear Mother! What is wanted is a human being who is good for something. But am I that, if I am to be honest about it?* In one of the "Seven Maxims" from the Spring of 1799 (*S* 14, 48), he appealed to "the profound feeling of mortality, change, life's temporal limits." A mournful sense of separation and loss always accompanied and perhaps even encompassed Hölderlin's meditation on unification, serving as its shifting horizon, its harrowing season. "For he has attained much who can understand life without mourning." Yet the point is not to try to attain too much, not to blast away at the horizon or season of mourning with hopes for too much. *I was always tempted to see you, and when I saw you it was only to feel that I could be nothing for you. . . . Because I wanted to be so much for you, I was forced to tell myself that I would be nothing for you.*

Every bit as early in his life as a thinker Hölderlin tried to meet the necessity of separation and loss with the force of remembrance, albeit not as containment and preservation. Human beings would elevate themselves above mere need and necessity only if they remembered with gratitude their destiny or proper "skill," "calling," or "sending" (*Geschick*). The "Fragment of Philosophical Letters" (from 1795–96; *S* 14, 36) invoked *In philosophical letters I want to find the principle that will explain to me the separations* [die Trennungen] *in which we think and exist* a memory of life that is thankful (*dankbar*), a "thinking that dares to enter into the more intense nexus of life [*den innigeren Zusammenhang des Lebens zu denken wagt*]" (*S* 14, 37). Every bit as early in his life as a poet, and certainly by 1797, the necessity of separation and the destiny of remembrance joined in a thinking of *tragedy.* In "*Das lyrische dem Schein nach idealische Gedicht*" ("On the Differences among the Kinds of Poetry"; *S* 14, 184; *B* 598–602), Hölderlin invoked his own version of the famous Fichtean-Schellingian "intellectual intuition," according to which tragic thinking depends upon insight *I almost believe that I am pedantic out of sheer love* into the unity of all life, life being the scene of love, separation, and loss.

Tragedy rises as a flame from what seems to be a "primally unified life," an Edenic state or an Empedoclean sphere in which everything encounters everything else and each receives its "rights," its "entire measure of life." At a certain point in primally unified life, at a certain *uncertain* point, which is to say, at each indeterminate and unbounded point of the infinitely present, separation invariably supervenes and disrupts the unity. Diremption occurs with, in, and through a feeling of *excess*. The parts that constitute the whole of life come to "feel too unified [*zu einig*]." The hyperbolic, ironic, excessive "too" (*zu*), which is not only hyperbolic but also hyperbolliptic *He must die, for he lived too well, / The gods all loved him overmuch. / . . . What can the son of god do? / Boundlessly the boundless one is struck* marks the moment of scission and separation at the putative point of most intense unity. In the "Grund zum Empedokles" Hölderlin will say: " . . . too intensely, too singularly." *Zu innig, zu einzig.*

When, where, and how does the excess transpire, disrupting unity at the point of life's supreme intensity? The parts of the unified whole of life separate not only when they wander from the center but also when they are "closer to the mid-point [*Mittelpunkt*] of the whole" (*S* 14, 185). At the fulcrum too, where the radius of every circle begins, and where beginning and end should be balanced for all eternity, disruption invariably occurs. The reign of the sky god, the celestial monarch who, born of the Titans, remains a child of Chaos, is periodically overthrown.

> *The Lord of Time, troubled in his enthroned rule,*
> *Scowls gloomily over all raging.*
> *His day is done, his lightning flashes,*
> *Yet what kindles above merely burns,*
> *While the striving below is savage discord.*

Hölderlin cites as the cause of such disruption and discord the necessitous free will or contingent arbitrariness—for *Willkür* means both—of Zeus, son of Cronos, lord of heaven, father of earth, and wielder of the lightning bolt: " . . . *in dieser notwendigen* Willkür des Zevs *liegt eigentlich der ideale Anfang der wirklichen Trennung.*" The moment or point of excess is the central point, the mid-point, of all life, where extremes meet; the point of excess and separation is none other than the central or middle point of unification. A smaller point burning at the center of every middle point, like the smoking axle of a wheel, and a still smaller point burning at the axle's center, in turn, and so on, into abyssal infinity. It is god. It is strife. It is the very life of life: death: miracle: mirage. *O mirage! It is gone forever!* It is truth: the lie. It is, as Hölderlin obsessively says, "both together."

Yet whatever else it is, the fiery point is *pain*, felt always in searing intensity. For even if nature and humanity affect one another reciprocally and harmoniously, as Hölderlin notes in "Das untergehende Vaterland," so that a new world and a new life germinate in the ashes of the old; and even if tragic dissolution can be felt only in a heart that senses the nascent though as yet undiscovered unification; it remains the case, as every hermit knows, that the modality of possibility remains fixed in mournful remembrance of what has dissolved and is lost forever to possibility. The access and the excess of *pain* *the best simply have to perish one way or the other* rise in the course of dissolution, drowning out any possible apprehension of the new life, up to the point at which a genuinely tragic language transforms amorphous pain into a tremor of terror. For the language of tragedy *O Greece, with your genius and your piety, where have you gone?* does not manage to communicate "the first pain of dissolution." (That modest phrase, "the first pain of dissolution," from "Becoming in Passing Away," a phrase that hides well its excess, Hölderlin later reworks to read: ". . . not the first, raw pain, *still too* unknown in its depths to those who suffer and those who observe [*nicht der erste rohe in seiner Tiefe dem Leidenden und Betrachtenden* noch zu *unbekannte Schmerz der Auflösung*]"; Beißner and Schmidt read: ". . . *dem Leidenden und Betrachtenden* noch zu *unbekannte* . . ." [*S* 14, 84, 94, 97; *B*, 642].) All of which suggests that *pain* is the celestial element of fiery excess that remains to be found, *das Aufzufindende,* which transcends all pure spiritual import and artistic form in the direction of the sign.

Pain, a sign?

No doubt, a sign that is not read, a sign undeciphered, a sign too isolated to be twisted and spun into a thread of narrative. *Zu ein(z)ig.* A sign too intense for any gleaning of meaning in and through the stuff of either historical narrative or drama. *Zu innig.* A sign seared of its sense, a sign graved in fire.

Passing away? And yet
To remain is like a stream chained
By frost. Foolish boy! Does the holy
Spirit of life sleep and keep itself anywhere
So that you might tie him down, the pure one?
The ever joyous one will never shudder anxiously
In prisons for you, or hesitate hopelessly on one spot.

A Digression on Heidegger and *Innigkeit*

Heidegger's avowed purpose in his lecture course of 1934–35 on *Hölderlin's Hymns, "Germanien" and "Der Rhein,"* is to prevent the word *Innigkeit* from collapsing into anything his students (and now his readers) might recognize.[7] Heidegger's avowal is both a gesture of fidelity to Hölderlin's exceptional legacy and a betrayal of Hölderlin's text. For as recalcitrant and resistant to interpretation as Hölderlin's own "fundamental attunement" may be (and *Grundstimmung* is also Hölderlin's word for *Innigkeit,* it is not merely Heidegger's, so that Heidegger is doubtless correct to associate these two words), Heidegger's own desire to prevent his students from "understanding" that attunement is both rigorously faithful and insidious. His reading, in terms of "the historical existence of a people and the decision touching them" (*GA* 39, 116), may well be the most terrifying betrayal, precisely because of the proximity of Hölderlin and Heidegger in the matter for "decision," to wit, "the sending of a people and their relation to the gods" (*GA* 39, 116–17). It is a proximity felt too intensely by Heidegger for him to ignore it, no matter how much farther down the raveling threads of time, history, national destiny, social order, and generation he may have been. It is also a proximity, incidentally (and obviously), never felt by Hölderlin toward Heidegger, inasmuch as no window opens onto the unbounded *future.* The same limitation applies to Heidegger and to ourselves, of course, even if we should feel, perhaps too intensely, a certain proximity to Heidegger. But who, we? Among other things, we who, like Hölderlin and Heidegger, have no window on the future, even and especially when we feel too intensely.

Nevertheless, let me at least try to cite a moment of difference in Heidegger's lectures that allows us to separate Hölderlin from Heidegger, without, however, dreaming of originals and innocents. The moment of difference emerges at the core of Heidegger's *double rejection* of the "usual" ways of reading *Innigkeit.* He begins: "The originally unified nexus of the most extensive conflict is what Hölderlin, especially in his later years, called by a single word of his own: *Innigkeit*" (*GA* 39, 117). Heidegger then refers us to a later moment in his lecture course, in which *Innigkeit* is identified as "the original unity of powers in the *Reinentsprungenen* [the purely engendered], and as the mystery of such being" (*GA* 39, 248ff.); indeed, for Heidegger the word *Innigkeit* recurs as his essential clue concerning the "endowment and assignment" of the German people and their own unbounded, or too terribly bounded, future (*GA* 39, 291ff.). But to continue:

> This word [*Innigkeit*] confronts us again and again in the most varied domains, in sundry transformations and configurations. It is one of Hölderlin's principal words. Naturally, a schoolbook definition cannot capture its import. However, let us immediately guard against a misunderstanding: *Innigkeit* does not mean simply the "interiority"

> [“*Innerlichkeit*”] of sensibility in the sense of the closing-off-in-itself of a “lived experience” [“*Erlebnisses*”]. Nor does it mean an especially high degree of “warmth of feeling” [“*Gefühlswärme*”].

In effect, these “two misunderstandings” are, in Heidegger’s view, but one: in the final era of metaphysical subjectivity, as portrayed in many if not all of Heidegger’s texts, including the *Beiträge zur Philosophie*,[8] all interiority is reduced to the tepid sentimentality of “lived experience.” If metaphysics begins with the yoking of *alētheia* under “correctness,” and continues in modernity with “certitude of representation,” it ends when the thinker exposes the mushy interiority of a psychologizing life-philosophy. Heidegger wants to rescue the poet’s word from the swamp of inwardness, whether in Descartes’s *cogito* or in life-philosophy’s “lived experience.”

Yet why do we sense that Heidegger is more troubled by the latter than by the former, that he is more resistant to “warmth of feeling” than to cogitation? *Gefühl* is by no means a word Hölderlin forbids himself to write. Does Heidegger’s trouble have to do with an allergic reaction not only against life-philosophy but also against the disquieted relationship of his own thought to all “other” forms of life, for example, animal and vegetable life *in this my life as a plant* “just-plain-life,” as he calls it in *Being and Time*, and even “divine life”—what, in a word, one might have to call *daimon* life?[9] But to continue: “Nor is *Innigkeit* a byword of the ‘beautiful soul’ and of the sort of attitude that soul takes toward the world. With Hölderlin, the word has nothing of the aftertaste of a dreamy and deedless sensitivity [*einer verträumten tatenlosen Empfindsamkeit*].”

To be sure, Hölderlin’s Empedocles pursues nothing other than an ideal deed, a full deed at the end—his speculative suicide—even if that deed is frustrated throughout the three versions of *Der Tod des Empedokles*. Yet what sorts of deeds is Heidegger thinking of? Why does he oppose them to dream-states, to which Hölderlin (and indeed Heidegger himself, who consistently favors the Apollonian over the Dionysian) is certainly not foreign? Why does Heidegger reenact with little or no refinement Hegel’s scornful reproach of *die schöne Seele*? Is Heidegger’s Hölderlin more Hegelian than we believed? Finally, why does Heidegger resist feeling, sensitivity, and sensibility, which Hölderlin himself never spurned, more than Hegel ever did? Whatever we may reply, Heidegger wants all these things reversed:

> Altogether to the contrary. It [*Innigkeit*] means first of all the supreme force [*höchste Kraft*] of Dasein. Secondly, this force proves itself in successful confrontation with the extreme conflict in beyng from the

> ground up [*diese Kraft bewährt sich im Bestehen der äußersten Widerstreite des Seyns von Grund aus*]. In short, it [*Innigkeit*] means the attuned, cognizant inherence in [*Innestehen*] and carrying out of [*Austragen*] the essential conflict of that which in the juxtaposition has an original unity, the "harmoniously juxtaposed. . . ." (*GA* 39, 117)

Heidegger prefers to persist within and to carry out from within, to confront, engage, withstand, settle, and survive the conflict surrounding what is essential. He prefers the original unity of the harmoniously juxtaposed. He prefers to be cognizant (*wissend*). He prefers supreme force, the point, and unity, over pain, fire, and dissolution. One might rejoin, to be sure, that Hölderlin prefers these as well, so that it is merely the tonality of the preference—and of its inevitable frustration—that constitutes the difference. At all events, with regard to the matter of *Innigkeit*, Heidegger *Also one of the wretched / Of this race, a mortal, like you* prefers what metaphysics always and everywhere prefers, and in the most traditional of metaphysical tones. "Openness for beings, letting ourselves into them [*das Sicheinlassen*] and persisting through their discordance, does not exclude *Innigkeit*; rather, it alone grants proper possibility to beings' power, a power that unifies on the basis of the ground [*zu ihrer aus dem Grunde einigenden Macht*]" (*GA* 39, 118).

Heidegger acknowledges that *Innigkeit* plays a decisive role in Hölderlin's *Grund zum Empedokles*, to which we shall soon turn, where the theme (in Heidegger's words) is "tragic being" as such. He cites Hölderlin's "most profound *Innigkeit*, expressed in the tragic-dramatic poem," and notes the poet's references to a variously "modest," "bold," and "excessive" *Innigkeit*. He then quotes the following cryptic lines from the *Grund*: " . . . for the *innigste* sensation is exposed to transiency precisely to the degree in which it does not repudiate the truly actual [or truly *temporal*][10] and sensuous relations (and therefore it is also a law of lyric poetry, if the *Innige* in itself is less dead [or less *profound*][11] there, thus easier to keep, to repudiate the physical and intellectual nexus)." Even though it is impossible for me here to recover the context of the quotation—inasmuch as the *Allgemeiner Grund*, from which it is taken, discusses the difficult and delicate negotiation of the poet's own experience with a foreign, analogous "stuff"—Heidegger's interpretation is bold, to say the least:

> Here it is said clearly that the nexus of beings, whose being is to be founded in poetry—in this case, the fundamental relation of an historical people to their gods—, that is to say, the fundamental attunement in the original unity of its conflict, must be repudiated precisely in order

> to preserve the "*innigste Empfindung,*" the fundamental attunement, in the face of transiency, of overhasty utilization and leveling. Thus the fundamental attunement is nothing that dare be made immediately "popular." (*GA* 39, 119)

No negotiation, nothing foreign, and thoroughgoing contempt for the *populär,* in a fatherlandish thinking that craves to heed, hold, and keep. If not to aggrandize, and boldly. How vastly different Hölderlin's own national pedagogy is from all this! While veiling and repudiation (*Verhüllung, Verleugnung*) are indeed essential to the tragic dramatist's search for the foreign analogue, these words sound remarkably different under Heidegger's pen ("—concealing preservation of being proper—," ". . . its concealing power," "Poetic saying of the mystery is *repudiation* [*die* Verleugnung]"), even before the word *Vaterland* comes to occupy him excessively. Excessively? *Zu innig, zu ein(z)ig.*

To be sure, *Vaterland* is a crucial word for Hölderlin as well, and not only in "Das untergehende Vaterland." A reading of the Heidegger/Hölderlin confrontation dare not stop with *Innigkeit.* It would have to double back on itself *and pray for the French* in order both to examine Hölderlin's national pedagogy more critically and to grant Heidegger's text its own irreducible strangeness and resistance to all narrative reductions—including the political reduction. Another time, perhaps. For the moment, it is enough if we affirm Heidegger's sense of *intensity* as something other than interiority—even if Heidegger's own confidence in historical decision and bold deeds was never touched by Hölderlin's profound sense of tragic dissolution. To see Heidegger escape unscathed from this aspect of Hölderlin, however, is to see Hölderlin escape Heidegger.

Hyperbollipsis

In *pure* life, nature and art are merely juxtaposed harmoniously, with the divine as the mid-point between the two. How nature and art confront or affront one another in an *impure* life, a life that is never transparently clear and never pristine, a life that always collapses back into the old confusions *uralte Verwirrung* after bypassing the illusory end-point: this is the principal question posed in Hölderlin's *Grund zum Empedokles,* with which these few points of mine will close. . . .

Even in *pure* life the divine mid-point *Now I can say that Apollo has struck me* would have to be the point of excessive intensity

(*Übermaß der Innigkeit*), the point-of-change for all things in unstable juxtaposition. The undulating wave of periodic alter(n)ation intersects the mid-point at each crest or peak of its apogee and at each valley of its nadir. The ruling divinity of every mid-point is *polemos*, as Heracleitus would have said; or, in Empedocles's vision, a vision that remains vital in Freud, Yeats, and countless others, *Neikos*, "Strife." Indeed, the broad, flattened "X" of Hölderlin's first sketch may depict the interpenetrating cones or vortices of Empedoclean Love and Strife. To dwell *in* the chiasmic mid-point is to be twisted aorgically *out* of it, and thus to dwell undecidably in the very midst of the to-be-found. Such is the case with Schelling's Archäus, who in spite of all that he can do is dislodged from the center of the circle, catapulted to its circumference, and then thrust back again, without respite. "In the middle," says Hölderlin's *Grund*, "lies struggle and the death of the individual" (*S* 13, 361). Thus the fulcrum, the central point and unifying moment of tragic drama (*der vereinende Moment*), appears as an illusion or mirage on the point of irretrievable evanescence (*wie ein Trugbild, [das] sich immer mehr auflöst*). In the final scene of the third draft of *Der Tod des Empedokles*, Manes taunts Empedocles himself as such a specter. *Trugbild!* he cries. If Manes, who is perhaps the old Egyptian priest of Neith, derives from the *Di Manes* or the *daimon*, that is, the tutelary genius of Empedocles, who is himself the tutor of young Pausanias, then the colorful philosopher-physician of antiquity is indeed, as Hölderlin says he is, no more than a "momentary unification" of extremes. Manes is therefore neither one nor the other extreme exclusively: neither Pausanias returned and wizened from his (impossible) regressive-progressive voyage to Imperial Rome, Sophoclean Athens, and antediluvian Egypt, nor Empedocles redoubled as his own opponent (*Gegner*), nor Solon's Egyptian priest fresh from the pages of *Timaeus*. Manes is nonetheless manifold: the very figure of figurative reading, Manes is these three, plus many more figures of di-manic reading.

For his part, Empedocles of Acragas is utterly duplicitous. His text on "nature" (fragment 17) contains the words *dipl' ereō*, "I shall tell a double tale," "I shall redouble my tale," "I, being double, shall tell. . . ." In his well-rounded sphere of truth he unites the extremes of *Philia* and *Neikos* "too intensely" (*zu innig*). Thus the "felicitous betrayal" (*der glückliche Betrug*) of unification—as though the knot of destiny *could* be either tied or cut once and for all—"is dissolved precisely to the degree that it was too intense and singular [*zu innig und einzig*]" (*S* 14, 361). As an individual, Empedocles must go down. As an individual uniting the extremes of his age, he must go down in the performance of an ideal deed, which the first draft calls "one full deed," accomplished "at the end." Such would be Empodocles's consummation, his speculative suicide, his historic and epochal sacrifice, inasmuch as *I am now full of parting* he is the avatar of his city's destiny and the destiny of all mortals.[12]

A visible, sensuous avatar of destiny, however, under the law of limit, can never resolve the *universal* problem of destiny, can never solve it visibly, sensuously, and individually—otherwise the life of an entire world would perish with a mortal who is but one of its particulars, however exceptional he or she may be. An odd situation results. Empedocles *must* be a sacrifice, he *must* go down, and yet he *cannot* do so. His suicide represents the double-bind of an imputed *hubris* and *nefas* that pertain undecidably to both mortals and gods. (As the later "Remarks" suggest, both mortals and immortals practice betrayal and infidelity.) For only a godlike child of godlike parents *Now, I fear, I must see to it that I do not end as Tantalos did, who became more of the gods than he could digest* could tantalize the gods. Thus no fateful resolution is possible, except as illusory (*scheinbar*), that is to say, as tragic. Solution and resolution dissolve in perpetual postponement and perplexity. The very excess of intensity and singularity in Empedocles makes every decisive solution (*Lösung*) sheer undecidable dissolution (*Auflösung*). The dramatic narrative of the death of Empedocles can be played out only as a thread that consists of points of fire, only as an ellipsis, only *in between* the gutted points that reproduce themselves to infinity *I've seen the sad and lonely Earth* within and without. As signs of pain. A fire burns out of control in the heart and hearth of each point and *blanc* of hyperbollipsis. . . .

Late in the *Grund zum Empedokles* Hölderlin indicates two traits of the tragic hero, the hero whose very excesses frustrate the excessive death in which the drama would otherwise culminate. The first trait seems at first to be a mere *epistemological* excess, the second an excess of *music* and *charm.*

In his fury to know, says Hölderlin, Empedocles had to tear himself from his own mid-point, penetrating his object so excessively (*so übermäßig penetrieren*) that he "lost himself in it, as in an abyss" (*S* 13, 365). In his ardor to penetrate all the points of cognition, Empedocles found himself swallowed up in them. Whether hyperbolic or elliptical, whether lunging too far or falling short, Empedocles was excessive in his drive to know. As the result of a bizarre reversal, he felt himself penetrated by the objects. He became "more infinitely receptive" (*unendlicher empfänglich*), more boundlessly gravid with things. He found in retrospect that he had always surrendered himself to people and things in erotic devotion (*hingegeben hatte*).[13] Hölderlin's words here suggest the reproductive act—an equivocal phrase, as we noted earlier, suggesting a remembrance and a coupling of life and work, a remembrance that in some eminent sense, a sense very difficult to determine, is *of woman.* Perhaps Hölderlin's Empedocles plays out the untold fate of the woman-man Teiresias, whose words in Sophocles's plays serve as the caesura of the dramatic action, that is, as the secret of the tragedies' dramatic *rhythm.*

The second excess, no doubt related to the first, has to do with the esteem in which the hero's people hold him. The citizens of Acragas, the jealous priest (Hermokrates), the archon-father of Panthea (Kritias-Mekades), the hero's brother (Strato), the women Panthea and Delia, the beloved Pausanias, and even the oriental alter-ego of Empedocles, Manes—all are ardently drawn to him, as though torn from their own distinct mid-points and dragged into the outermost orbit of his life. Hölderlin explains: "Nature . . . appeared with all its melodies in the spirit and in the mouth [*im Geiste und Munde*] of this man, and so intensely and ardently and personally." One is reminded of Hölderlin himself, in the circle of his own friends: a secondary-school teacher describes him in an official report as *venusta,* "*liebreizend,*" that is to say, as stimulating or inspiring love. (It must be difficult sometimes to be a secondary-school teacher: Heidegger says that teaching is more difficult than learning, because the teacher must let the pupils learn.) Hölderlin tells us of Empedocles's *Anmut,* usually rendered as "grace," although a reading of one of Hölderlin's most important sources, Schiller's *Über Anmut und Würde,* would teach us to render the word *I only wish I could show you her picture, then I wouldn't need to say a word* as "charm" or "attractiveness" or "stirring beauty," meaning the stunning beauty of a sexed creature.

They worshipped him, they all accepted him, says Hölderlin of the "foreign" yet analogous personage of Empedocles, who is to be the stuff of Hölderlin's own raveling tragedy. Among those people he lived for a time, supremely independent, yet always in supreme intensity, always teaching his doctrine of excess. *Oh, give yourselves to nature, before she takes you!* He drew them all toward himself, and they gathered about his fire. Yet because he appeared among them too conspicuously, too outrageously, and ultimately too sensuously, too threateningly, *zu sichtbar und sinnlich erschien* *the most familiar virtues and faults of the Germans can be reduced to a rather dull-witted domesticity* he had to go down. Or, rather, he had to *remain* in downgoing, to *persist* on the brink, precisely because his teaching was all about *not* persisting, *not* remaining. He had to express himself in "some one most determinate point." Which point? "In a point where they were most in doubt concerning the unification of the extremes in which they lived" (*S* 13, 367). In the end, he had to express himself out of the open point of his beautiful mouth, singing its flow of excessive words.

Like Schelling's God, "whose every path culminates in embodiment,"[14] Hölderlinian and Empedoclean divinity, on its path of infinite dissolution, must undergo perpetual alter(n)ation of sexes and sexualities. *How is it with us? are you so certain of what you see?* The first words of the earliest manuscript of *Der Tod des Empedokles* (*S* 13, 30; 179) are *Panthea. Rhea.* Panthea we recognize: she is the woman cured by the physician Empedocles, the woman whose mid-point never went cold.[15] However, who is Rhea?

Rhea is Hölderlin's original name for the woman he eventually called Delia, associated with the Antigone of Sophocles's Athens. Panthea Rhea. Their conjoined names reverberate with the saying of one of Empedocles's forebears, for in it we can hear Heracleitus's *panta rhei.*[16] All divinity flows. It is as if the points of fire in Hölderlin's Empedocles meant to take us in the direction of fluid mechanics, the molten mechanics of divinity and woman.[17]

Rhea, the consort of C(h)ronos, or Time, is the mother of all the primary Olympians—of the brothers, Zeus, Poseidon, and Hades, as well as of Hera, the sister and queen of Zeus. Rhea is the great titaness of the earth, Magna Mater, Kybele. If she disappears from the manuscript of *Der Tod des Empedokles,* it is not because she is one of the "accidents" to be eliminated from the play as a result of Hölderlin's "repudiation of everything accidental" (*B* 903–6). Rhea recurs. In the flow of every fiery point.

Panthea Rhea. All divinity flows. The great titaness returns as the fiery magma of Etna. She stretches out her arms to Empedocles, the son of Aither, of supernal, celestial fire, in order to reclaim him. *You too must go down, / You beautiful star! and it won't be long now.* Fire will ultimately join fire, in an act of ultimate fidelity to the earth. As Françoise Dastur says in a striking phrase, "The fire of spirit rises toward the heights, but love and pain, which are the mortals' lot, bend the flame back [*courbent la flamme*] to earth."[18]

> *To me too life became a poem.*
> *For your soul was in me, and openly, like you,*
> *My heart gave itself to the earnest Earth,*
> *The long-suffering, and often in the sacred night*
> *I swore it to her, unto death,*
> *Without fear: faithfully to love her who is fateful.*

To be sure, Hölderlin's Empedocles never takes the plunge. His full deed at the end remains a deed on the verge, suspended among the points of hyperbollipsis . . . threading points of fire . . . through the needle's eye of dissolution. Fidelity to the earth is not a bold deed done at one go, not a leap of faith or thought. It could take one hundred years of solitude.

The tapestry or *stuff* of tragedy ravels to the *thread* of finitely finite historical time. It frays at the precise *point* of excessive intensity, consumed forever in that beautiful mouth—the mouth of Rhea, the mouth of Venus—where the ardor of unification bursts into the *fire* of an utterly precise dissolution.

> Forgive me, dearest Mother! if I cannot make myself altogether clear to *you.* I repeat to you courteously what I was able to have the honor to say. I beg our good Lord, inasmuch as I speak as a learned person, that he help you in every way, and me. Take care of me. Time is precise, down to the letter, and all-merciful.
>
> For the nonce,
> your
> most obedient son,

10

Stone

John Sallis

The old Jewish cemetery in Prague is a jumble of gray and brownish stones crowded into a small, walled-in area in what was once the Prague ghetto. The stones are packed in so densely that one knows, even before reading of it, that several thousand are buried here. Now nearly all the stones are leaning, protruding at various inclinations from the black earth, a spectacle of utter disarray. Some are leaning at such a sharp angle that they seem ready to topple over. One has the impression that their thrust, though persistent, has grown feeble with the passing of time, that even stone, thrusting upward into the open, is drawn back toward the earth, toward the silence of those who, though dead and gone, would be memorialized by the stones.

At first one cannot but meet this strange sight with silence. It is not so much that words are lacking, but rather that one feels the need to hold them back, not to let them intrude, uninvited, upon the silent spectacle, like alien ghosts trampling over the graves of an unknown people. It is as if the very strangeness of the sight would be violated if brought back prematurely to the familiarity of one's native tongue. And so, at first one just looks at the disarray of tombstones, matching it with a stony gaze, silence on both sides. Not that all the inscriptions are effaced. On a few of the stones the names or symbols are still quite legible, and one notices how these stones make visible the individuality of the memorialized one by setting in the light of day something marking that individual as such. But on most of the stones one can see only that such marks were once inscribed, and the dead whom they still memorialize come to light only anonymously, as more general individuals, former inhabitants of the

Prague ghetto. Along the vertical edges of several of the stones there are sculpted columns or half-columns with elaborate capitals, and one is struck by the sharp contrast between this appearance of architectural-like support and the actual state of the cemetery. And yet, precisely because these stones show the wear of time, they can evoke an awareness of the peculiar temporality of stone: stone is ancient, not only in the sense that it withstands the wear of time better than other natural things, but also in the sense that its antiquity is of the order of the always already. Stone comes from a past that has never been present, a past unassimilable to the order of time in which things come and go in the human world; and that nonbelonging of stone is precisely what qualifies it to mark and hence memorialize such comings and goings, births and deaths. As if stone were a sensible image of timelessness, the ideal material on which to inscribe marks capable of visibly memorializing into an indefinite future one who is dead and gone.

By being walled-in, the cemetery forms a kind of ghetto within the ghetto—or rather, within what was once the ghetto, one so well-known that Hitler chose it as the site where he planned to build a museum to an extinct race. Now, of course, there is no longer a ghetto in Prague. Not that the place has been destroyed, this place once closed off as the place of the other, this place where the other remained other within, yet separated from, the otherwise selfsame city. Now it is preserved and opened up to all, made a scene for all to visit, generating return on the capital used to open and preserve it. Now it is assimilated to an economy that tolerates no closing off, an economy that assimilates all, a politics that declares as its imperative: Let there be no more ghettos! Let there be no more walls!—except perhaps around old cemeteries with their worn, worthless old stones. Let these sites of the absolutely unassimilable, of death and the dead, remain walled-in—the better to be assimilated to the economy of assimilation. Yet as, after the holocaust, a politics of the ghetto has become absolutely unthinkable, the need has become all the more urgent to recognize that assimilation too is violent and that it becomes more violent the more the other resists assimilation, the more decisively other the other is or becomes. To say nothing of the capacity of this economy to enlist in its service the violence of technology. The question is whether we today can think beyond this all-too-symmetrical opposition between the ghetto that would enforce otherness and the assimilation that would enforce sameness. An ancient question, this question of same and other, ancient like stone.

But I have wandered. Let us return to the old cemetery and linger just a bit longer within its walls, closing out the sounds of the city, listening to the silence within. Here one hears with one's eyes, hears the silent appeal of the stones for a kind of remembrance. What kind? Not a remembrance in which one would call up an image of someone once seen, actually or in an image, or even once read of in a narrative about the Prague ghetto, fictional or otherwise. It is in no sense a calling from within oneself but rather a call coming from the stones themselves as their silent presence begins to announce that someone whose earthy remains lie buried below has once lived and died, someone whose name or other identifying mark may or may not still be legible on the stone, in any case a stranger whose absence is utterly sealed. And yet, without violating that seal, the stones bring the dead back; they summon the dead in the very announcing of the seal that forever deprives the dead of presence. Thrusting upward into the light of day, catching even some rays of sunlight, the shining stones produce a simulacrum of rebirth, of the rebirth of those long dead, of those who, in being reborn, remain nonetheless dead, absent, silent.

Eventually one will break the silence, though reluctantly and only after having lingered for some time within the walls. For if any sight could make one experience the need to be addressed before speaking, the need to speak only responsively, it is the sight of the old cemetery. When the moment finally came, I would venture only a single word, one not quite native, foregoing still the assimilation of the sight to the familiarity of the mother tongue. The word uttered finally in response to the sight, the first word evoked by the disarray of gravestones closed off within the great Baroque city where, even still, as a foreigner one most often speaks German—the word is: *vorbei.* First of all, in the common sense: it's past, it's over and done with. As one says of winter when it finally begins to recede: it's over, it's gone. But also in the sense that Heidegger released in the word, an inherently unstable sense, which he kept in play for only a brief time, in some early drafts for what eventually became *Being and Time.*[1] During this time *das Vorbei* is the name of death: Dasein's being toward its own death is a matter of its comporting itself to its own goneness, *das Vorbei.* It is a matter of its running up against its own goneness, that future that will never be present. And yet, common sense insists that what is gone, what is over and done with, is the past; and as soon as one begins to apply this measure, the measure of presence, to *das Vorbei,* it begins to name the past rather than one's ownmost possibility at the limit of the future.

The word might, then, be left suspended, while at the same time being turned responsively to the sight of the old cemetery. Then it would say—bringing everything back now, finally, to the native tongue: dead and gone. And yet, also: brought back—in the word itself, in the appeal to which it responds, in the accord of the word to the appeal. Brought back, even if still only as dead and gone. As, in this double sense, past.

Hegel said almost the same of art, that it is for us something past. His declaration of the pastness of art is in play from the very outset of the lectures on fine art (*schöne Kunst*) that he presented several times during the 1820s at the University of Berlin. For these lectures Hegel used the title *Aesthetics*, as did his student H. G. Hotho, who edited the lectures after Hegel's death and published them for the first time in 1835. Yet Hegel grants the title only as a concession to common speech, noting at the very beginning that it "is not wholly suitable, since *aesthetics* means more precisely the science of sense, of feeling [*Wissenschaft des Sinnes, des Empfindens*]."[2] The proper title would be, instead, philosophy of art, for in the concept of art that the lectures develop it is not a matter only of sense and feeling but also of truth. It is precisely this double bond that leads Hegel to declare the pastness of art.

Art is for us something past. More than a century later Heidegger will insist that a decision has still not been reached regarding this declaration, that the pastness of art remains still undecidable. A measure, no doubt, of the decisiveness of Hegel's lectures, which Heidegger will call "the most comprehensive reflection on the essence of art that the West possesses."[3]

Art is for us something past. Art, says Hegel, "no longer fulfills our highest needs. . . . Art no longer grants that satisfaction of spiritual needs that earlier ages and nations sought in it and found in it alone." Thus he concludes: "In all these respects art, considered in its highest determination [*Bestimmung*], is and remains for us something past [*ein Vergangenes*]" (*A* 1, 21f.). Hegel knew of course that the great art of the past would continue to speak to mankind; but its speech would have become foreign, no longer satisfying the highest needs of mankind. Such art would be past in a double sense, doubly an art of the past, stemming from a past age and sufficient to the highest needs of past ages only. Hegel also knew of course that works of art would continue to be created in the future; but he insisted that there would never be, in the most decisive sense, an artwork of the future, but only artworks that, even before being created, would already have become something past. To all art, past and future, Hegel would say and would have humanity say: *nicht mehr*, "we bow our knees no longer" (*A* 1, 110). Art is something past. Art is *vorbei*, dead and gone, as far as the highest needs of mankind are concerned. Even if its ghosts return. Even if they spring up from the soil of the future.

Yet along with the ghosts of art there are other specters whose words do still speak to the highest needs of mankind, now and into the future, specters that do not merely return to haunt a world to which they no longer truly belong, specters in whom, on the contrary, the spirit of art is reborn in new shapes, speaking new tongues. These specters both banish art and replace it. In them the spirit of art is reborn, and this ressurrection of what is otherwise dead and gone is the highest testimony that, in Hegel's words, "the life of spirit is not the life that shrinks from death and keeps itself untouched by devastation, but rather the life that endures it and maintains itself in it. It wins its truth only when, in utter dismemberment, it finds itself." Such is the magic of spirit, its magical power (*Zauberkraft*), that from the negativity of death it can bring itself back into being: "Spirit is this power only by looking the negative in the face and tarrying with it. This tarrying is the magical power that turns it around into being."[4] What that magic produces from art is religion and philosophy. These are the other shapes of spirit that come to displace art, sealing its consignment to the past while themselves arising from its very dismemberment.

All three figures belong to the same sphere. But within the limits of the *Aesthetics*, Hegel does not trace the turnings of these circles so as to delimit the figures in a rigorous way, that is, so as to display the magic by which spirit returns from death to life in ever higher shapes. Within the limits of the *Aesthetics*, even the concept of art is merely taken up lemmatically, not rigorously derived as such; it is "a presupposition given by the system of philosophy" (*A* 1, 35). And so, at the outset Hegel delimits the sphere common to art, religion, and philosophy in a way that foregoes, or at least defers, the circlings of spirit: the sphere common to the three figures he simply identifies as that in which are expressed the most comprehensive truths of spirit. What distinguishes art specifically is that it presents these truths in sensible form, in a configuration palpable to sense, bringing these most comprehensive truths nearer to sense and feeling. But precisely for this reason art is not the highest shape in which to express these truths. Because of its sensible form, it is limited to a specific content: art can present spirit only down to a certain level, not in its depth. The multidirectionality of Hegel's discourse, even the contrariety of its directionalities, should not go unnoticed here: the *higher* shapes of spirit are those that express the *deeper* levels of the truth of spirit, and the depth of spirit to which art cannot reach is, in turn, the most *interior*, the inwardness of spirit, which is thus opposed to the exteriority in which art is at home. For art is at home only at the level at which spirit can go forth truly into the sphere of sense, remaining adequate to itself there, submitting fully to enclosure within a sensible configuration. Hegel refers to the Greek gods as constituting such a content, in distinction from the deeper comprehension of truth achieved through Christianity and the development of reason, a comprehension of spirit at a depth where it is no longer so akin to sense as to be appropriable to such material as art has for configuring it. The absolute inwardness of spirit proclaimed by Christianity occurs at that depth, as does the modern detachment of the universal from the sensible, the separation by which the universal can come to govern the sensible as a rational law or maxim outside it. Because art cannot reach to this depth unfolded in the spirit of the modern world, it is for us something past.

Nonetheless, art does—even today, even now that it is for us something past—present the truth of spirit. It presents spirit in the guise of spirit, not in the disguise, for example, of nature. It presents spirit as spirit, even if not in its full depth. This is why it belongs to the sphere of absolute spirit, along with religion and philosophy. Indeed, at those junctures in the *Aesthetics* where Hegel sets forth in full generality the vocation of art and the essence of art as determined by that vocation (*die Bestimmung der Kunst*—in the double sense), he invariably refers to the presentational character of art, to its character as *Darstellung*. In one formulation, it is the vocation of art to present "the truth in the form of sensible artistic configuration [*der sinnlichen Kunstgestaltung*]" (*A* 1, 64). Or, again: "Art has no other vocation but to bring before sensible intuition [*sinnliche Anschauung*] the truth as it is in spirit" (*A* 2, 16). Both formulations mark clearly the double bond of art: on the one hand, its bond to the truth of spirit, which it is bound to present; on the *other* hand, its bond to the sensible, in an artistic configuration of which it is bound to shape its presentation. One of the most remarkable accomplishments of the *Aesthetics* is the way in which it goes about systematically determining the specific character of the sensibleness (*Sinnlichkeit*) to which art is bound. Even at the most general level, where the differentiation between the various forms of art and that between the individual arts has not yet come into play, Hegel rigorously distinguishes the artistic bond to the sensible from other types of relatedness that spirit can assume to the sensible. Among those other, nonartistic types of relatedness he includes: first, sensible apprehension, which merely looks on; second, desire, which uses and consumes things, gaining self-realization in them; and, third, theoretical intelligence, which goes straight for the universal, detaching it so thoroughly that the sensible loses all further relevance. By contrast, the artistic configuration, the artwork, is cherished, yet without becoming an object of desire. It counts neither in its immediate material existence nor in its pure universality, but rather as what Hegel calls *Schein.* I will not translate but only transliterate this word, linking to this first mention of the word *shining* a reminder of the polysemy that it is to take over from the German.

Listen, then, to the remarkable passage, near the beginning of the *Aesthetics*, in which Hegel tells how the sensible enters into the artwork:

> For in the sensible aspect of the artwork [*im Sinnlichen des Kunstwerks*], spirit seeks neither the concrete material stuff, the empirical inner completeness and development of the organism, which desire demands, nor the universal and purely ideal thought. Rather, what it wants is sensible presence [*sinnliche Gegenwart*], which indeed should remain sensible, but freed from the scaffolding of its mere materiality. Therefore, the sensible in the artwork [*das Sinnliche im Kunstwerk*], in comparison with the immediate existence of things in nature, is elevated to pure *shining* [*zum bloßen* Schein], and the artwork stands in the *middle* between immediate sensibleness and ideal thought. (*A* 1, 48)

The sensible character of the artwork is thus to be thought as shining. So is its beauty: when, later in the *Aesthetics*, Hegel comes to develop a rigorous determination of beauty, he defines it as "the sensible shining of the idea" (*A* 1, 117).

One could say that it is this sensible, shining character of the artwork that destines art to have become something past. And yet, the bond of art to the sensible has this effect only because it is not the only attachment that art has. Art is also bound to present the truth, and it is only because, as sensible, it cannot present the truth in its full depth that it is destined to become something past, that it has become something past for us today for whom the full depth of spirit has unfolded. In more precise terms, then, one can say that the pastness of art is determined by art's double bond, by its being bound both to truth and to the sensible, the dynamics of this double bond making it a double bind. Caught in this bind, art becomes for us something past. The depths of spirit cannot, in the end, be brought fully to the light of day, made to shine.

Recollecting the entire history of art, the *Aesthetics* marks the pastness of art in various connections. For that becoming-past—the end of art, as it were—is no simple event, and one would have missed the point entirely if one thought it only a matter of pointing to a linear time-scale, indicating the point in time where art becomes something past. For in the art of poetry, for instance, the passing that would consign art to the past is always already broached: poetry is not tied down to sensible material in the decisive way that other arts are, and, as its sound dies away, the passing enacts a self transcendence of art, letting art pass away and become something past (see *A* 1, 94). In romantic art there is also operative a certain self-transcendence, a passing that will have come into play with the end of classical art (see *A* 1, 87).

The Hegelian recollection gathers art in its history in such a way as to distribute it along two axes, that of its forms (symbolic, classical, romantic) and that of the individual arts (architecture, sculpture, painting, music, poetry). Throughout this recollection the end is in play, and there is perhaps no corner of the *Aesthetics* where one cannot at least catch a glimpse of the eventual pastness of art. For the discourse of the *Aesthetics*, for the discourse that gathers and distributes art in its history, art has already passed away. It is almost as if that discourse were an extended funeral oration. It is almost as if the *Aesthetics* were an inscription written for the gravestone that would memorialize art, calling it back now that it is dead and gone.

Stone also figures prominently in that inscription, especially in its beginning.

Art, recollected in its history, displays its pastness. Most remarkably, it displays that pastness even in its beginning, in the stone (that most ancient material) from which art in its beginning shapes its work. For in the Hegelian recollection of its history, architecture counts as the beginning of art. Even though, within the recollection, the primary concern is to establish architecture as the beginning by so deriving it from the essence of art (this, says Hegel, is what *we* have to do), Hegel insists also that architecture is the art that came first in the order of existence, in fact developing earlier than sculpture, painting, and music. And yet, beginning with this beginning, Hegel is careful from the beginning to interrupt all tendencies to valorize such beginnings: he declares the beginning insignificant and parodies those who are so simple as to think that the simple beginning of something reveals that thing in its concept and origin (*in ihrem Begriffe und Ursprunge*) (*A* 2, 23). It is not in the architectural beginning that one is to seek the origin of the artwork.

But how does architecture display the pastness of art? It does so by showing almost from its beginning a propensity to be appropriated to religion, which will finally, in the form of Christianity, exceed art so decisively as to consign it to being something past. At the simplest level Hegel notes that "the beginning of art stands in the closest connection with religion (*A* 1, 311). Within the specific developments of the forms of architecture, Hegel shows how the architectural edifice itself comes to be degraded (*herabsetzt*) into providing the enclosure for spiritual meanings quite independent of architecture as such. This degradation of architecture itself is realized most perfectly, if also paradoxically, in classical architecture, in the Greek temple, which serves perfectly the purpose of enclosing the statue of the god. Indeed, the beauty of classical architecture consists in its appropriateness to this purpose, its purposiveness, its serving perfectly the purpose of religion. Its beauty is not only that it is in this respect purposive but also that it shows this purposiveness, lets it shine forth from the edifice itself. But to provide enclosure—even the open enclosure of a temple—requires bearing weight, providing support, and the peculiarity of Greek architecture lies in its way of giving shape to this supporting as such, namely, by employing the column as the fundamental element. Hegel says of the Greek columnar orders: "Neither earlier nor later was anything discovered more architecturally beautiful or purposive" (*A* 2, 64f.). Whatever material may have been used in the earliest stages, certainly the great classical temples to which Hegel refers—he mentions the temple at Paestum, presumably the same one that will command Heidegger's attention a century later, though one cannot be sure, for there are in fact three temples at Paestum—certainly such temples are built of stone. Especially in the stone columns the beauty of such temples shines forth. In the very same stone, that shell for the spacing of religion, there is displayed the pastness of art.

But what about the beginning? For architecture does not begin by building classical temples. What does it build in the beginning? And with what material does it construct its first buildings?

The character of what is built in the beginning is determined, in part, by the essence of beginning as such, of the devalorized Hegelian beginning. A beginning is as such something immediate and simple, and so in the beginning architecture can only have erected buildings with independent significance, buildings that bear their meaning within themselves rather than finding it in some other purpose that they would serve. So, then, in the beginning the buildings are simple and integral, almost like sculptures except that they can bear their meanings only symbolically.

With what material are these first buildings constructed? Hegel refers to an age-old dispute as to whether architecture begins building with wood or with stone. He grants the importance of the question, conceding that the character of the material will affect the fundamental architectural forms. And yet, he justifies putting the question aside—or rather, deferring it—since it is linked to a question of external purposes, wood being used to build huts for human shelter, stone being used in temples built to house gods. To decide for wood or for stone would be to introduce purposiveness into the beginning where it cannot yet take place, where it cannot yet take over the place that would be built, degrading architecture as such.

Not, then, at the beginning, but only when that degradation has been recollected—the perfect degradation exemplified in the Greek temple—only then does Hegel really address the age-old dispute as to whether building began with wood or with stone. He accords to wood a certain natural advantage, an appropriateness for building: it does not require extensive workmanship, since it occurs by nature in regular, linear pieces that can be directly put together; whereas stone, not occurring in such a firmly specific shape, must be split and chiseled into shape before the individual pieces can be laid atop one another so as to construct an edifice. Since a great deal of work is required before stone comes to have the shape and utility that by nature wood has from the beginning, building will have begun—so it seems—with wood. And yet, at the very point where Hegel seems ready to settle the dispute once and for all in favor of building in wood, he turn abruptly away from the natural solution to a certain distribution of the two building materials to architecture in each of its three forms, symbolic, classical, and romantic. Here is the point on which the turn is made: since stone is relatively formless at the start, it can be shaped in any and every way, and therefore "it offers suitable material both for symbolic as well as romantic architecture and the latter's more fantastic forms." Wood's natural advantage turns out to pertain only to classical architecture, in which its naturally rectilinear form "proves directly more serviceable for the stricter purposiveness and reasonableness [*Verständigkeit*] that are the basis of classical architecture." Hegel declares, then, contrary to what one would have expected, that building in stone is especially predominant in independent, i.e., symbolic architecture. In the beginning architecture will have built predominantly in stone—as it will also, hardly less so, when in romantic form it comes to erect Gothic cathedrals. And even if, at some undeveloped stage, classical architecture built temples of wood, Hegel insists that it "does not stop at all at building in wood but proceeds, on the contrary, where it develops into beauty, to build in stone" (*A* 2, 55). It will always have been in stone that architecture will have let the truth shine forth.

But especially in the beginning. First of all, in Babylon, in those blocks of stone assembled for building the Tower of Babel. Then in those enormous solid columns of stone, those phallic columns, that were erected in ancient India in worship of the procreative force. Then in Egypt, where the obelisks, standing freely and independently, are symbols meaning the rays of the sun, as Hegel says, "sunrays of stone" (*A* 2, 35).

But hardly less at the end, in the final form, romantic architecture. In the Gothic cathedral the independence of symbolic architecture is united with classical purposiveness. More thoroughly than the Greek temple, the cathedral forms an enclosure, a space of worship, a place of tranquility closed off from nature, indeed from everything mundane. And yet, Christian worship is not only tranquil enclosedness but also elevation above the finite, and this elevation is what, beyond all purposiveness, determines the independent architectural character of the cathedral, which is thus built so as to express elevation toward the infinite, its spires soaring into the heavens. In romantic architecture it is no longer, as in the Greek temple, the supporting as such that provides the basic form of the building; for in the cathedral the walls have the appearance of striving upward, and the very difference between load and support comes to be cancelled. The beauty of the cathedral is not only its aspect of purposiveness but also its shining forth in such a way as to give the appearance of free ascent, its stone shining as if in ascent. Little wonder that the romantic architect comes, as Hegel says, "to refuse validity to the material . . . in its materiality and to interrupt it everywhere," for instance, with elaborate decorations. Hegel says of Gothic architecture: "There is no other architecture that with such enormous and heavy masses of stone . . . preserved nonetheless so completely the character of lightness and grace" (*A* 2, 82). Stone made to shine as if, renouncing its ancient heaviness, it now soared into the heavens. Or rather, not *now* but *then*, in the time of Gothic architecture, for us something past.

Heidegger too writes of the shining of stone. Most notably, in a text first presented as a lecture in Freiburg in 1935 (exactly a century after the publication of Hegel's *Aesthetics)*. An expanded version of the lecture was presented in Frankfurt in 1936 and finally published in 1950 as "The Origin of the Work of Art." In certain respects Heidegger's text is written in the shadows, most decisively, in a certain withdrawal from the brilliant sunlight that has shone on the stone of the temple at Paestum since ancient times. Most overtly, it is written in the shadow of Hegel's *Aesthetics*, in the shadow cast by Hegel's declaration of the pastness of art. Heidegger insists that a decision regarding Hegel's declaration has still not been reached, thus leaving this colossal question suspended over his text, like a giant question mark casting its shadow across the text.

Here is how Heidegger begins to write of stone and its shining: "Standing there, the building rests on the rocky ground" (UK, 28). There—granting a place where, as with every artwork, truth can take place—there it is, above all, a matter of standing, of the support that allows something like a temple at Paestum to stand. But now it is no longer, as in the Hegelian recollection, the shining of such support shaped into classical columns that is underwritten. It is not with the form of the work itself that Heidegger begins, but rather with a double support through which the work is linked to what lies beneath it and what opens above it. Beneath it, supporting it, is the rocky ground (*Felsgrund*): in being supported, in resting on the rock, the temple draws up from the rock the darkness of its massive support, thus bringing to the light of day, thus letting shine, that obscure, massive ground, letting shine forth the very darkness of the rocky support. Heidegger says that this supporting is not impelled to anything (*zu nichts gedrängten*): it is utterly without prescribed purpose, utterly unpurposive, in starkest contrast to the columns on which Hegel fixes his gaze and in which he sees the purposive support given shape and made to shine. Whereas columns are designed to support a temple, the rocky ground on which the temple is erected can support any and every kind of edifice. Heidegger continues: "Standing there, the building withstands the storm raging above it and so first makes the storm itself manifest in its violence" (UK, 28). The temple not only is supported by the rocky ground but also bears its support within itself, standing there under the raging storm, making manifest, as Heidegger says, the storm, the force of the storm, but also, in its resistance to that force, letting its own self-support become manifest.

Then it is as if the thunderstorm had passed, the sun now reappearing from behind the dark clouds, shining upon the stone of the temple, still dripping with rain, glistening as the rays of sunlight strike it. Now, after the storm, Heidegger writes of the shining of stone: "The luster [*Glanz*] and gleam [*Leuchten*] of the stone, itself shining, it seems, only by the grace of the sun [*anscheinend selbst nur von Gnaden der Sonne*], nonetheless first brings the light of day, the breadth of the sky, the darkness of night to shine forth [*bringt . . . zum Vorschein*]" (UK, 28). Heidegger adds: "The temple's firm towering makes visible the invisible space of the air." Nothing that Heidegger ever wrote is more contrary to sound common sense than what he writes here about the shining of the temple's stone. Not only does it invert common sense, but—in a figure that it would be difficult to compose—it also inverts in the same move precisely what Hegel delimited as the inversion of common sense, namely, metaphysics, philosophy as such. For both common sense and metaphysics would take it for granted that there is, first of all, the open space of the air and sky within which the light of day would shine forth in natural alternation with the coming of the darkness of night. Despite all inversion, despite all the magical power to turn the negative into being, even Hegel's metaphysics would still take being for granted, as granted in the granting of a beginning; still it would take for granted the "there is"—both in the sense of the *es gibt* (something is given, granted) and in the sense of there being already a *there,* a place, a *Da,* in which then something like the stone of the temple could come to shine. Heidegger reverses this—or, more precisely, sets it revolving, circling. Even if the shining of the temple's stone seems to require—and in a sense certainly does require—the shining sun, still it is the shining of the artwork that opens and sustains the space of air and sky in which things can come to the light of day and recede into the darkness of night. It is through the shining of the artwork that there is an open place in which things can come and go. Such coming and going, Heidegger notes, is what the Greeks called *physis,* which Heidegger translates as *Aufgehen.* Let me, without pretending to translate, simply say: *coming up* (as the sun comes up each morning and as a plant comes up from the seeds planted in the ground); but also *opening up* (as when a rose blossoms). And let me, instead of pretending to explain, merely refer to what Heidegger writes in a contemporaneous text, *An Introduction to Metaphysics:* "*physis* as *Aufgehen* can be experienced everywhere, e.g., in celestial occurrences (the rising of the sun), in the rolling of the sea, in the growth of plants, in the coming forth of man and animal from the womb."[5]

Recalling the fateful translation of *physis* as *natura,* nature, one realizes suddenly that Heidegger is reversing, setting into revolution, the relation between art and nature that has remained in force since the Greeks, the relation in which art as mimesis is subordinated to nature. The secondariness thus ascribed to art from the beginning of metaphysics is only compounded when in German idealism nature is thought as the other of spirit and artistic *mimesis* then redetermined as the presentation of spirit in a natural, sensible material. All art would be made in the image of those Egyptian obelisks that Hegel discusses in the *Aesthetics,* those "sunrays in stone," as he calls them. For us all art would be, like them, something past.

Heidegger would reverse the relation, would set its terms circling. Neither nature nor spirit would precede art, consigning it to the secondariness of mimesis. Not even truth would precede art, neither the truth of nature, nor the truth of spirit, nor the truth that Heidegger thinks as *aletheia,* as first opening the space in which anything like nature and spirit can come forth, come and go.

Heidegger's remarkable little discourse on the shining of the temple's stone concludes by delimiting a ground. He characterizes it as the ground of human dwelling and delimits it in reference to that coming and going that the Greeks called *physis.* This ground he proposes to call *earth.* It is, he says, that to which the things that come up, that open up into the light, are brought back and sheltered, secured. Almost as those who have lived and died are brought back and their memory secured by the gravestones in the Prague cemetery. For, indeed, what is more properly *of the earth* than stone? Perhaps even when its materiality is interrupted. Perhaps even when its shine makes it appear to renounce its ancient heaviness and to soar into the heavens.

Reversing the relation between art and nature, undermining the classical concept of art as *mimesis,* Heidegger regards the temple as opening the space of air and sky, as freeing the expanse in which things can come up into the light of day. Thus opening a world, the temple also brings forth the earth as that to which the things that come up into the light are brought back and secured. In Heidegger's words, "The temple-work, standing there, opens up a world and at the same time sets this world back again on the earth which itself only thus comes forth as home ground [*als der heimatliche Grund*]" (UK, 28).

Heidegger extends his discourse on the temple, weaving it back and forth between world and earth, delimiting the artwork as the being through which world is set up (*aufstellen*) and earth set forth (*herstellen*), more precisely, as the being that gives place to the strife of world and earth, to their *polemos*. It is as such that truth takes place in art. Not that truth somehow first subsists in itself—heaven knows where!—and then comes to be exemplified or presented in the artwork. On the contrary, *there is* such truth only insofar as a being, the artwork, is brought forth so as to give place to truth. The truth *of* art comes about only as the truth *in* art, only insofar as truth sets itself to work in the work. Art does not present a truth that would precede it (as an original precedes an image) or that would exceed it and be capable finally of consigning it to secondariness, making it for us something past. Art is the taking place of truth, a way in which truth happens.

As Heidegger weaves his discourse there are several turns at which it is drawn back to stone, almost as if to borrow the support, the weight. As the discourse turns around world, it is, for instance, declared that stone is worldless, and a contrast is drawn with men, who have a world in which they are open to other beings and themselves, and even with plants and animals, which, though they have no world as such, are linked to a surrounding (*Umgebung*). I shall not pause to return to the extended meditation (in Heidegger's lecture course of 1929–30) from which this schema of differences results nor to evoke the critical discussion that Derrida and others have brought to bear upon it. For in the present context it suffices to note the sense of the differences and on that basis to observe the following: that stone is worldless does not mean that it cannot enter a world, that it cannot be taken up into a world that opens around it or above it. One can say of stone in particular what Heidegger says of everything: that through the opening up of a world it gains its lingering and hastening, its remoteness and proximity, its breadth and narrowness.

But what is decisive is the way in which stone enters a world when something is made of that stone, when, for instance, an artwork is made from such material (*Werkstoff*), when something like the temple at Paestum is set forth (*herstellen*) from stone, made (as we say) out of it. Heidegger contrasts such making with that involved in fabricating equipment:

when stone is used for making an ax, it is used up, in the sense that its materiality disappears into the serviceability of the ax, and the material is more suitable the less it resists being absorbed into the equipmental character of the ax. What matters is not the stoneness of the ax, but only its serviceability for performing its function. This is why, with technical advances, one has not the slightest hesitation about replacing a stone ax with the more serviceable one that can be made from metal. Indeed, in more technically advanced countries one no longer finds stone axes, if even axes at all; in the half-century since Heidegger chose this now almost quaint example, stone axes have been replaced by more serviceable equipment, have passed out of use, have become for us something past, hardly even to be called back, recalled.

The stone of the temple at Paestum is utterly different: "By contrast the temple-work, in setting up a world, does not let the material disappear, but rather lets it come forth for the very first time, to come into the open of the work's world" (UK, 32). In the temple, then, the stone does not disappear but, on the contrary, is set forth into the very world that the artwork opens up; it comes to show itself as such in that world, to shine forth as stone. And even if, with the advance of technology, other materials prove more serviceable or even more artistically pliant, even if eventually all buildings are made of steel, glass, and concrete, there will still be need to call back buildings of stone, to remember the temple at Paestum. Even though it could never have soared into the heavens like a Gothic cathedral, to say nothing of the skyscrapers that now tower above our cities—like those enormous phallic columns erected in ancient India, like the obelisks of ancient Egypt, perhaps even like the Tower of Babel, but now built without being impeded by the untractableness of stone, built so as almost to appropriate the material (steel, glass, concrete) to the work, built so as almost to make it disappear in these colossal machines fabricated for housing human life, these machines for living, as Le Corbusier called them.

But the temple at Paestum is different: it lets the stone shine forth as stone in the very world opened up by the temple. It does so precisely because of its way of being made of stone: the stone of the temple comes to light as bearing its weight, as supporting, not simply in the aspect of the columns, but rather, says Heidegger, "as the work sets itself back into the massiveness and heaviness of stone" (UK, 32). He adds: "That into which the work sets itself back and which it lets come forth in the setting back of itself we call earth." He concludes: "The work brings the earth itself into the open of a world and keeps it there. The work lets the earth be an earth." But again, what is more properly *of the earth* than stone? This, then, is what the temple at Paestum does: it lets stone be stone. And if one would know what stone is, the most propitious way would be to recall the temple, to bring oneself before its ancient stones, to let their silence resound.

But what is stone that it comes to be disclosed precisely in this way, in the artwork? Could it not be known more directly, by being simply brought to light, opened up to view? Heidegger writes:

> The stone presses downward and manifests its heaviness. But while this heaviness presses against us, it denies us any penetration into it. If we attempt such a penetration by breaking the rock to pieces, it still does not display in its pieces anything inward and opened. The stone has instantly withdrawn again into the same dull press and bulk of its pieces. (UK, 33)

Yet, one may then try another, less direct, seemingly less violent way. Heidegger continues:

> If we try to grasp the stone's heaviness in another way, by placing the stone on scales, we merely bring the heaviness into the form of a calculated weight. This perhaps very precise determination of the stone remains a number, but the press of its heaviness has withdrawn from us [*das Lasten hat sich uns entzogen*]. . . . It shows itself only when it remains undisclosed and unexplained. Earth thus shatters every attempt to penetrate into it.

Thus does earth escape, despite all devastation, the calculative assault of technology.

Like the earth to which it belongs, stone shows itself only when it is brought into the open *as* self-secluding, as closed off, as self-closed. This is what the artwork and only the artwork can do; this is what the temple does precisely by its way of being made of stone.

Because it is made of stone, the temple sets forth earth into the open, the world, and thus gives place to that strife of world and earth that Heidegger identifies as the truth of art. No longer is its stoneness something that would limit the temple's capacity to present truth in its proper depth, that would, hence, prevent the temple from bringing the truth to one at that depth, consigning it to the past, making the temple for us something past. On the contrary, its stoneness is precisely what allows it to present—or rather, to give place to—the impenetrable depth of truth, the self-closure of earth, the self-concealing concealment that constitutes the *lethe* of *aletheia*. For through the shining of the temple's stones—its beauty—that which is dead and gone, that which is *vorbei*, that whose absence is sealed, closed off, is nonetheless brought to light.

Notes

John McCumber, Introduction: Transforming Thought

1. Aquinas accomplishes this by what I call the "docilization" of matter: see my *Diakena: Metaphysics, Oppression, and Heidegger's Challenge,* forthcoming.

2. I have discussed this in more detail in my *Poetic Interaction* (Chicago: University of Chicago Press, 1989), 247ff.

3. Cf. Rodolphe Gasché, *The Tain of the Mirror* (Cambridge: Harvard University Press, 1986); for Gasché's account of Derrida, of course, the tain is not stable but rather a differantial infrastructure of destabilization.

4. To be sure, such self-creation had for Kant to proceed in accordance with rules, in order to qualify as "rational." But the rules in question inhered in reason's own nature: reason could choose to be itself or not to be itself, and remained free to create itself or surrender to "inclination."

5. Richard Boyd, Philip Gasper, and J. D. Trout, "Introduction" to Boyd, Gasper, and Trout, *The Philosophy of Science* (Cambridge: MIT Press, 1991), xiii.

6. G. W. F. Hegel, *Werke,* 20 vols., ed. Eva Moldenhauer and Karl Markus Michel (Frankfurt: Suhrkamp, 1970–71), vol. 13, 24, 142; English translation, Hegel, *Aesthetics,* 2 vols. with consecutive pagination, trans. T. M. Knox (Oxford: Oxford University Press, 1975), 10, 103. For further discussion of the "death of science," see *The End of Science?* ed. Richard Q. Elvee (Lanham: University Press of America, 1992), especially the papers by Ian Hacking, Mary Hesse, and Gunther Stent. Sheldon Glashow delivers precisely the kind of "lament" that Hegel refers to here.

7. Hegel, *Enzyklopädie,* in Hegel, *Werke,* vol. 9, para. 393 Zus.; paragraph numbers are valid for the English translation, *Hegel's Philosophy of Nature,* ed. M. J. Petry (London: Allen and Unwin, 1970); Martin Heidegger, *Die Selbstbehauptung der deutschen Universität* (Frankfurt: Klostermann, 1983).

8. See my *Poetic Interaction,* 216f.

9. See Hegel, *Phänomenologie des Geistes,* 6th ed., ed. Johannes Hoffmeister (Hamburg: Meiner, 1952), 229f., 362f.; English translation, Hegel, *Phenomenology of Spirit,* trans. A. V. Miller (Oxford: Oxford University Press, 1979), 187, 308f. Also see my *Poetic Interaction,* 63–86.

10. For an account of this see my *The Company of Words* (Evanston: Northwestern University Press, 1993), chapter 11, passim.

11. See my *Poetic Interaction,* 380ff.

12. Hegel, *Werke*, vol. 7; English translation, Hegel, *Philosophy of Right*, trans. T. M. Knox (Oxford: Oxford University Press), 23.

13. Martin Heidegger, *Die Selbstbehauptung der deutschen Universität*, 17.

14. Ibid., 14f.

Dominique Janicaud, Heidegger-Hegel: An Impossible "Dialogue"?

1. Among the numerous allusions to Hegel in the *Grundprobleme der Phänomenologie*, the two most significant appear to contradict each other: "The overcoming [*Überwindung*] of Hegel is the necessary step which must be made in the development of Western philosophy, if the latter is to remain alive at all." Martin Heidegger, *The Basic Problems of Phenomenology*, trans. Albert Hofstader (Bloomington: Indiana University Press, 1982), 178. Elsewhere, however (in a passage pointed out by Michel Haar), we read that "Hegel saw all that it was possible to see . . ." (ibid., 282). In fact, these two assertions are not incompatible: the context of the latter allows us to determine its precise meaning and to unravel the apparent contradiction. Hegel brought the presuppositions of Platonism to their completion, but the finitude [*Endlichkeit*] of the system remains to be comprehended, by beginning again from the "radical center of philosophy" as such. It is not a matter of outdoing Hegel on his own ground, but of "going beyond him" by allowing his philosophy "to come to itself" [*zu sich selbst zu kommen*]. This last problematic is already present *in ovo*, but in a particularly elliptic manner, especially in that "fundamental ontology" is still thought as a further deepening [*approfondissement*] of philosophy. The later *Kehre* [turning] will allow *thinking* as such to be distinguished from philosophy and from metaphysics.

2. Heidegger, *Hegel's Phenomenology of Spirit*, trans. Parvis Emad and Kenneth Maly (Bloomington: Indiana University Press, 1988), 28.

3. Homage is paid to Hegel as early as *Die Kategorien- und Bedeutungslehre des Duns Scotus* (1915).

4. Heidegger, *Nietzsche* (Pfullingen: Neske, 1961), vol. 1, 9; English translation, Heidegger, *Nietzsche*, trans. David Farrell Krell (San Francisco: Harper and Row, 1984), vol. 1, xv.

5. See Heidegger's "Letter on Humanism," in *Basic Writings*, trans. David Farrell Krell (New York: Harper and Row, 1976), 193–242.

6. Heidegger, "Die onto-theo-logische Verfassung der Mataphysik," in *Identität und Differenz* (Pfullingen: Neske, 1957), 37; *Identity and Difference*, trans. Joan Stambaugh (New York: Harper and Row, 1969), 42.

7. Hegel, *Philosophy of Nature*, trans. M. J. Petry (New York: Humanities Press, 1970), § 258, 229; G. W. F. Hegel, *Enzyklopädie der philosophischen Wissenschaften im Grundisse*, in Hegel, *Werke*, ed. Eva Moldenhauer and Karl Markus Mechel (Frankfurt: Suhrkamp, 1970–71), vol. 9, 48.

8. See Heidegger, "Letter on Humanism," in *Basic Writings*, 242.

9. Heidegger, "Hegel und die Griechen," in *Die Gegenwart der Griechen im neueren Denken* (Tübingen: Mohr, 1960), 43.

10. "Die Vollendung der Metaphysik beginnt mit Hegels Metaphysick des absoluten Wissens als des Willens des Geistes." Heidegger, *Vorträge und Aufsätze* (Pfullingen: Neske, 1954), 76; "The completion of metaphysics begins with Hegel's metaphysics of absolute knowledge as the Spirit of will." Heidegger, "Overcoming Metaphysics," in *The End of Philosophy*, trans. Joan Stambaugh (New York: Harper and Row, 1973), 89.

11. Heidegger, *Identity and Difference*, 49; *Identität und Differenz*, 45.

12. Ibid., 37; 42.

13. Ibid.

14. Ibid., 41; 45.

15. Ibid.

16. Ibid., 39; 44.

17. Hegel, *Wissenschaft der Logik* (Hamburg: Meiner, 1934), vol. 2, 32–34; Hegel, *Science of Logic*, trans. A. V. Miller (New York: Humanities Press, 1976), 417.

18. See Heidegger, "Hegels Begriff der Erfahrung," in *Holzwege* (Frankfurt: Klostermann, 1963), 161; *Hegel's Concept of Experience* (New York: Harper and Row, 1970), 105. On the Hegel-Heidegger confrontation concerning *difference*, see §IV of "Heideggeriana," in D. Janicaud and J.-F. Mattei, *Heidegger from Metaphysics to Thought*, trans. Michael Gendre (Albany: SUNY Press, 1995), 15–38.

19. Heidegger, *Identity and Difference*, 59; *Identität und Differenz*, 56.

20. Ibid., 41; 45.

21. Heidegger, *Holzwege*, 177; *Hegel's Concept of Experience*, 132.

22. See Heidegger, "Hegel und die Griechen."

23. This rupture is effected and explained in § 82 of *Being and Time*, trans. J. Macquarrie and E. Robinson (New York: Harper and Row, 1962), 480–86.

24. Heidegger, *Hegel's Phenomenology of Spirit*, 146.

25. Ibid., 145.

26. Heidegger, "The Anaximander Fragment," in *Early Greek Thinking*, ed. David Farrell Krell and Frank A. Capuzzi (San Francisco: Harper and Row, 1975), 25–27; "Der Spruch des Anaximander," in *Holzwege*, 310–11.

27. Heidegger, "Summary of a Seminar on the Lecture, 'Time and Being,'" in Heidegger, *On Time and Being*, trans. John Stambaugh (New York: Harper and Row, 1972), 50. "Protokoll zu einem Seminar über den Vortrag "Zeit und Sein," in *Zur Sache des Denkens*, 53.

28. Heidegger, *On Time and Being*, 49; *Zur Sache des Denkens*, 53.

29. Heidegger, *Identity and Difference*, 47–48; *Identität und Differenz*, 43–44.

30. Hegel, *Science of Logic*, 581; *Wissenschaft der Logik*, vol. 2, 217.

31. Hegel, *Science of Logic*, 581. "Die wahrhafte Widerlegung muss in die Kraft des Gegners eingehen und sich in den Umkreis seiner Stärke stellen." Hegel, *Wissenschaft der Logik*, vol. 2, 218.

32. Heidegger, *Identity and Difference*, 48; *Identität und Differenz*, 44.

33. Hegel writes: "Only in its consummation is it the absolute" (*Science of Logic*, 829). "Nur in seiner Vollendung ist es das Absolute" (*Wissenschaft der Logik*, vol. 2, 490).

34. See Heidegger, *On Time and Being*, 48; *Zur Sache des Denkens*, 52.

35. Hegel, *Logic*, trans. William Wallace (Oxford: Clarendon, 1975), 3; *Enzyklopädie*, in *Werke*, vol. 8, § 1, 41. Note particularly the last sentence: "The difficulty of making a *Beginning* immediately comes up, because any beginning, as something *immediate*, makes a presupposition—or, rather, is one" (translation altered). See also § 6.

36. On the speculative import of "authentic scepticism," see Hegel, "Verhältnis des Skeptizismus zur Philosophie," in *Werke*, vol. 2, 213–72.

37. See Hegel, *Science of Logic*, 389; *Wissenschaft der Logik*, vol. 2, 3.

38. On the complex relations among the Hegelian thinking of destiny, its rational determinations and its "unthought," see Dominique Janicaud, *Hegel et le destin de la Grèce* (Paris: Vrin, 1975), 317.

39. See Heidegger, *Identity and Difference*, 45; *Identität und Differenz*, 41.

40. Ibid. "But inasmuch as Hegel's thinking belongs to a period of history (this does not mean at all that it is belongs to the past) . . ." "Insofern nun aber Hegels Denken in eine Epoche der Geschichte gehört (dies meint beileibe nicht zum Vergangenen)."

41. " . . . niemals im Geheimnis die Weisheit liegt." Hegel, *Vorlesungen über die Philosophie der Weltgeschichte* (Hamburg: Meiner, 1923), vol. 3, 569.

42. "Das zuerst verborgene und verschlossene Wesen des Universums hat keine Kraft, die dem Mut des Erkennens Widerstand leisten könnte . . ." Hegel, *Einleitung in die Geschichte der Philosophie* (Berlin: Akademie-Verlag, 1966), 6; *Lectures on the Philosophy of History*, trans. J. Sibree, vol. 1 (London: G. Bell, 1894), xliii.

43. Hegel, *Science of Logic*, 389; *Wissenschaft der Logik*, vol. 2, 3.

44. Hegel, *Enzyklopädie*, §20, 71; *Logic*, 29.

45. Hegel, *Wissenschaft der Logik*, vol. 2, 496; *Science of Logic*, 836.

46. See Heidegger, "The Thinker as Poet," in *Poetry, Language, Thought*, trans. Albert Hofstadter (New York: Harper and Row, 1975), 5, 9; *Aus der Erfahrung des Denkens*, 17, 9.

47. Heidegger, *On the Way to Language*, trans. Peter D. Hertz (San Franciso: Harper and Row, 1971), 3; *Unterwegs zur Sprache*, 88.

48. Heidegger, *Identity and Difference*, 72; *Identität und Differenz*, 71.

49. Ibid., 72.

50. Heidegger, *Early Greek Thinking*, 14; *Holzwege*, 298.

51. Michel Haar, "The History of Being and Its Hegelian Model," in this volume.

52. I am borrowing an expression from Jacques Taminiaux, who demonstrated, from another angle (the aesthetic), the "respective implications of the hermeneutical and speculative circles," and also the unavoidable tension that exists for Heidegger between "attention to the enigma" and the "solution to the philosophical problem of the essence of art." See Jacques Taminiaux, "The Hegelian Legacy in Heidegger's Overcoming of Aesthetics," in this volume.

53. Haar, "The History of Being," 46–47.

54. I have questioned this connection in Janicaud and Mattéi, *Heidegger from Metaphysics to Thought*, 37.

55. Hegel, *Science of Logic*, 588. "... *die Philosophie soll keine Erzählung dessen sein, was geschieht sondern eine Erkenntnis dessen, was wahr darin ist.*" Hegel, *Wissenschaft der Logik* vol. 2, 22.

56. Michel Haar, "Structures hégéliennes," 48.

57. Ibid.

58. Heidegger, *Hegel's Phenomenology of Spirit*, 74.

59. As I have already suggested in *Powers of the Rational: Science, Technology and the Future of Thought*, trans. Peg Birmingham and Elizabeth Birmingham (Bloomington: Indiana University Press, 1994), 216.

60. Heidegger, *Hegel's Phenomenology of Spirit*, 24.

61. Ibid., 30, 41.

62. Heidegger, *Hegel's Concept of Experience*, 85; "Hegels Begriff der Erfahrung," *Holzwege*, 150.

63. Heidegger, *Being and Time*, § 7, 50.

64. Heidegger, *Hegel's Phenomenology of Spirit*, 24.

65. Ibid., 75.

66. Ibid., 97. See also Heidegger, *Hegel's Concept of Experience*, 27: "The first section names the matter of philosophy" (translation altered). "Hegels Begriff," *Holzwege*, 117: "*Der erste Abschnitt nennt die Sache der Philosophie.*"

67. Heidegger, *Hegel's Concept of Experience*, 132; *Holzwege*, 177.

68. Heidegger, *Hegel's Phenomenology of Spirit*, 100.

Michel Haar, The History of Being and Its Hegelian Model

1. Martin Heidegger, *Zur Sache des Denkens* (Tübingen: Niemeyer, 1969), 84; hereinafter *ZSD*.

2. Martin Heidegger, *Holzwege*, 5th ed. (Frankfurt: Klostermann, 1979), 298; hereinafter *HW*.

3. Martin Heidegger, *Identität und Differenz*, 5th ed. (Pfullingen: Neske, 1976), 39.

4. Martin Heidegger, *Nietzsche*, 2 vols. (Pfullingen: Neske, 1961), 2:489; hereinafter *N*.

5. *ZSD*, 56.

6. *HW*, 307.

7. Hegel, *Leçons sur l'histoire de la philosophie*, trans. Gibelin (Paris: Gallimard, 1959), 156.

8. Hegel, *Die Vernunft in der Geschichte, A: Die Bestimmung des Geistes*, ed. J. Hoffmeister (Hamburg: Felix Meiner, 1955), 59.

9. Preface to Martin Heideger, *Vorträge und Aufsätze*, 3d ed. (Pfullingen: Neske, 1967); hereinafter *VA*. The opposition of *Vergangenes/Gewesenes* was already made in Heidegger, *Sein und Zeit*, 14th ed. (Tübingen: Niemeyer, 1977), 328: " 'So long' as Dasein factically exists it is never past, though indeed it has always already been in the sense of 'I have-been.' " See also Heidegger, *Gesamtausgabe* (Frankfurt: Klostermann, 1975–), vol. 24: *Grundprobleme der Phänomenologie* (hereinafter *GP*), 411 on "the ordinary concept of the past."

10. See *HW*, 295: "The whole of what has-been (das Ge-n~esene) is what has the character of a Geschick."

11. *N*, 2:481.

12. Cf. Martin Heidegger, "Principes de la pensée," *Martin Heidegger: Cahiers de l'Herne* 45 (1983), 75.

13. *N*, 2:388.

14. Martin Heidegger, "Was ist Metaphysik," in *HW*, 52.

15. *N*, 2:487.

16. Martin Heidegger, *Erläuterungen zu Höiderlins Dichtung* (Frankfurt: Klostermann, 1951), 106; hereinafter *EHD*.

17. Ibid., 84. "Gesetzt, dies Andenken denkt voraus, dann kann auch das Zurückdenken nicht ein 'Vergangenes' denken, dem nur der Bescheid des Unwiderruflichen zu leihen wäre. Das 'Denken an' das Kommende kann nur das 'Denken an' das Gewesene sein, worunter wir im Unterschied zum nur Vergangenen das fernher noch Wesende verstehen" "Given that thinking thinks forward, then thinking-back cannot think something 'gone by,' to which only the distinction of the irrevocable would be proper. Thinking 'of' what is coming can only be thinking 'of' what is past, by which, in distinction to what is merely 'gone by,' we mean what still holds sway" (translation John McCumber).

18. Martin Heidegger, *Was Heißt Denken?* (Tübingen: Niemeyer, 1954–), 95; hereinafter *WHD*.

19. *N*, 2:481.

20. *N*, 2:420.

21. "Every epoch of philosophy has in itself its own necessity." Martin Heidegger, *Die Technik und die Kehre* (Pfullingen: Neske, 1962), 66.

22. *VA*, 76.

23. *ZSD*, 56.

24. Martin Heidegger, *Der Satz vom Grund* (Pfullingen: Neske, 1962), 154.

25. *ZSD*, 56 (emphasis added).

26. Ibid.

27. *WHD*, 98.

28. For example, *N*, 2:444.

29. *N*, 2:435.

30. Ibid.

31. *N*, 2:428.

32. Called to mind as "vesperal," the planetary epoch is occasionally named "hesperial" (from the Greek *hespera*, evening), which means the twilight of the destiny of Being.

33. *N*, 2:423.

34. Emphasis added. Cf. *HW*, 223.

35. See Heidegger, "Der Spruch Anaximanders," in *HW*, 302.

36. Ibid.

37. Ibid.

38. *ZSD*, 44.

39. *ZSD*, 57.

40. "Nachwort" to "Was ist Metaphysik?"
41. *ZSD*, 25.
42. Ibid., 44.
43. *N*, 2:262.
44. Ibid.
45. Martin Heidegger, "The Overcoming of Metaphysics," in *VA*, 71.
46. *VA*, 36: cf. also *ZSD*, 58.
47. Martin Heidegger, *Gelassenheit* (Pfullingen: Neske, 1959), 37.
48. *N*, 2:202.
49. *HW*, 300.

David Kolb, Circulation and Constitution at the End of History

1. References to Hegel's works will be made in the text according to paragraph numbers in *E* (*Encyclopedia*), and *PR* (*Philosophy of Right*), and according to pages in the German and English editions in *WL* (*Science of Logic*, the Meiner *Gesammelte Werke* vol., page from the Oxford Miller translation). Some translations have been modified. I am grateful to John Burbidge, Rebecca Comay, David Cummiskey, John McCumber, and John Russon for comments on earlier versions of this essay.

2. A pair of 1989 articles by Francis Fukuyama in *Nation's Interest* helped fuel recent debate about Hegel's views on the end of history.

3. Unlike Hegel, Marx does not describe the structure of the final society in any detail; the future self-determining community should establish its own structures. Such communal voluntarism is anti-Hegelian. Habermas could also be seen as discussing the unblocking of circulation. While he doesn't believe that this is the end of history, he does share the view that in our age it is possible to remove barriers to fuller communal will-formation and self-determination. He differs from the earlier views of Adorno, Horkheimer, and Benjamin, for whom history has become at least stalled, if not ended, in our protean system of domination.

4. See for example Richard Rorty, *Contingency, Irony, and Solidarity* (Cambridge: Cambridge University Press, 1989).

5. See the discussions in my *The Critique of Pure Modernity: Hegel, Heidegger, and After* (Chicago: University of Chicago Press, 1987), and "What Is Open and What Is Closed in the Philosophy of Hegel," *Philosophical Topics* 19, no. 2 (Fall 1991). There I try to see what kind of closure is appropriate to Hegel's theory, and suggest an argument that such closure cannot be achieved.

6. On a sufficient level of generality, this description would include Max Weber's theory of modernization.

7. "The individual is more than merely an entity bounded on all sides, but *this more belongs to another sphere of the concept;* in the metaphysics of being, the individual is simply a determinate something" (*WL* 21, 100f./113f., my emphasis).

8. There is an analogy in the language of physics: there can be many trajectories through a state space; the end of history cannot merely be the end of

one such trajectory; it must be itself specially related to the dimensionality and metric of the state space.

9. Hegel summarizes the different types of infinities that occur in the first part of the logic during his discussion of measure (*WL* 21, 370/371). Elsewhere in the *Logic* Hegel makes caustic remarks about those who find the infinite depths of space and time conceptually significant. They provide only more and more stars, more of the same kind of facts. What should be impressive is the relations of measure and law which allow the grasping of these immensities (see *WL* 21, 222/228). Presumably he would make similar remarks about those who would exclaim over the depth and variety of history without seeking its underlying pattern.

10. The ordered series arrives in Hegel's second discussion of the bad infinite. During the logical treatment of quantity a certain generative relation produces the infinite number series. But the series of the integers, while ordered, is not yet teleological. The series is once more an alternating affirmation of identity and otherness, without any cumulation or finality. Because at this stage quantity is being thought in abstraction from quality, each unit of the series is thought as abstractly similar in quality to the others. There are no resources here for thinking history or finality.

11. After quantity and quality are joined in the category of "measure" another infinite arises. After the famous treatment of quantity changing into quality comes a sub-section devoted to "the measureless" (*WL* 21, 369/371). This describes a measureless substrate that remains while the measure ratios of associated quantities vary. As the quantitative ratios alter, the associated qualities change. Further quantitative changes then lead to further qualities, and so on. The individual phases can be ordered through their measures, and unified because of their substrate. So the series as a whole can be conceived as ordered and as having a direction of quantitative growth.

12. In addition, there is the problem of justifying the choice of one measure among the many available. Also, this procedure contains no assurance that the qualities associated with the quantitative ratios will themselves show any interesting order.

13. It may seem curious that in the second major part of the *Logic*, on essence, the bad infinite makes only one major appearance, as a directionless wandering through a space of possible grounds among which explanation meanders until the category of "complete ground" is established to put limits on what can count as a legitimate ground (*WL* 11, 311/466). However, all of the categories of the essence section attempt to think a totality in which particular determinations stem from an inner essence. This is an advance because it allows that the field of possible states is not simply given but is dependent on some deeper principle. But the categories of essence fail to stabilize the relation between the inner essence and the field of possible determinate manifestations.

14. Hegel connects *Repulsion* to *abstoßen* and *aussersichkommen*. Repulsion is not a force, but a logical category providing the conceptual condition for thinking a multiplicity of identical units that might be subject to some empirical force (*WL*

21, 156/168). It is very important that repulsion is not an example of becoming, since it is not a transition from being into nothing or vice versa. It is an explication of the self-relation of being-for-self; "a self-subsistent whole of this kind, just because it is a real being-for-self, is at the same time a repulsion into distinct self-subsistent somethings" (*WL* 21, 344/347). In the section on quality repulsion occurs to the being-for-self unit. In the treatment of quantity repulsion occurs before the infinite number series; it affects the enclosed quantitative unit and so allows the infinite series to be thought. In the treatment of measure repulsion affects the enclosed measures that correlate with qualities, and so makes possible the categories of the nodal line and the measureless substrate.

15. Cf. Jacques Derrida, *La Dissémination* (Paris: Éditions du Seuil, 1972).

16. "Determinateness (*Bestimmtheit*) as such belongs to being and the qualitative [in the first part of the logic]; as determinateness of the concept [in the third part of the logic] it is particularity (*Besonderheit*). It is not a limit, as though it were related to an other beyond it; on the contrary . . . it is the proper, immanent moment of the universal; in particularity, therefore, the universal is not with an other (*bei einem Anderen*), but utterly with itself (*schlechthin bei sich selbst*)" (*WL* 12, 37/605).

17. "The concept, when it has developed into a concrete existence that is itself free, is none other than the I or pure self-consciousness" (*WL* 12, 17/583).

18. "The concept is absolute power just because it can freely abandon (*entlassen*) its difference (*Unterschied*) to the shape of self-subsistent diversity (*selbständiger Verschiedenheit*), outer necessity, contingency, caprice, opinion, which however must not be taken for more than the abstract aspect of nothingness" (*WL* 12, 39/608).

19. In Hegel's more technical terms, a syllogism is required whose middle term is not the particular (as in civil society), but the universal (as in the state). It turns out that the civil society is not an alternative to the state but a subordinate aspect of the more concrete unity. See my *The Critique of Pure Modernity,* chapters 4 and 6.

20. Most well known are Hegel's remarks on the intractable problems of poverty with its increasing disparities of wealth and the creation of a rabble of disaffected citizens. "The important question of how poverty is to be abolished is one of the most disturbing problems which agitate modern society" (*PR* §244A). He also worries about problems connected with interest group democracy. In party politics any group will be seen as only representing a particular set of interests, and so as exercising arbitrary power. The government is "opposed by the advocates of liberty as the mandates of a particular will, and branded as displays of arbitrary power. The will of the many expels the ministry from power and those who had formed the opposition fill the vacant places; but the latter having now become the government, meet with hostility from the many, and share the same fate. Thus agitation and unrest are perpetuated. This collision, this nodus, this problem is that with which history is now occupied and whose solution it has to work out in the future" (Hegel, *Philosophy of History,* trans. John Sibree [New York: Dover, 1956], 452).

21. The passage continues: "The fixity of the determinateness into which the understanding seems to run, the form of the imperishable, is that of self-relating universality. But this belongs properly to the concept; and consequently in this universality is to be found expressed, and infinitely close at hand, the dissolution of the finite. This universality directly refutes the determinateness of the finite and expresses its incongruity (*Unangemessenheit*) with the universality" (*WL* 12, 42/611).

22. It is in this way that I would attempt to include Hegel's remarks about the scene of world history moving to the Americas.

23. Notably missing in both thinkers is that Nietzschean or Darwinian memory that holds traces of earlier uses and former teleologies that were abruptly redirected by evolution or the will to power.

24. I have discussed the different movements of Hegel's and Heidegger's stories of history leading to the modern age in *The Critique of Pure Modernity.*

25. Many deconstructive accounts do tell a dominant final story that is classically modernist: that there are conditions that make possible meaning and discourse and society, and we have just recently become explicitly self-aware of these conditions, and that self-awareness will change our world henceforth. I have made some tentative steps toward distinguishing various ironic and nonironic stories and attitudes toward the (formal and other) conditions of discourse and society in *Postmodern Sophistications: Philosophy, Architecture, and Tradition* (Chicago: University of Chicago Press, 1990).

Robert Bernasconi, "We Philosophers": *Barbaros mēdeis eisitō*

Abbreviations

GA 32 Martin Heidegger, *Hegels Phänomenologie des Geistes, Gesamtausgabe* vol. 32 (Frankfurt: Klostermann, 1980).

HBE Martin Heidegger, "Hegels Begriff der Erfahrung," in *Holzwege*, Frankfurt: Klostermann, 1972, 105–92.

HCE Martin Heidegger, *Hegel's Concept of Experience* (New York: Harper and Row, 1970).

HG Martin Heidegger, "Hegel und die Griechen," *Wegmarken* (Frankfurt: Klostermann, 1967), 255–72.

HPS Martin Heidegger, *Hegel's Phenomenology of Spirit*, trans. P. Emad and K. Maly (Bloomington: Indiana University Press, 1988).

I G. W. F. Hegel, *Introduction to the Lectures on the History of Philosophy*, trans. T. M. Knox and A. V. Miller (Oxford: Oxford University Press, 1985).

IaD Martin Heidegger, *Identity and Difference*, trans. J. Stambaugh (New York: Harper and Row, 1969).

ID Martin Heidegger, *Identität und Differenz* (Pfullingen: Neske, 1957).

PG G. W. F. Hegel, *Phänomenologie des Geistes*, ed. W. Bonsiepen and R. Heede, *Gesammelte Werke*, vol. 9 (Hamburg: Meiner, 1980).

PS G. W. F. Hegel, *Phenomenology of Spirit*, trans. A. V. Miller (Oxford: Oxford University Press, 1977).
V6 G. W. F. Hegel, *Vorlesungen über die Geschichte der Philosophie.* Teil 1, Vorlesungen 6, ed. Pierre Garniron and Walter Jaeschke (Hamburg: Meiner, 1994).

1. In a note appended to the text, Heidegger explains that *Hegel's Concept of Experience* arose from seminars and lectures from the academic year 1942–43 (HBE, 344; *HCE*, 155).

2. See further R. Bernasconi, "Comment on Religion and Culture in Hegel," in *Hegel's Philosophy of Action*, ed. L. S. Stepelevich and D. Lamb (Atlantic Highlands: Humanities Press, 1983), 115–23.

3. See also *Vorlesungen über die Geschichte der Philosophie*, vol. 2, Theorie Werkausgabe 19 (Frankfurt: Suhrkamp, 1975), 44; *Lectures on the History of Philosophy*, vol. 2, trans. E. S. Haldane and Frances H. Simson (London: Routledge, 1968), 34.

4. It was the second edition, prepared after Hegel's death by Johannes Schulze, which first adopted the now familiar title *Phänomenologie des Geistes.* Hegel already announced this change in the second edition of the *Science of Logic* (1832) when he added in a footnote to the preface to the first edition which read "This title will not be repeated in the second edition which will be published next Easter." *Wissenschaft der Logik*, in *Gesammelte Werke*, vol. 21, ed. F. Hogemann and W. Jaeschke (Hamburg: Meiner, 1985), 9 n.; *Science of Logic*, trans. A. V. Miller (London: Allen and Unwin, 1969), 29 n.

5. For a discussion of this ambiguity, especially insofar as Hegel addresses it in the preface, see John Sallis, "Hegel's Concept of Presentation," *Hegel-Studien* 12 (1977), 129–56. Under the title "the double position of the Phenomenology of Spirit," this is the focus of Heidegger's reading of Hegel in the 1930–31 lecture course (*GA* 32, 12ff.; *HPS*, 9ff.).

6. F. Nicolin, "Zum Titelproblem der *Phänomenologie des Geistes*," *Hegel-Studien* 4 (1967), 125–76.

7. See P.-J. Labarrière, *Structures et mouvement dialectique dans la Phénoménologie de l'esprit de Hegel* (Paris: Aubier, 1985), 209.

8. K. R. Dove, "Hegel's Phenomenological Method," *Review of Metaphysics* 23, no. 4 (1969–70), 635.

9. Ibid., 640–41.

10. W. Marx, *Hegel's Phänomenologie des Geistes* (Frankfurt: Klostermann, 1971), 94, 100; *Hegel's Phenomenology of Spirit*, trans. Peter Heath (New York: Harper and Row, 1975), 78, 84.

11. Joseph Flay, *Hegel's Quest for Certainty* (Albany: State University of New York Press, 1984), 240.

12. David M. Parry, *Hegel's Phenomenology of the "We"* (New York: Peter Lang, 1988), 228–29. Parry hesitates to identify the "we" simply with absolute knowing, in a way that is perhaps somewhat similar to Heidegger's hesitation in the 1930–31 lecture course as I shall show it later. However, Parry's discussion is curtailed

and somewhat unclear because he seems to sense at this point the problem of the double reading of the *Phenomenology* without having developed the resources to develop it further. Ibid., 229–30.

13. Otto Pöggeler in a subclause identifies the "for us" as "for us philosophers who are already familiar with the whole of the speculative philosophy," but this phrase seems to suggest the whole system and so begs the question of the introduction to science that the "we" and the "for us" address: Pöggeler, *Hegels Idee der Phänomenologie des Geistes* (Freiburg: Alber, 1973), 244. Clearly the issues raised here can only be clarified by a rereading of the *Phenomenology*, in the absence of which I refer to two of my early efforts to indicate what that means for the interpretation of certain pages within the text. See "Hegel and Levinas. The Possibility of Forgiveness and Reconciliation," *Archivio di Filosofia* 54 (1986), 325–46; and "Persons and Masks: The Phenomenology of Spirit and Its Laws," in *Hegel and Legal Theory*, ed. Drucilla Cornell, Michel Rosenfeld, and David Gray Carlson (New York: Routledge, 1991), 78–93.

14. The sense of "double reading" being introduced here should not be confused with the employment of the same phrase in a similar context by Jacques Taminiaux. "D'une ontologie fondamentale à l'autre: la double lecture de Hegel," in *Lectures de l'ontologie fondamentale* (Grenoble: Millon, 1989), 193–210; *Heidegger and the Project of Fundamental Ontology*, trans. Michael Gendre (Albany: SUNY Press, 1991), 145–59.

15. An important implication of the interpretation being developed here is that it casts severe doubt on the numerous articles about the *Phenomenology* in which one stage of the dialectic is examined in isolation from the remainder of the book. Such articles restrict themselves methodologically to the observations of a first-time reader of the book insofar as they demand that Hegel should deduce the next form of consciousness from the one which immediately preceded it. Sometimes the writers of these articles follow the method rigorously and, focusing on the book's first few chapters, give no indication at all of having read to the end of the book.

16. It is certainly true that the "we" and the "for us" are most prominent in the first chapter of the book, but an analysis of their occurrences shows that they do not diminish in importance as the work develops, even where the frequency is somewhat less. For a list of Hegel's uses of these terms, see J. Gauvin, *Wortindex zur Phänomenologie des Geistes, Hegel-Studien* 14 (1984). A detailed analysis of the "for us" is to be found in J. Gauvin, "'Für Uns' dans la Phénoménologie de l'Esprit," *Archives de Philosophie* 33, (1970), 829–54.

17. For a similar view which emphasizes the "Unterwegscharakter" of the "for us," see K. Tsujimura, "Das Hegelsche 'für uns,'" *Kant oder Hegel?*, ed. D. Henrich (Stuttgart: Klett-Cotta, 1983), 376.

18. In commenting on Heidegger's acknowledgment of the ambiguity of Hegel's description of a science that is itself an appearance (HBE, 129; *HCE*, 48), Timothy Bahti observes how Heidegger "converted Hegel's ambiguity and its twofold character into a single, proper meaning through its referral to us as the observers of the appearance and the locus of its meaning," but Bahti does not

interrogate Heidegger's interpretation of the "we" to see how it reconstitutes the ambiguity in another way. "The Indifferent Reader: The Performance of Hegel's Introduction to the *Phenomenology*," *Diacritics* 11 (1981), 75–76.

19. There is therefore a parallel between Heidegger's interpretation of Hegel (no Absolute without us) and Heidegger's own problematic: no Being without human being, no Being without us. See *Der Ursprung des Kunstwerkes* (Stuttgart: Reclam, 1967), 100; *Poetry, Language, Thought,* trans. A. Hofstadter (New York: Harper and Row, 1971), 87.

20. For the contrast between Hegel's and Heidegger's relation to the past as *Erinnerung,* see Dennis Schmidt, *The Ubiquity of the Finite* (Cambridge: MIT Press, 1988), 151; and Robert Bernasconi, *The Question of Language in Heidegger's History of Being* (Atlantic Highlands: Humanities Press, 1985), 9–12.

21. Andrzej Warminski in his instructive reading of *Hegel's Concept of Experience* marks some of those differences in detail. He has highlighted some of the places where Heidegger no longer says "we" to include Hegel. He also shows how Heidegger appropriates Hegel's "we" for his own thought, as when he identifies it as those who skeptically pay heed to the Being of beings. Warminski has less to say, however, on the "we" that is constituted in the course of Heidegger's reading of Hegel, and that is my interest here. "Parentheses: Hegel by Heidegger," in *Readings in Interpretation* (Minneapolis: University of Minnesota Press, 1987), 112–62.

22. The phrase is Adriaan Peperzak's from his "Einige Fragen zum Thema 'Hegel und Heidegger,'" in *Heideggers These vom Ende der Philosophie,* ed. M. F. Fresco, R. J. A. van Dijk, and H. W. Peter Vijgeboom (Bonn: Bouvier, 1989), 61. One cannot fail to recall other, earlier, contexts in which Heidegger said "we" and meant "we Germans." See Robert Bernasconi, "'I will tell you who you are.' Heidegger on Greco-German Destiny and Amerikanismus," in *From Phenomenology to Thought, Errancy, and Desire,* ed. Babette E. Babich (Dordrecht: Kluwer, 1995), 301–13.

23. M. Heidegger, *Was ist das—die Philosophie?* (Pfullingen: Neske, 1963), 13; *What Is Philosophy?* trans. W. Kluback and J. T. Wilde (London: Vision, 1972), 31. See also Heidegger, *Was heisst Denken?* (Tübingen: Niemeyer, 1971), 136; *What Is Called Thinking?* trans. F. D. Wieck and J. Glenn Gray (New York: Harper and Row, 1968), 224. However, there are other passages that indicate that Heidegger at least thought it worth asking if Occident and Orient alike might not be overwhelmed "transcending what is merely European" (*Holzwege,* 300). See Robert Bernasconi, "Heidegger and the Invention of the Western Philosophical Tradition," *Journal of the British Society for Phenomenology,* 26, no. 3 (October 1995), 240–54; and "Heidegger's Other Sins of Omission," *American Catholic Philosophical Quarterly,* 69, no. 2 (1995), 333–50.

24. Heidegger cites the famous inscription from the entrance to Plato's Academy, "*Ageōmetrētos mēdeis eisitō,*" in *Die Frage nach dem Ding* (Tübingen: Niemeyer, 1962), 58; *What Is a Thing?* trans. W. B. Barton and Vera Deutsch (Chicago: Regnery, 1970), 75.

25. There is a history of controversy surrounding the identification partic-

ularly of the first of the religions discussed by Hegel. The proposal that Judaism was meant is argued by Walter Jaeschke. See *Vernunft in der Religion* (Stuttgart-Bad Cannstatt: Frommann-Holzboog, 1986), 209–15; *Reason in Religion,* trans. J. Michael Stewart and Peter Hodgson (Berkeley: University of California Press, 1990), 198–204.

26. This claim is modified or more precisely complicated in Robert Bernasconi, "With What Must the Philosophy of World History Begin?" in *Nineteenth Century Contexts,* forthcoming.

27. See Robert Bernasconi, "The Anglican Bishop and the Pagan Priests: Warburton and the Hermeneutics of Egyptian Hieroglyphs," *Archivio di Filosofia* 60 (1992), 131–44; and "Krimskrams," in *Interrogating the Tradition,* ed. J. Sallis and C. Scott (Albany: SUNY Press, forthcoming). For discussions of the Egyptian philosophy and religion that Hegel knew and copied in his youth, see G. W. F. Hegel, *Frühe Exzerpte,* ed. F. Nicolin, in *Gesammelte Werke,* vol. 3 (Hamburg: Meiner, 1991), 113–14, 175–76. For Hegel's mature view of Egypt, see Jay Lampert, "Hegel and Ancient Egypt: History and Becoming," *International Philosophical Quarterly* 35, no. 1 (1995), 43–58.

28. Hegel, *Vorlesungen über die Geschichte der Philosophie.* Teil 2, Vorlesungen 7, ed. P. Garniron and W. Jaeschke (Hamburg: Meiner, 1989), 1.

29. "Nur noch ein Gott kann uns retten," *Der Spiegel* 23 (1976), 217; "*Der Spiegel* Interview with Martin Heidegger," trans. Lisa Harries, in *Martin Heidegger and National Socialism,* ed. Gunther Neske and Emil Kettering (New York: Paragon House, 1990), 63.

30. K. Rosenkranz, *Hegel als deutscher Nationalphilosoph* (Leipzig: Duncker and Humbolt, 1870). For some of the background, although Rosenkranz's book is not mentioned, see Domenico Losurdo, *Hegel und das deutsche Erbe* (Köln: Pahl-Rugenstein, 1989).

31. The most important sources for an understanding of this issue in Heidegger was his lecture courses on Hölderlin, *Hölderlins Hymnen "Germanien" und "Der Rhein"* (Frankfurt: Klostermann, 1980); *Hölderlins Hymne "Andenken"* (Frankfurt: Klostermann, 1982); and *Hölderlins Hymne "Der Ister"* (Frankfurt: Klostermann, 1986). See Robert Bernasconi, " 'Poet of Poets: Poet of the Germans,' " in *Heidegger in Question: The Art of Existing* (Atlantic Highlands: Humanities Press, 1993), 135–48.

32. A somewhat generous defense of Hegel along these lines was developed by W. H. Walsh in "Principle and Prejudice in Hegel's Philosophy of History," in *Hegel's Political Philosophy,* ed. Z. A. Pelczynski (Cambridge: Cambridge University Press, 1971), 181–98, esp. 193.

33. The reference is, of course, to Hegel's description of Africa. See *Vorlesungen über die Philosophie der Weltgeschichte,* vol. 1: *Die Vernunft in der Geschichte,* ed. J. Hoffmeister (Hamburg: Meiner, 1980), 234; *Lectures on the Philosophy of World History,* trans. H. B. Nisbet (Cambridge: Cambridge University Press, 1975), 190. See Robert Bernasconi, "Hegel at the Court of the Ashanti," in *Hegel after Derrida,* ed. Stuart Barnett (London: Routledge, 1998), 41–63.

34. Hegel, *Grundlinien der Philosophie des Rechts* (Frankfurt: Suhrkamp,

1978), § 166, 318–20; *Elements of the Philosophy of Right*, trans. H. S. Nisbet, (Cambridge: Cambridge University Press, 1991), 206–7. See further Susan M. Easton, "Hegel and Feminism," in *Hegel and Modern Philosophy*, ed. David Lamb (London: Croom Helm, 1987), 30–55.

35. Martin Heidegger, *Unterwegs zur Sprache* (Pfullingen: Neske, 1971), 87, 131; *On the Way to Language*, trans. P. D. Hertz (New York: Harper and Row, 1971), 3, 37.

36. The reading of Hegel outlined in the second and third sections of this paper was worked out in my course on the *Phenomenology of Spirit* that was given at Essex University almost every spring term between 1979 and 1988 and at Vanderbilt University in the fall semester of 1987. I am grateful to the students for their participation and forbearance. This reading was summarized in lecture form in papers delivered at St. John's College, Annapolis, and to the Department of Comparative Literature at the State University of New York at Buffalo in the fall of 1987. Earlier versions of the whole paper were given at DePaul University and the University of Toronto in January and February 1992 respectively. I would like to thank both audiences, and particularly Nahum Chandler, Rebecca Comay, Stephen Houlgate, David Krell, Amit Sen, and Peter Simpson, for their questions and comments, which have contributed to the final form of this essay. Rebecca Comay's comments on the penultimate draft of the essay were especially helpful to fine-tuning the argument and its presentation. For its publication now I have added references to some recent essays in which I have since developed in more detail certain themes of the paper. I hope the excessive degree of self-citation will be excused by the reader as simply an effort to show that since writing this paper I have indeed tried to cash some of my promissory notes. I propose to take the issues further in a work in progress tentatively entitled *Philosophy's Paradoxical Parochialism.*

Dennis J. Schmidt, Ruins and Roses: Hegel and Heidegger on Sacrifice, Mourning, and Memory

Abbreviations

Texts by Hegel:

PG — *Phänomenologie des Geistes* (Hamburg: Meiner, 1952) (followed by paragraph number)
VPG — *Vorlesung über die Philosophie der Geschichte* (Hamburg: Meiner, 1971)
WL — *Wissenschaft der Logik* (Hamburg: Meiner, 1971)
PR — *Philosophie des Rechts* (Frankfurt: Suhrkamp, 1970)
FS — *Frühe Schriften* (Frankfurt: Suhrkamp, 1972)

Texts by Heiddegger:

WM — "Was ist Metaphysik?" *Wegmarken* (Frankfurt: Klostermann, 1972)
H — *Holzwege* (Frankfurt: Klostermann, 1972)
GA — *Gesamtausgabe* (Frankfurt: Klostermann, various years) (followed by volume number and page number)

US	*Unterwegs zur Sprache* (Pfullingen: Neske, 1975)
EM	*Einführung in die Metaphysik* (Tübingen: Niemeyer, 1966)
SA	*Die Selbstbestimmung der Deutschen Universität* (Frankfurt: Klostermann, 1983)

Other:

Theses	Walter Benjamin, "Über den Begriff der Geschichte," *Gesamme Þte Schriften* (Frankfurt: Suhrkamp, 1972) (followed by paragraph number)
Höl	Friedrich Hölderlin, *Samtliche Werke* (Berlin: Propyläen Verlag, 1923) (followed by volume number and page number)

1. Given Hegel's remarks about the speculative meaning of the skull as one of the ways in which Spirit comes to objectify and elaborate itself as "body" (see esp. *PG*, 328 on the skull as the *caput mortum*), this might qualify as one of the greatest puns in the history of philosophy.

2. Martineau, unpublished manuscript, 34.

3. Karl Löwith, *Mein Leben in Deutschland vor und mach 1933* (Frankfurt: Fischer, 1989).

4. William Richards, *Heidegger: Through Phenomenology to Thought* (The Hague: Nijhoff, 1967).

5. Though Kierkegaard does discuss Antigone. See esp. *Either/Or*, vol. 1, 153–63. Of special interest in his discussion are the remarks about Antigone's "secret" and the "pain of her solitude."

6. See Georges Bataille, "Hegel, la Mort et le sacrifice," in *Deucalion* 5 (1955), 21–43.

7. Here see David Farrell Krell, "Lucinde's Shame: Hegel, Sensuous Woman, and the Law," *Cardozo Law Review* 10, no. 5–6 (March–April 1989), 1673–86.

8. Ernst Bloch, *Natural Law and Human Degnity*, trans. D. Schmidt (Cambridge: MIT Press, 1986).

9. Luce Irigaray, *Speculum of the Other Woman*, trans. G. Gill (Ithaca: Cornell University Press, 1987).

10. For a more detailed discussion of the significance of the question of translation, see my "Hermeneutics and the Poetic Motion," in *Hermeneutics and the Poetic Motion*, ed. Dennis J. Schmidt (Albany: SUNY Press, 1990), 1–17.

11. For more detailed discussions of that claim see my "Poetry and 'the' Political," in *Festivals of Interpretation*, ed. K. Wright (Albany: SUNY Press, 1990); and "Black Milk and Blue: Heidegger and Celan on the Politics of Language" in *Word Traces*, ed. A. Fierettos (Baltimore: John Hopkins University Press, 1990).

12. I do not believe that it is an accident that Heidegger concludes the "*Tatsache und Gedanken*" with a reference to the "catastrophe" that broke in upon the Germans(!).

Jacques Taminiaux, The Hegelian Legacy in Heidegger's Overcoming of Aesthetics

1. Martin Heidegger, "The Origin of the Work of Art," in Heidegger, *Poetry, Language, Thought*, trans. Albert Hofstadter (New York: Harper and Row, 1971), 79. Hereafter cited as OWA.

2. *Les implications de cette ambigüité.*

3. In the original text, the German word for "real" is *wirklich.*

4. G. W. F. Hegel, *Sämtliche Werke*, vol. 18 (Berlin: Dunckes und Humbold, 1832–45), 321. Hereafter cited as *SW.*

5. G. W. F. Hegel, *Phenomenology of Spirit*, trans. A. V. Miller (Oxford: Oxford University Press, 1977), §§397–418, 237–52. Hereafter cited as *PS.*

6. English text translated from G. W. F. Hegel, *Leçons d'esthétique*, vol. 1, trans. S. Jankelevitch (Paris: Aubier, 1979), 11. Hereafter cited as *LA.*

7. Martin Heidegger, *Being and Time*, trans. J. Macquarrie and E. Robinson (New York: Harper and Row, 1962), 28 English/8 German. Hereafter cited as *BT.*

8. *Existentialia.*

9. Martin Heidegger, *Nietzsche*, vol. 1, trans. David Krell (New York: Harper and Row, 1979), 77ff. Hereafter cited as *N.*

10. Martin Heidegger, *The Question concerning Technology*, trans. William Lovitt (New York: Harper Torchbooks, 1977), 35.

Martin Donougho, Hegel's Art of Memory

1. Droysen in his *Historik* (1857) writes that "no one before, roughly, the middle of our century would have thought to speak of a history of music"; the claim is discussed by Carl Dahlhaus in his *Foundations of Music History* (Cambridge: Cambridge University Press, 1983), 40.

2. On this see J. M. Bernstein, *The Fate of Art: Aesthetic Alienation from Kant to Derrida and Adorno* (University Park: Pennsylvania State University Press, 1992), especially chapter 22, which deals with Heidegger. Bernstein points out (79) that Heidegger's attempt at overcoming aesthetics is more radical than Gadamer's, which takes aim principally at eighteenth-century theories of taste.

3. Martin Heidegger, *Holzwege*, in *Gesamtausgabe*, vol. 5 (Frankfurt: Klostermann, 1977), 68 (66 in the original edition); further citations in text as *H.* Cf. *Nietzsche: Der Wille zur Macht als Kunst* (1936/37), in *Gesamtausgabe*, vol. 43 (1985), 99–100.

4. John McCumber, *Poetic Interaction: Language, Freedom, Reason* (Chicago: University of Chicago Press, 1989), 13–14.

5. Cf. Barnett Newman's famous put-down of Susanne Langer: "Aesthetics is to art what ornithology is to the birds." Worse, ornithology is at least good for *something*, whereas aesthetics . . . ?

6. Paul de Man, "Hegel on the Sublime," in *Displacement: Derrida and After*, ed. Mark Krupnick (Bloomington: Indiana University Press, 1983), 139–53, 141

for the quotation following. De Man was working on Hegel at the time of his death, and one can only regret that more has not been published. He was the sort of critic of whom you could say that with enemies like that, who needs friends?

7. Peter Szondi, *Poetik und Geschichtsphilosophie,* vol. 1 (Frankfurt: Suhrkamp, 1974), "Hegel's Lehre von der Dichtung," 392f. For Szondi's understanding of "dialectic," cf. *On Textual Understanding and Other Essays* (Minneapolis: University of Minnesota Press, 1986), in a note on 189: "we use the words 'dialectic' and 'dialectical' in a way that confirms Hegel's usage but without accepting the implications of his system . . . [this would involve, e.g.,] the unity of contradictory terms, the turning of one term into its opposite, the act by which one term posits the negation of itself, and self-division."

8. I use "Romantic" with a capital letter to distinguish *our* usage from that current in Hegel's time, which understood "romantic" as (broadly speaking) Christian, Roman, medieval, etc. The former dates only from the mid- to late nineteenth century; see, e.g., René Wellek, *Essays of Criticism* (New Haven: Yale University Press, 1963), 136ff.

9. Martin Heidegger, *What Is Called Thinking?* (New York: Harper and Row, 1968), 11; translation amended.

10. See Heidegger, *Was heißt Denken?* 2d ed. (Tübingen: Niemeyer, 1961), 159 (20 June 1952); for some reason, the passage is not translated in the English edition. The immediate occasion is a recommendation to visit an exhibit in Freiburg on prisoners of war, to hearken to their "soundless voice." One wonders what "this annihilation" refers to, the war, or the effects upon Germany (division, imprisonment).

11. Hegel's emphasis tends to be universalist, however, as in the following: "The past belongs to memory [*Erinnerung*], and memory succeeds in clothing characters, events, and actions in the garment of universality, through which single external and contingent particulars do not penetrate." G. W. F. Hegel, *Vorlesungen über die Ästhetik,* in Hegel, *Werke,* 20 vols. (Frankfurt: Suhrkamp, 1970–71), vol. 13, 248; *Hegel's Aesthetics: Lectures on Fine Art,* trans. T. M. Knox (Oxford: Clarendon Press, 1975), 189. Henceforth cited in text as *LA* and *HA.*

12. See David Kolb, *The Critique of Pure Modernity: Hegel, Heidegger, and After* (Chicago: University of Chicago Press, 1986), passim.

13. *System of Ethical Life (1802/3) and First Philosophy of Spirit (1803/4),* trans. Henry Harris and T. N. Knox (Albany: SUNY Press, 1979), 221; *Gesammelte Werke,* vol. 6 (1975), 287. Mnemosyne was (is) mother of the muses.

14. See Harris and Knox, *System of Ethical Life,* 254–55 (quoting Rosenkranz).

15. The *Propaedeutic* is Rosenkranz's compilation of notes for Hegel's students. 1810–11 was the first year that Hegel lectured specifically on "psychology." An English translation of the 1817 *Encyclopedia* is now available in the series "The German Library," vol. 24, ed. Ernst Behler (New York: Continuum, 1990), 45–264.

16. G. W. F. Hegel, *Phänomenologie des Geistes,* in *Werke,* vol. 3, 188; *Phenomenology of Spirit,* trans. A. V. Miller (Oxford: Clarendon Press, 1977), 148. (Citations in text use these editions.) The context is significant: Rational consciousness declares that the world is *its* world, using the "pure," "abstract," or "empty"

mein/Meinen (my/opinion). The activity of remembering instances constitutes the first step toward proving that reality is rational and subjective—for me. Proleptically we may point to the relation between the subject and names, discussed below: there too the self is master, in that it lays down the ordering of names, yet must lay itself open to that order—must act empirically, that is.

17. See Jacques Derrida, "The Pit and the Pyramid," in Derrida, *Margins of Philosophy* (Chicago: University of Chicago Press, 1982), 69–108; and the second lecture ("The Art of Mémoires") in his *Mémoires for Paul de Man* (New York: Columbia University Press, 1986), 45–88. The latter self-consciously "commemorates" de Man's "Sign and Symbol in Hegel's *Aesthetics*," *Critical Inquiry* 8, no. 3 (1982), 761–75. See also John Sallis, "Ending(s): Imagination, Presentation, Spirit," in his *Spacings: Of Reason and Imagination in Texts of Kant, Fichte, and Hegel* (Chicago: University of Chicago Press, 1987), 132–57, 167–71; David Farrell Krell, *Of Memory, Reminiscence, and Writing: On the Verge* (Bloomington: Indiana University Press, 1990), chapter 5: "Of Pits and Pyramids," 204–39, replete with—a nod to Derrida—"Poe-faced" interruptions; and Deborah Chaffin, "Hegelian Dialectic and the Limits of Representation," in *The Textual Sublime: Deconstruction and Its Differences*, ed. Hugh Silverman and Gary Aylesworth (Albany: SUNY Press, 1990), 85–95. Not least, there is John McCumber, *The Company of Words: Hegel, Language, and Systematic Philosophy* (Evanston: Northwestern University Press, 1993), 220–38.

18. On which see now Mary Carruthers's remarkable *The Book of Memory: A Study of Memory in Medieval Culture* (Cambridge: Cambridge University Press, 1990), as well as Frances Yates, *The Art of Memory* (Chicago: University of Chicago Press, 1966). Hegel will argue that memory (as *Gedächtnis*) needs no help from sense or imagination.

19. G. W. F. Hegel, *Enzyklopädie der philosophischen Wissenschaften im Grundrisse* (1830), § 456 Zus. Elsewhere Hegel ranges art under "intuition," religion under "representation," and philosophy under "thought." But at § 449 Zus. he notes that the artist cannot be treated "merely as intuitive" (*bloß anschauend*), since he has to recollect and reflect a great deal.

20. See *Hegel's Philosophy of Subjective Spirit*, vol. 2: *Anthropology*, trans. Michael Petry (Dordrecht: Reidel, 1978), 412.

21. Cf. the earlier account of the mechanism of memory and selfhood in the 1805/6 "Philosophy of Spirit," which reads like a run-through for the later *Encyclopedia* version. Hegel speaks of the image as owned by the self, as "mine," preserved within the self, which is master. See *Gesammelte Werke*, vol. 8, 186–87. Hegel goes on: "Man is this night, this empty nothing, which contains everything within its simplicity—a wealth of infinitely many representations and images, none of which occur to him—or which are not current. This night, the interior of nature here existing—*pure self*—the enveloping night filled with phantasmagorical representations." (After having written this, I was delighted to come across the same passage cited by Slavoj Žižek in his *Looking Awry: An Introduction to Popular Culture through Jacques Lacan* [Cambridge: MIT Press, 1991], 87. He applies it to the strange shapes bodying forth from the eyes of Madeleine/Kim Novak in the title sequence of Hitchcock's *Vertigo*. Žižek's entire

account of how, for both Lacan and Hegel, the self is constructed from the outside in is apt here.)

22. In his edition (vol. 2, 495), Petry notes that "*Schacht*" was originally a measuring rod.

23. The *Propaedeutic*, besides having more to say on active imagination in dreams, somnambulism and madness, notes (under "productive imagination," its third division) that "poetic phantasy" serves not contingent states and moods but Ideas and spiritual truths, drawing out and configuring the essence of things; and further that "symbolizing" puts upon images a construction different from what they express, but one that nevertheless bears an "analogous" relation to them (§ 154). Hegel adds that the poet (*Dichter*) is a deep spirit, a "seer" apt to be misunderstood by common sense—and he repeats his own quip about no man being a hero to his valet.

24. Cf. the 1827 edition (*Gesammelte Werke*, vol. 19, 336), which speaks of "productive memory (Muse, Mnemosyne)" as well as the 1805/6 system (*Gesammelte Werke*, vol. 8, 189): "That ego looks on the thing only as sign, its essence however as ego, as meaning, as introreflected, is accordingly itself *ob*ject [*Gegenstand*]. . . . This is *language*, as *name-giving power*" (in the margin—"remembrance, creativity"). Kant's "productive imagination" left a rich legacy for Fichte and the Romantics.

25. I note in passing that this does not contradict what Hegel says in the *Aesthetics* (*LA*, 459; *HA*, 356), where the pyramid is thematized as "the simple image" of symbolic art. For what the image captures is the "truth" of the symbolic art-form, namely, that there is *no* iconic resemblance between the material of the signifier and what it signifies: the iconic image points to the arbitrary basis of semiotic resemblance!

26. Cf. again 1805/6, where Hegel writes (in a marginal note) that despite its simplicity, ego has many names. How can this be? Hegel's tortured syntax indicates the difficulty of thinking it. In brief, ego in its restlessness must continually attain fixity, as *fixed* (*befestigen*) plurality, as *order* (*Ordnung*) (192–93). Hegel paints a Schopenhauerian picture of indeterminate ego attaining individuation, like fate, not knowing what it wills. The ego exists as things, names, the deposit of order: "it makes itself *thing*, for it fixes within itself [*in sich*] the ordering of names; it fixes it *within itself*, i.e., it makes itself into this thoughtless order which has only the semblance of an order—in the *semblance* of *order* lies the ego—necessity, [the] self of aspects" (194). At the same time, the thing is implicitly nothing but ego; and Hegel adds in a marginal note (194) that working with names becomes *repetition*, for intelligence is indifferent to any sensuous differentia.

27. McCumber, *The Company of Words*, 384–85, with reference to the death of (representational) meaning, and rightly pointing out that Hegel does not—pace Derrida, Nancy, and others—locate progression in sublation (*Aufhebung*).

28. For example, *LA*, 399; *HA* 307–8. Hegel goes on to state that classical art is neither symbol nor sign; yet as we shall see, he is forced to call that particular bluff too.

29. *LA*, 395; *HA*, 304. This passage was dubbed by de Man ("Reply to Raymond Geuss," *Critical Inquiry* 10, no. 2 [1983], 383–90, at 386) "*the* canonical

sentence of Hegel's *Aesthetics*," though in the course of a dispute over "canonical" (i.e., literal) versus "literary" (here, deconstructive) reading of Hegel's texts—what he "means" and what he "says." That is to say, the passage is a *crux*, whose ambiguity is a challenge. I cannot go into this "*Auseinandersetzung*," save to suggest that de Man shows the methodological limitations to Geuss's orthodox exegesis.

30. De Man, "Sign and Symbol," e.g., 766, 770. As to de Man's further displacement, his argument, very schematically, is as follows: Hegel in effect has memory (as *Gedächtnis*) "efface" recollection (*Erinnerung*), rather than dialectically recuperating it. If art is nevertheless held to be an internalizing of the sensuous (or conversely, the sensuous shining of the Idea), as Hegel supposes (together with modern "Hegelian" interpreters of Romanticism), this position can be squared with the realization that thoughtful memory has dissolved any such interpenetration by suggesting that art is for us something past (see, e.g., 773). Hegel tries to have his aesthetic cake and dialectically—in thought—eat it too. De Man sees through this "ideology" of the aesthetic.

One should note that such a strategy of "resistance to Hegelian critical theory" (cf. his approach to the sublime, below) rests on the moot assumption that the *Aesthetics* is "[d]edicated to the preservation and the monumentalization of classical art"(773), i.e., an aesthetic recuperation still.

31. Croce brings that out very well in his attack on the theory of genre; and see the trenchant analysis in Francis Sparshott, *The Theory of the Arts* (Princeton: Princeton University Press, 1982), especially chapter 11. And just to put de Man in the picture, Hegelian dialectic cannot so easily be assimilated to a movement of "internalization" or "self-recuperation."

32. See *Lectures on the Philosophy of Religion*, vol. 2: *Determinate Religion* (Berkeley: University of California Press, 1987), where Hegel gives his elucidation of the text, including the words "The fruit of my loins is Helios," i.e., Apollo. Lacoue-Labarthe is mistaken in referring to Hegel's "jubilation" at this unveiling of Apollonian truth, of self-awareness; see his "La verité sublime," *Po&tique* 38 (1986), 83–116, at 100. One is tempted to speak rather of Lacoue-Labarthe's jubilation here at being able to put Hegel in his place.

33. I attempt that in an unpublished paper entitled "On the Hegelian Sublime," where essentially I take issue with de Man's ingenious reading of Hegel as a "prosaic" thinker, reducing figure to thought.

34. See, e.g., McCumber, *Poetic Interaction*, 313–14; Gary Shapiro, "From the Sublime to the Political: Some Historical Notes," *New Literary History* 16, no. 2 (1985), 213–35, especially 213f. and 223f. (noting Hegel's fusion of the two); and Lacoue-Labarthe, "La verité sublime."

Although Heidegger never uses the term, his descriptions of a Greek temple or a Van Gogh painting, say, do invoke certain effects, of the sublime and of desublimation alike. The artwork happens in the gap opened up between earth and world, a gap never quite closed. At the same time, Heidegger marshalls such language so as to (try and) *dis*place representation, *de*center the stable subject (e.g., of the Kantian sublime).

35. See Dieter Henrich, "Der Begriff der Schönheit in Schillers Ästhetik," *Zeitschrift für philosophische Forschung* 11 no. 4 (1957), 527–47, especially 546f.

36. Following Thomas Weiskel's influential *The Romantic Sublime: Studies in the Structure and Psychology of Transcendence* (Baltimore: Johns Hopkins University Press, 1976). Ironically, it is Weiskel who gives a speculative reading of the Kantian sublime, not Hegel himself.

37. Cf. de Man, "Sign and Symbol," 775: "Allegory functions, categorically and logically, like the defective cornerstone of the entire system." De Man reads the sublime as another such cornerstone; he blames Hegel, more precisely philosophical judgment, for this reduction of representation to prosaic terms—it forms part of the dialectical machine from which he wants to escape.

38. A point Walter Jaeschke makes with characteristic thoroughness in his "Kunst und Religion," in *Die Flucht in den Begriff: Materialen zu Hegels Religionsphilosophie*, ed. F. W. Graf and F. Wagner (Stuttgart: Klett Cotta, 1982), 163–95, especially 185f.

39. Hegel, *Vorlesungen über die Philosophie der Geschichte, Werke*, vol. 12 (Frankfurt: Suhrkamp, 1970–71), 293–94.

40. Lacoue-Labarthe calls it the "aestheticization" or "fiction" of the political: see *Heidegger, Art and Politics* (translation of *La Fiction du politique* [1987]) (Oxford: Blackwell, 1990), e.g., 66–70. He also cites Nancy's term, "immanentism."

41. Although communal memory gets a mention in the "*Geistphilosophie*" of 1804 (see above, n. 13), it no longer functions as an ideal; art enters in a very different—and ironic—guise in the fragment on "absolute consciousness" entitled "*ist nur die Form.*" Hegel, *Gesammelte Werke*, vol. 8, 279.

42. I speak of "him," because Hegel does, and the Greek tragedians were male; but we should recall that one of the players in this Hegelian drama, Antigone, is female, and it is woman who uncovers the subjectivity—or rather subjectivism—at the foundations of community.

43. Even here the painter is the "Zauberer" behind the scenes of *Entzauberung*, evoking the reaction "*He* can paint!" (see *LA*, 226; *HA*, 598).

44. Strictly speaking, the account of the persona/person process comes in the following chapter on religion.

45. True, both men came in time to question the integrity of self-reflexive subjectivity.

46. It is a little like Lacan's "what I want to say is what I am saying" or his consciousness of the analyst as the master to truth ("Moi, la Vérité, . . .")—which shows precisely the *im*possibility of escape from the slipperiness of positionality into an authentic self "beneath" or "behind" linguistic give and take.

47. *LA*, 237; *HA*, 607. See my "Remarks on 'Humanus heißt der Heilige' " in *Hegel-Studien* 17 (1982), 214–25. In the 1823 Lectures, "Humanus" enters instead as the supposed hero of an epical world history—a contradiction in aesthetic terms, Hegel declares, since such a figure would verge on the abstractly allegorical.

48. Dieter Henrich, *Hegel-Studien* 11 (Stuttgarter Hegel-Tage, 1970) (Bonn: Bouvier, 1974), 295–301; Henrich interprets Hegel's 1828–29 remarks on the end of romantic art as diagnosing such a Biedermeier-izing of art. See also his

"Kunst und Kunstphilosophie der Gegenwart," in *Immanente Ästhetik. Ästhetische Reflexionen*, ed. W. Iser (Munich: Paderborn, 1966), 11–32, for an extrapolation of Hegel to modern art, arguing that it must be postaesthetic, a formal play of imagination. Biedermeier should be seen as an important cultural tendency, if only because there is more post-Romantic art—local idyll, disillusioned irony (Byron, Heine)—than Romantic! See Virgil Nemianou's rehabilitation of the term in his *The Taming of Romanticism: European Literature and the Age of Biedermeier* (Cambridge: Harvard University Press, 1984), e.g. 37: "epigonism, doubt, and empiric reduction are characteristic of the age and its peculiar kind of greatness. It is a greatness achieved by accommodation and dialectical perspective."

49. Annemarie Gethmann-Siefert has detailed this historicizing process in her *Die Funktion der Kunst in der Geschichte* (*Hegel-Studien, Beiheft* 25 [Bonn: Bouvier, 1984]), and elsewhere. At the same time, she regrets Hegel's shift away from utopian, Schillerian thinking, and blames his systematizing tendencies for this gradual disillusionment.

50. Charles Baudelaire, *Selected Writings on Art and Artists*, trans. P. E. Charvet (Harmondsworth: Penguin, 1972), 408, in a section called "Mnemonic Art": the tension for the painter is to recall everything while giving a clear and instantaneous impression of the whole.

51. A good survey may be had in Stephen Bungay, *Beauty and Truth: A Study of Hegel's Aesthetics* (Oxford: Oxford University Press, 1984), 71ff.; see also Annemarie Gethmann-Siefert, "Eine Diskussion ohne Ende: Zu Hegels These vom Ende der Kunst," *Hegel-Studien* 16 (1981), 230–43. Hegel does not speak of the "death" or "end" of art, but rather claims that "for us," and within the perspective of his system, art "considered in its highest vocation is a thing of the past" (*LA*, 25; *HA*, 11): (1) we no longer "bend the knee" to art as cultic practice, and (2) our interest is "reflective" or scientific or philosophical rather than a living involvement with its production. That is not to say that art will not continue, only that it is of no religious importance.

52. Peter Bürger, *Theory of the Avant Garde* (Minneapolis: University of Minnesota Press, 1984). Luhmann speaks of "autopoiesis," by which art is considered as a social system; see his *Essays in Self Reference* (New York: Columbia University Press, 1990), chapters 1 and 11, especially 193–214.

53. Here the *locus classicus* is Paul Oskar Kristeller, "The Modern System of the Arts" (1951–52), reprinted in his *Renaissance Thought*, vol. 2: *Papers on Humanism and the Arts* (New York: Columbia University Press, 1965), 163–227.

54. For Blumenberg, see especially " 'Nachahmung der Natur': Zur Vorgeschichte der Idee des schöpferischen Menschen," in *Studium Generale* 10 (1957), 266–83; reprinted in *Wirklichkeiten in denen wir leben* (Stuttgart: Reclam, 1981), 55–103. Blumenberg takes the mimetic cosmology of Plato's *Timaeus* as exemplary for a whole tradition, including Aristotle's idea that mimesis can "complete" nature, and Christian notions of "creatio ex nihilo"—there was always a schema that God had to follow. Beginning with the Renaissance, and with Nicholas of Cusa in particular, this schema of a preordained schema came under attack. This account forms part of Blumenberg's larger view of modernity as

"self-maintaining," i.e., not as a displacement or imitation of divine generation. Cf. my "Creativity, Before and After" (XI World Congress of Philosophy, Brighton, 1988).

55. See Robert Pippin, *Modernism as a Philosophical Problem* (Oxford: Blackwell, 1991).

56. "Absorption" or "presentness" derives from Heidegger, via Cavell, it is worth noting. And I'd note further that the rather phenomenological method Fried adopts is hardly a way out.

57. Theodor W. Adorno, *Ästhetische Theorie* (Frankfurt: Suhrkamp, 1973), 129—art is deceptive, perhaps even in its promise of redemption!

58. Following Blanchot, Derrida speaks in favor of enfranchising a literary mode as a form of *écriture*, yet in fugitive mode, well short of seeing it institutionalized and legitimated as "Literature." See also Philippe Lacoue-Labarthe and Jean-Luc Nancy, *L'Absolu littéraire* (1978), translated as *The Literary Absolute: The Theory of Literature in German Romanticism* (Albany: SUNY Press, 1988), which shares a Heideggerian inspiration; also Lacoue-Labarthe, "The Caesura of the Speculative" (1978), in *Typography: Mimesis, Philosophy, Politics* (Cambridge: Harvard University Press, 1989), 208–35. De Man too began with Heidegger, but moved toward a position that sees poetic naming (of self and and literature alike) as linguistic artefacts. His 1982 essay, "The Resistance to Theory," included in his *The Resistance to Theory* (Minneapolis: University of Minnesota Press, 1986), 3–20, has a different account again: art is posited by a philosophical aesthetics, and both mark exhibiting "resistance" to rhetoric, a resistance itself rhetorical, manifesting as it does a certain will to power, a pull to "totalization," etc. I might wheel in here an odd hybrid—indeed confusion—with the first, socially reactive account, Terry Eagleton's *The Ideology of the Aesthetic* (Oxford: Blackwell, 1990), which likewise sees "art" as an effect of the discourse that would study it. And I'd even mention the Rortian barometer that sees philosophy in the nineteenth century as a form of "literature."

59. Paris: Gallimard, 1949—translated in *The Gaze of Orpheus and Other Literary Essays* (Barrytown: Station Hill, 1981), 21–62.

60. Lacoue-Labarthe and Nancy, *The Literary Absolute*, 34.

61. Derrida, "The Ends of Man," in *Margins of Philosophy*, 109–36, at 123.

62. Hegel, *Phenomenology of Spirit*, 455—it is "Fate" that puts them in the museum, one supposes.

63. See, e.g., Peter Bürger, "Aporias of Modern Aesthetics," *New Left Review* 184 (1990), 46–56, and more generally, his *Prosa der Moderne* (Frankfurt: Suhrkamp, 1988), and *Postmoderne: Alltag, Allegorie und Avant-garde*, ed. C. and P. Bürger (Frankfurt: Suhrkamp, 1987).

64. Jürgen Habermas, *The Philosophical Discourse of Modernity* (Cambridge: MIT Press, 1987), lectures 1 and 2, especially 16–17.

65. See Vincent Descombes, *Philosophie par gros temps* (Paris: Minuit, 1989), 182–83; *The Barometer of Reason*, trans. Stephen Schwartz (New York: OUP, 1993), 181. I borrow this all the more happily because many of the conclusions I draw from his book do not match his own.

Kathleen Wright, Heidegger on Hegel's Antigone: The Memory of Gender and the Forgetfulness of the Ethical Difference

1. Heidegger's 1935 reading is to be found in Martin Heidegger, *Einführung in die Metaphysik* (Tübingen: Niemeyer, 1953), 112–26; in English as *An Introduction to Metaphysics*, trans. Ralph Manheim (New York: Anchor Books, 1959), 123–38. The 1935 reading will be cited in the text as *EM*, followed by page number for the German, and *IM*, followed by page number for the English. All translations from *EM* are my own. Heidegger's 1942 reading is to be found in Martin Heidegger, *Hölderlins Hymne "Der Ister,"* ed. Walter Biemel, vol. 53 of his *Gesamtausgabe* (Frankfurt: Klostermann, 1984), 63–152; in English as *Hölderlin's Hymn "The Ister,"* trans. by William McNeill and Julia Davis (Bloomington: Indiana University Press, 1996), 51–122. The 1942 reading will be cited in the text as *GA* 53, followed by page number for the German, and *HHI*, followed by page number for the English. All translations from *GA* 53 are my own. I have discussed the textual strategy of these two readings and how this bears on the substance of Heidegger's account in "Grenzen der Weisheit: Heideggers Sophokles-Interpretation 1935/1942," trans. Aleida Assmann, in *Weisheit: Archäologie der literarischen Kommunikation*, vol. 3, ed. Aleida Assmann (Munich: Fink, 1991), 537–46.

2. Hegel's most detailed reading is to be found in G. W. F. Hegel, *Phänomenologie des Geistes*, ed. Johannes Hoffmeister (Hamburg: Meiner, 1952), 317–42; in English, *Phenomenology of Spirit*, trans. A. V. Miller (Oxford: Oxford University Press, 1977), 266–89.

3. Elizabeth Wyckoff, trans., *Sophocles' Antigone*, in *Sophocles I* from *The Complete Greek Tragedies*, ed. David Grene and Richard Lattimore (Chicago: University of Chicago Press, 1954), 171.

4. R. C. Jebb, translation and notes in part 3, "The *Antigone*", of his *Sophocles: The Plays and the Fragments* (Cambridge: Cambridge University Press, 1891), 77–78.

5. G. W. F. Hegel, *Aesthetics: Lectures on Fine Art*, vol. 2, trans. T. M. Knox (Oxford: Clarendon Press, 1975), 1218; In German, *Vorlesungen über die Asthetik*, vol. 15 of *Theorie Werkausgabe*, ed. Eva Moldenhauer and Karl Markus Michel (Frankfurt: Suhrkamp, 1970), 550.

6. Martin Heidegger, *Hölderlins Hymnen "Germanien" und "Der Rhein,"* ed. Susanne Ziegler, vol. 39 of his *Gesamtausgabe* (Frankfurt: Klostermann, 1980), 216. A. C. Bradley makes a related point when he remarks that "Greek tragedy represents the total Greek mind more fully than modern tragedy can the total modern mind." See his "Hegel's Theory of Tragedy," in *Hegel on Tragedy*, ed. Anne and Henry Paolucci (New York: Harper and Row, 1962), 388.

7. Hegel, *Aesthetics*, vol. 1, 464; in German, *Theorie Werkausgabe*, vol. 14, 60.

8. G. W. F. Hegel, *Philosophy of Right*, trans. T. M. Knox (Oxford: Clarendon Press, 1952), 114–15; in German, *Grundlinien der Philosophie des Rechtes*, vol. 7 of *Theorie Werkausgabe*, ed. Eva Moldenhauer and Karl Markus Michel (Frankfurt: Suhrkamp, 1970), 319.

9. Jacques Derrida, "Choreographies: An Interview with Jacques Derrida," trans. and ed. Christie V. McDonald, in *Diacritics*, 12, no. 2 (Summer 1982), 74.

Derrida makes a similar point in *Spurs: Nietzsche's Styles,* trans. Barbara Harlow (Chicago: University of Chicago Press, 1979). Selections from both works are reprinted in part 4, entitled "Sexual Difference in Philosophy," of *A Derrida Reader: Between the Blinds,* ed. Peggy Kamuf (New York: Columbia University Press, 1991).

10. Jacques Derrida, "Geschlecht: Sexual Difference, Ontological Difference," in *A Derrida Reader,* 380–402. Derrida also discusses Heidegger's mention of *Geschlecht* (sexuality) in "Language in the Poem," published in 1953. See his "Geschlecht II: Heidegger's Hand," trans. John P. Leavy, Jr., in *Deconstruction and Philosophy: The Texts of Jacques Derrida,* ed. John Sallis (Chicago: University of Chicago Press, 1987), 161–96.

11. Heidegger claims that "If there is someplace where reading in the problematic of *Being and Time* is completely absurd, then this place is Hegel." See his *Hegels Phänomenologie des Geistes,* ed. Ingtraud Görland, vol. 32 of his *Gesamtausgabe* (Frankfurt: Klostermann, 1980), 209.

12. Liddell-Scott lists the following for the adjectival *deinon:* (1) fearful, terrible, dread, dire; (2) with a notion of Force or Power mighty, powerful; (3) the sense of powerful, wondrous passed into that of able, clever, skillful. See *An Intermediate Greek-English Lexicon* (Oxford: Clarendon Press, 1964), 176–77. Heidegger translates *deinon* as "*un-heimlich*" (*EM,* 115; *IM,* 126). Ralph Manheim uses "strange" in his translation of Heidegger's 1935 reading of the "Ode to Man." McNeill and Davis prefer "uncanny' " in their translation of Heidegger's 1942 reading. However the English "uncanny," because it is associated with Freud's concept of the uncanny and the male's castration complex, fails to bring out the feminization of the term *to deinon* that takes place when Antigone becomes for Heidegger the paradigm case of *to deinon.*

13. A possible exception would be the choral lyric of Corinna, especially that concerned with Hesiodic material as well as with the story of Orestes.

14. Friedrich Nietzsche, *Menschliches, Allzumenschliches,* vol. 2 of his *Sämtliche Werke,* ed. Giorgio Colli and Mazzino Montinari (Munich: de Gruyter, 1980), 213.

15. See Patricia Jagentowicz Mills, "Hegel's Antigone," in *The Owl of Minerva,* 17, no. 2 (Spring 1986), 131–52, for a critique of Hegel's account. New studies on Hegel's reading of the *Antigone* have appeared after my essay was accepted for this volume. See, e.g., Kelly Oliver, "Antigone's Ghost: Undoing Hegel's *Phenomenology of Spirit,*" *Hypatia* 11, no. 1 (Winter 1996), 67–90.

16. "We should not however see Oedipus only as the human being who suffered a downfall. We must comprehend in Oedipus that figure [*Gestalt*] of Greek *Dasein* in which the fundamental passion of the Greeks ventured into the farthest and most wild [i.e., undomesticated domain], the passion to disclose being, i.e., the struggle [*Kampf*] for the sake of being itself" (*EM,* 81; *IM,* 90).

17. *EM,* 112; *IM,* 123. Heidegger is ultimately concerned with the being of human being for the Germans in 1935 as well as later in 1942. He understands the Germans to stand in a privileged relationship to the Greeks: both are the originators of Western history, the Greeks of the first beginning and the Germans of the new beginning. A discussion of how Heidegger conceives of the Greek and German mission would take us into Heidegger's politics. See my essay "Heidegger

and the Authorization of Hölderlin's Poetry," in *Martin Heidegger: Politics, Art, and Technology,* ed. Karsten Harries and Christoph Jamme (New York: Holmes and Meier, 1994), 164–74.

18. By experience, I mean *Erfahrung,* a rigorous working through, and not *Erlebnis,* a superficial impression. This distinction is Heidegger's. See *GA* 53, 128, 142; *HHI,* 103, 114. McNeill and Davis miss Heidegger's dismissive tone when he uses the word "*Erlebnis,*" which they translate (and interpret) as "lived experience."

19. George Steiner praises Heidegger's 1935 reading of the choral ode as "one of the most vivid encounters we know of between the Sophoclean chorus and the western imagination after Athens." He does not mention Antigone's absence or the masculinist content of this reading. See his *Antigones* (Oxford: Oxford University Press, 1984), 174. Steiner does not discuss Heidegger's 1942 reading in *Antigones* probably because vol. 53 of Heidegger's *Gesamtausgabe* was published in the same year as his *Antigones.*

20. McNeill and Davis fail to appreciate the significance of this new and third characteristic of *to deinon* when they translate "*das Ungewöhnliche*" as "the inhabitual." They stress instead "*das Ungeheure*" ("the extraordinary") in their translation, thereby missing the sexual difference Heidegger is introducing in his 1942 reading of Sophocles's *Antigone.*

21. *GA* 53, 147; *HHI,* 118. Friedrich Hölderlin, *Poems and Fragments,* trans. Michael Hamburger (Cambridge: Cambridge University Press, 1980), 605. Heidegger does not mention that Hölderlin refers here to the life of Oedipus.

22. According to H. J. Rose, "to the mythologist pure and simple there is not much that is interesting about Hestia, for she has practically no myth: she is the child of Kronos and Rhea, and she chose to remain virgin," in *A Handbook of Greek Mythology* (New York: E. P. Dutton, 1959), 167. See also Jean-Pierre Vernant, "Hestia-Hermes: The Religious Expression of Space and Movement among the Greeks," *Social Science Information* 8, no. 4 (1969), 131–68.

23. Wyckoff, trans., *Sophocles' Antigone,* 174.

24. On this topic, see my "Heidegger and the Mo(u)rning of History," in *Philosophy Today* 37, no. 4 (Winter 1993), 423–35.

David Farrell Krell, Stuff • Thread • Point • Fire: Hölderlin on Historical Memory and Tragic Dissolution

1. See David Farrell Krell, *Of Memory, Reminiscence, and Writing: On the Verge* (Bloomington: Indiana University Press, 1990), chapters 5 and 6, where I have discussed the cases of Hegel and Heidegger, respectively. I am grateful to my students and colleagues at DePaul University, especially Anna Vaughn and Paul Davies, and to colleagues at the Collège International de Philosophie, especially Françoise Dastur, for their willingness during the fall of 1990 to listen to the thoughts contained in this essay and to help them along. The essay appears in somewhat altered form, and in a different context, in Krell, *Lunar Voices: Of Tragedy, Poetry, Fiction, and Thought* (Chicago: University of Chicago Press, 1995), chapter 2. On Hölderlin and Empedocles, see also chapter 1.

2. For Hölderlin's texts I shall employ two editions: first, *Hölderlin Werke und Briefe*, ed. Friedrich Beißner and Jochen Schmidt (Frankfurt: Insel, 1982 [1st ed., 1969]), hereafter cited as *B;* second, *Friedrich Hölderlin Sämtliche Werke: Kritische Textausgabe*, ed. D. E. Sattler, vols. 12–14 (Frankfurt: Luchterhand, 1986 [based on the FHA, Verlag Roter Stern, 1985]), hereafter cited as *S.* While I accept Sattler's as the authoritative text today (and one must emphasize the *today*, inasmuch as each year seems to bring us yet another Hölderlin edition), the Beißner-Schmidt edition remains extremely useful, especially (but not only) because of the selection of letters. The intrusions in my text *he only mourns* are from either Hölderlin's letters or the three drafts of *Der Tod des Empedokles*. The translations throughout are my own. Note that for the most part I am limiting myself in what follows to the theoretical writings of the Jena, Frankfurt, and Hamburg periods; thus I shall have very little to say about Hölderlin's later "Remarks" on his Sophocles translations—on which so much of the contemporary discussion has focused. My reading of Hölderlin's *Der Tod des Empedokles* will at times intersect that of Andrzej Warminski, *Readings in Interpretation: Hölderlin, Hegel, Heidegger* (Minneapolis: University of Minnesota Press, 1987), chapters 1–2, especially 11–22. Like Warminski, I am interested in reading the final scene of the (truncated) third draft, the Manes scene, reading it "a little longer," reading it "*as* a scene of reading" (13). Like Warminski, I take it to be disconcerting and yet undeniable that "the transition from one world and time to another"—the transition that is *history*—hinges and unhinges "simultaneously" on "radical forgetting and radical remembering" (16). The themes of *fire* and *intensity*, themselves burning through the distinctions between Hesperian (Christian-Germanic), Greek, Egyptian, and Oriental, I take to be themes particularly appropriate to such radicality of reading.

3. See F. W. J. Schelling, *Über das Wesen der menschlichen Freiheit*, in vol. 7 of the *Sämmtliche Werke* (Stuttgart, 1830), 367 n.

4. See *regulae* 3 and 7 in Descartes's *Rules for the Direction of the Human Mind*, in Descartes, *Œuvres et lettres*, ed. André Bridoux (Paris: Pléiade, 1953), 44–45, 57–61.

5. Hölderlin, *B*, 729–36, 783–90; Walter Benjamin, part 3 of "Goethes Wahlverwandtschaften," in *Illuminationen* (Frankfurt: Suhrkamp, 1977), especially 116–19; Maurice Blanchot, *L'espace littéraire* (Paris: Gallimard, 1955), 374–75; and Philippe Lacoue-Labarthe, *L'imitation des modernes: Typographies II* (Paris: Galilée, 1986), especially 59–69. Lacoue-Labarthe calls *hyperbologic* what one would perhaps also have to think in terms of *ellipsis*. That is to say, Hölderlin's "regression" from a classic Aristotelian (i.e., mimetological and cathartic) to a more Sophoclean reading (and writing, and directing) of tragedy, insofar as it speaks regressively as a *speculative* discourse, always both falls too short and goes too far with regard to Aristotelian tragedy. Hence the confusions of Lacoue-Labarthe's own account—of Hölderlin's paralysis, dislocation, immobility, interdiction, distention, suspension, split, spiral hollow, foundering, and "spasm." While I cannot follow Lacoue-Labarthe's reading of the three drafts of *Der Tod des Empedokles* as precise stages of such a regression (60–62), and while I regret his acceptance of the traditional reading of *Innigkeit* as *l'intériorité* (62–64), I

celebrate his search in Hölderlin for a logic of excess, a logic of alternance, a logic of what—in recognition of tragic dissolution—I will here call *hyperbollipsis.*

6. On the caesura, see both Lacoue-Labarthe, *L'imitation des modernes,* and the following from Andrzej Warminski:

> What Hölderlin means by "caesura" is a very peculiar "cutting off," for it is an interruption that, in brief, allows the tragedy to continue. . . . It is what Hölderlin calls "the pure word.". . . Like the Manes scene, the caesura is the place where the tragedy explicitly turns upon itself, where, in short, representation represents itself *as* representation. That this turning is not the reflection of a Subject (absolute or otherwise) but rather of a text is clear from Hölderlin's using explicitly linguistic terms to name it: that is, caesura, the pure word. Indeed, rather than allowing the human subject to recognize himself in his own other, the caesura rips him out of his own sphere of life, out of the center of his own inner life, and carries him off into an other world and tears him into the eccentric sphere of the dead. (Warminski, *Readings in Interpretation,* 17)

7. Martin Heidegger, *Hölderlins Hymnen "Germanien" und "Der Rhein,"* in Heidegger, *Gesamtausgabe,* vol. 39 (Frankfurt: Klostermann, 1980), cited in the body of my text by volume and page. My thanks to Will McNeill of DePaul University for the reference and for his own work on Heidegger's Hölderlin. Warminski's brief treatment of Heidegger's course reduces its reading of "holy mourning" as Hölderlin's "grounding mood" [*Grundstimmung*] to a mere "ontologizing" gesture on Heidegger's part (Warminski, *Readings in Interpretation,* 64–71). Yet it is a mistake to see in Heidegger's reading of the "Not" of *Germanien* a mere retreat to the mood of dread or anxiety in the fundamental ontology of *Being and Time* or "What Is Metaphysics?" One would have to discuss Heidegger's extensive development of the theme of *Grundstimmung* after the period of *Being and Time,* for example, the fundamental mood of the 1929–30 lecture course, which is somewhere between "profound boredom" and "melancholy" (*die tiefe Lange-weile; Schwermut*). One would then have to take up Heidegger's explicit reference in the *Germanien* lecture course to the founding mood of Hölderlin's *Empedokles,* namely, *Innigkeit.* Quite surprisingly, Warminski neglects these pages of Heidegger's *Germanien* course, the very pages that might have proved to be most important for his own project. For the 1929–30 course, see Martin Heidegger, *Die Grundbegriffe der Metaphysik: Welt—Endlichkeit—Einsamkeit,* in Heidegger, *Gesamtausgabe,* vols. 29/30 (Frankfurt: Klostermann, 1983), especially 270–71, on melancholy, and the entire first part of the course, on profound boredom. Will McNeill and Nicholas Walker have beautifully translated the volume into English: see *The Fundamental Concepts of Metaphysics: World—Finitude—Solitude* (Bloomington: Indiana University Press, 1995).

8. Martin Heidegger, *Beiträge zur Philosophie (Vom Ereignis),* in Heidegger, *Gesamtausgabe,* vol. 65 (Frankfurt: Klostermann, 1989), passim.

9. See David Farrell Krell, *Daimon Life: Heidegger and Life-Philosophy* (Bloomington: Indiana University Press, 1992), passim.

10. Beißner-Schmidt and Sattler alike read *wahren zeitlichen* rather than Hellingrath's *wahren wirklichen.* See *S* 13, 359; *B,* 572.

11. Beißner-Schmidt and Sattler read *weniger tief* rather than Hellingrath's *weniger tot.* Ibid.

12. "Hölderlin's Empedocles, reaching by voluntary steps the very edge of Etna, is the death of the last mediator between mortals and Olympus, the end of the infinite on earth, the flame returning to its native fire, leaving as its sole remaining trace that which had to be abolished precisely by his death: the beautiful, enclosed form of individuality. After Empedocles, the world is placed under the sign of finitude, in that irreconcilable, intermediate state in which reigns the Law, the harsh law of limit. The destiny of individuality will be to appear always in the objectivity that both manifests and conceals it, both denies it and forms its basis: 'Here too the subjective and the objective exchange faces' " (Michel Foucault, *The Birth of the Clinic: An Archaeology of Medical Perception,* trans. A. M. Sheridan [London: Tavistock, 1973], 198).

13. On *Hingebung* in Friedrich Schlegel's *Lucinde,* and in Hegel's polemic against that novel, see David Farrell Krell, "Lucinde's Shame: Hegel, Sensuous Woman, and the Law," *Cardozo Law Review* 10, nos. 5–6 (March–April 1989), 1673–86; reprinted in *Hegel and Legal Theory,* ed. Drucilla Cornell, Michel Rosenfeld, and David Gray Carlson (New York: Routledge, 1991), 287–300; also revised and reprinted in *Re-reading the Canon: Feminist Interpretations of Hegel,* ed. Patricia Jagentowicz Mills (University Park: Penn State Press, 1995), 89–107.

14. F. W. J. Schelling, in his *Stuttgarter Privatvorlesungen* of 1810, quoted in David Farrell Krell, "The Crisis of Reason in the Nineteenth Century: Schelling's Treatise on Human Freedom (1809)," in *The Collegium Phaenomenologicum: The First Ten Years,* ed. John Sallis, Giuseppina Moneta, and Jacques Taminiaux (Dordrecht: Kluwer Academic Publishers, 1988), 25.

15. See David Farrell Krell, *Postponements: Woman, Sensuality, and Death in Nietzsche* (Bloomington: Indiana University Press, 1986), 45–46, 111.

16. I am grateful to Dr. Andrea Rehberg for this suggestion.

17. See chapter 6, "The 'Mechanics' of Fluids," in Luce Irigaray, *This Sex Which Is Not One,* trans. C. Porter with C. Burke (Ithaca: Cornell University Press, 1985), especially 108–9, 117–18.

18. Françoise Dastur, *Hölderlin: Tragédie et modernité* (La Versanne: Encre marine, 1992), 52.

John Sallis, Stone

1. Most notably in the lecture that Heidegger gave in July 1924 to the Marburger Theologenschaft: *Der Begriff der Zeit* (Tübingen: Niemeyer, 1989), 17–21.

2. G. W. F. Hegel, *Ästhetik,* vol. 1, ed. Friedrich Bassenge (Berlin: Verlag das europäische Buch, 1985), 13. Hereafter *A,* followed by volume and page numbers.

3. Martin Heidegger, "Der Ursprung des Kunstwerkes," in *Holzwege*, vol. 5 of *Gesamtausgabe* (Frankfurt: Klostermann, 1977), 68. Hereafter UK, followed by page number.

4. G. W. F. Hegel, *Phänomenologie des Geistes*, ed. J. Hoffmeister (Hamburg: Meiner, 1952), 29f.

5. Martin Heidegger, *Einführung in die Metaphysik*, vol. 40 of *Gesamtausgabe* (Frankfurt: Klosterman, 1983), 16.

Notes on Contributors

Robert Bernasconi is the Moss Professor of Philosophy at the University of Memphis.

Rebecca Comay is a professor in the Department of Philosophy at the University of Toronto.

Martin Donougho is an associate professor in the Department of Philosophy at the University of South Carolina, Columbia.

Michel Haar is a professor of philosophy at the University of Paris, Sorbonne.

Dominique Janicaud is the director of the Centre de Recherches d'Histoire des Idées at Université de Nice.

David Kolb is the Charles B. Dana Professor of Philosophy at Bates College.

David Farrell Krell is a professor of philosophy and the founding director of the Humanities Center at DePaul University in Chicago.

John McCumber is a professor in the Department of German at Northwestern University.

John Sallis is the Liberal Arts Professor of Philosophy at Pennsylvania State University.

Dennis J. Schmidt is a professor in the Department of Philosophy at Villanova University, Pennsylvania.

Jacques Taminiaux is the Adelmann Professor of Philosophy at Boston College and the former director of the Center for Phenomenological Studies at the University of Louvain-la-Neuve.

Kathleen Wright is a professor of philosophy at Haverford College in Pennsylvania.